The Logik of the Heart

To those special heart-thinkers
scattered around the world
who are seeking *Ueber-logikal* thinking.

The Logik of the Heart:

The Organic Templates of Spiritual Writers, Rudolf Steiner, and *The Philosophy of Freehood*

Mark Riccio

Mark Riccio, my email: Mhamatz@yahoo.com
Heart-logik website: www.organicthinking.org
To obtain copies: www.waldorfbooks.com

TO GET A PDF FILE OF THE BOOK'S DIAGRAMS IN **COLOR,** SIMPLY SEND ME AN EMAIL!

Acknowledgments
I would like to thank Ruth Foster who was completely supportive when I started the research process in 2007. Next in line was the tireless effort of editing and discussion with Angela Beltrani who helped me to find a better voice and to revise the entire earlier draft. More recently Paul Schlarman, Helena Mitchell, Nigel Lumsden, and Alexandra Riccio did editing for which I am very thankful.

I have to thank especially my estranged teacher, Florin Lowndes, for the countless hours he spent answering questions about life, Rudolf Steiner, and the logik of the heart. I was privileged to meet man with an incredible biography and continuous brilliant insights into Steiner's work.

Finally, and foremost, I thank my devoted father who supported me, when need be, during this lengthy process.

Some Introductory Words

In writing <u>The Logik of the Heart</u> my purpose has been two-fold. The first purpose is to give spiritual thinkers a powerful form of communication and organizing ideas that has remained mostly unconscious. New Age writers could enhance their already dynamic and spiritual frame of mind with this way of conceptualizing. <u>The Logik of the Heart</u> gives in a potent dose the organicism, depth, and clarity that authors are looking for. Spiritual writers can find the right form for their thoughts!

The second purpose is to give Anthroposophical individuals the keys for unlocking Rudolf Steiner's work. Much has been written about Rudolf Steiner, but hardly anything about the heart-logik forms he used in composing his books. Even though Rudolf Steiner (1861-1925) tried desperately to introduce this new form of thinking and writing, his friends and followers in the Anthroposophical Society movement never took it up. I would like to dedicate this book to the Waldorf teachers who have kept Anthroposophy (the idea of heart-thinking) alive. Without them, Steiner's work would have surely fallen into obscurity. Waldorf teachers now have a method book which supports Steiner's pedagogical suggestions and may also open up discussion on to how evolve Waldorf education.

I have spent many years writing and rewriting this book. I wanted to write about this new logik in order to make it easy for a wider audience. I have attempted to write in heart-thinking patterns. I hope my enthusiasm in writing this book makes up for what I was lacking in heart-thinking artistry. In this edition the diagrams are unfortunately black and white, however to enjoy them in color simply email me for the PDF, or reconstruct them yourself using colored pencils.

Each chapter has a very distinct character and function. The first four chapters present the Heart Logik in terms of writing and thinking. Each chapter grows in detail and complexity with chapter four covering sentence level analysis of the heart-thinking. Chapter Five presents some heart-logikal perspectives on Waldorf Education, Christianity, and more practical applications. Most importantly, Chapter Five has a special meditation (Pranic Tube) for those who are interested in working in a deeper way with meditating on heart-thinking forms. There is a Logik of the Heart Study Guide attached to this book which explains how to approach Steiner's main heart-logik text, <u>The Philosophy of Freehood</u>. It describes how to read systematically in order to discover heart-logik forms in other authors' writing. There are many gems not only in the main body of the Study Guide, but also in the Appendices.

Table of Contents

Chapter One, What is living form?

Did you ever wonder if your favorite book affected you the way it did because of some inherent movement in the words and stories, a special form, or "living form," that eluded you because you were not sure what to look for? These special forms are the topic of this book and are called by various names such as the logik of the heart, creation logik, and heart-thinking, living thinking, and even Christ-thinking. This book describes an organic method of organizing books, articles, and a variety of other types of writing that will imbue these works with the very essence of life and living processes. Some famous authors (and some not so famous) have tapped into this form of thinking which flows like waves through a series of ideas or storylines. Only one author, Rudolf Steiner, is known to have deliberately used this method of writing and intended his books as training manuals for others. After studying these archetypal patterns of writing in Steiner's work, I uncovered these same forms in Plato's <u>Republic</u>, the *New Testament*, and other well-known works. This wave-like manner of structuring ideas, books, and prayers seems to have been in use for several thousand years, however never consciously.

Yet these wave-like patterns are not limited to Steiner's work or other great pieces of literature. We can see them in the natural world, science, philosophy, religion, and literally in every action that we take. This model has many applications for changing the way we think, not only about life, but about education as well. Although this book does not intend to be exhaustive on the topic of living form and the logik of the heart, it does give the fundamental principles for a renewal of how to work with structure in books and writing.

My heartfelt intention is to share the knowledge of living form so that readers can be empowered in their own work. An understanding of the logik of the heart will enliven and broaden the vision of those working creatively. I cannot answer all questions and points about living form, but I can point to some places where living form is obvious so that it can become a universal method of creating and writing.

What value does this living form have? In a new age of dynamic thinking we are seeking new ways of expressing ourselves and our ideas. Even though we find living form in some ancient texts, this living form has applications which are helpful to our modern mind-frame and learning style. Living form captures what our "distractible" minds are already doing; in our modern consciousness we are actively surveying and scanning the whole and the parts. Our general lack of attention now becomes an advantage for learning living form because living form only makes sense to those who can already think dynamically, i.e., in levels and intervals. In addressing the needs of the ADD (attention deficit disorder) culture, thinking in living-form may someday be the leading idea in educational models.

The idea of living form seems to be wide-spread in our culture, but remains unconscious for the most part. (Later in the book, I uncover examples in popular texts, prayers, and poems and thus give an overview of authors whose work intuitively incorporated living form.) The conscious application of living form was accomplished by Rudolf Steiner - the founder of Waldorf education, the creator of biodynamic farming, the architect of the Goetheanum, the author of numerous books on freedom philosophy, a speech and drama teacher, Vasily Kandinsky's personal mentor and so on – who used living form in all of his projects. George O'Neil, a close friend of Ernest Hemingway, was the first person to figure out the technique of living form Steiner used in his books and other works. O'Neil's student, Florin Lowndes, published Steiner's compendium of living forms. Both O'Neil and Lowndes then analyzed various books, essays, advertisements, and speeches. They found that again and again these living forms were decipherable in such classics <u>The Scarlet Letter</u> and the *Gettysburg Address* as well as in articles of lesser known writers who tapped into these archetypal patterns. I have drawn on their work and have applied it to further examples, and in addition, distilled aspects of living form so that the public can utilize it more effectively.

This volume presents many examples from various spiritual sources, which is no accident, since these are reflective of my own interests. I felt that there is a lack of concrete examples of what could be called a "spiritual" or "Christian" writing style. Thus I presented examples from the Christian corpus whose living form was originally mentioned by Steiner and/or systematically worked out by the Bible scholar, Bullinger. If I were a scientist or musician, then the book would have been included examples out of the sciences and musical composition. I would first like to cover examples of the logik of the heart that are easily grasped   as a kind of warm up before I enter into more complicated thought-forms in later chapters.

*

Goethe and Living Form: Goethe can be seen as a father of living form in so far as its very origins are based upon observations he made about the plant world. His famous Urpflanze or Archetypal Plant was realized in a series of sketches covering the delicate stages of plant growth: from seed to leaf, bud to flower, pistil and stamen to fruit, and finally new seed. These seven stages are the first concrete representation of living form. Goethe claimed to have a living knowledge of the *idea* of a plant which gave him the capacity to see in his mind's eye the metamorphosis of a plant. The process of metamorphosis in this archetypal plant contains four laws or relationships that need to be considered in order for the plant's development to be grasped. *These laws are rhythm, enhancement (intensification), polarity, and inversion.*

All living things unfold according to these four principles of nature. Thus we see in the seven major steps in the life of a plant how each step expands and contracts in rhythmical forms, how the plant becomes more complex (enhances) in its manifestations, and how aspects of the plant stand in polarity to other aspects, and finally how the plants moves from external processes and inverts into hidden processes. The four-leveled diagram of the archetypal plant shows the four interrelationships of the one Idea of living form.

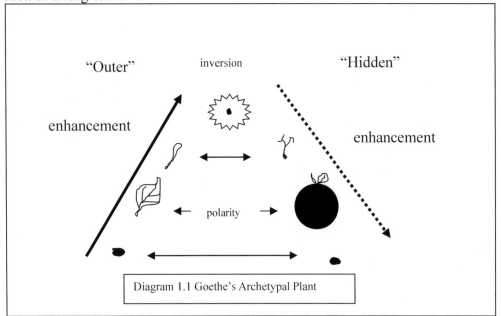

Diagram 1.1 Goethe's Archetypal Plant

This one *idea* comes to meet us in our biology text books, however, in a slightly modified form in the double helix of genetics. Formally speaking, one can see a similarity between the four levels, polarity, and the inverting of the DNA strands. Is it possible that there is some transcendent element or idea contained in all truly living models? And could this transcendent element be then referred to as "God's living form."

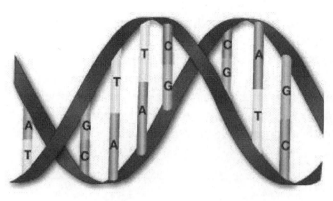

Thymine (Yellow) = T   Guanine (Green) = G

Adenine (Blue) = A   Cytosine (Red) = C   Diagram 1.2

Fritjof Capra writes in his <u>Web of Life</u> that "from Pythagoras to Aristotle, to Goethe, and to the organismic biologists, there is a continuous intellectual tradition that struggles with the understanding of pattern, realizing that it is crucial to the understanding of living form." (p.158) In other words, it is the pattern which aids us in understanding life itself; we are not limited to analyzing just the parts but seeing the whole and finding the inter-connections. So a new thinking about nature requires us "to understand things systemically [which] literally means to put them into a context, to establish the nature of their relationships." (p.27) As we shall see later, in order to comprehend and practice living form, we need this capacity of surveying from the whole to the parts and from the parts to the whole always looking for patterns.

*

The Seven Fold Model of Spiritual Traditions: Living form is also found in many spiritual traditions. By the term "living form," I am referring to ideas which are structured according to the same interrelationships as Goethe's Archetypal Plant. The most basic (and in most traditions forgotten) was the idea that human beings have four fundamental energy bodies (or energy systems) plus three higher potential energy fields. The theosophical and anthroposophical spiritualist theories claim that human beings have seven bodies or members, and this idea can be traced from the earliest of religious ideas in ancient Hinduism through Judaism and Christianity. All peoples and religions have some notion that all human beings have the same fundamental constitution (seven aspects). In light of these religious beliefs, the goal of every individual is to cultivate these three higher potential energy fields through a spiritual education.

Generally speaking, most new age spiritualists and ancient traditions recognize these four main energy bodies: the physical body, life or etheric body, astral or feeling body, and the I-body; plus the three potential higher bodies Spirit-Self, Life-Spirit, and Spirit-man. The differences between the traditions tend to be the varying nomenclature and slightly different perception of the function of the energy of each particular body/field. The form of the seven fold human being is identical to the archetypal plant with its seven aspects/stages of development. The difference between a human and a plant is that the latter three aspects/stages of the plant occur naturally over time while humans must develop the three higher aspects through working on themselves. In the seven-fold human being diagram, the three lower bodies are transformed into three higher bodies with the "I" at the top doing the work. Also added are the Ancient Indian terms of Manas, Buddhi, and Atman next to the Christian principles.

All religions share this one Idea that the human being has the task of ennobling his lower energy fields by addressing and altering his diet, habits, feelings, and thoughts in order to unfold the higher energy bodies and fields of knowing. In Christianity the three higher members were represented as the Holy Spirit, the Christ, and the Father[1] and in Judaism as the six pointed Star of David symbolizing the ego transforming of the lower three points into three higher members. The menorah also brings this to mind with the six candles being lit by the "higher" candle, a perfect metaphor for how the ego, or I, transforms the other bodies. (The Hanukah Menorah has nine candles reflective of the even a more complex understanding that the human being consists of nine energy fields/bodies.) This model now becomes a seven fold model with four distinct levels: a physical level, life level, a feeling level, and a thinking or ego level.

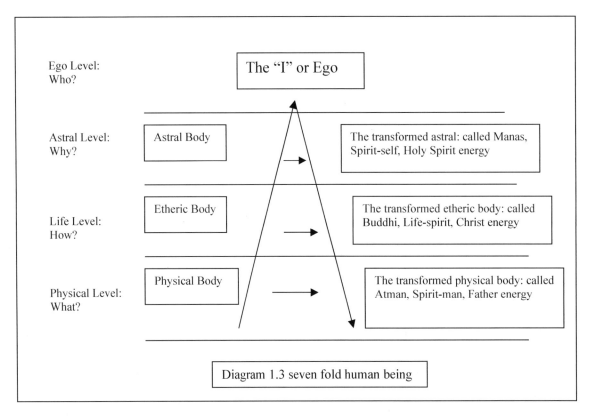

Diagram 1.3 seven fold human being

The form of the seven fold human being can be adapted to reflect a model of the Logik of the Heart (God's living form). We still see the same interrelationships of intensification and polarity. What was once held as a spiritual truth can now be used as a model for organizing thoughts.

*

Philosophy and the Four-fold Logic: The seven fold model of the human being has four main levels and perspectives: **what? how? why? and who?** These questions can be applied to ideas and actions. And their application becomes a model for analyzing existing structures and breaking down the creative process. Let us look at some examples of this four-fold logic.

---

[1] Rudolf Steiner said: We have to distinguish then in Christian esotericism, first, the Holy Spirit (Christians have as much of the Holy Spirit in them as they have ennobled their astral bodies); second, the Son, the Logos, the Word (Christians have as much of the Son, the Logos, the Word within them as they have transformed their etheric bodies); and third, the Father (Christians have as much of the Father in them as their physical bodies have been transformed and made immortal). Only initiates or very advanced human beings can have the Father consciously within them.

Each object has four general attributes: form and material, function, design, and idea/name. A chair generally consists of:

a what? wood, nails;

a how? sitting, it is shifted back and forth at the table;

a why? it has a certain design (kitchen chair has a different function and design than a lounge chair),

and a who? it has a name (or can be a designer's plan, an idea).

A university consists of:

a who? a name (technical, medical university);

a why? research professors;

a how? graduate students researching;

and what? the building designed for research.

A car consists of:

a what? the materials and form of the car;

a how? the way it drives and its functions (lights, doors, seats);

a why? the purpose of its design, a family car or sports car;

a who? its name brand or type.

There is no definitive way of analyzing and breaking down existing structures and once you start to experiment with this new logic you may make some quite wonderful and original schema.

Additionally, all actions (plans carried out) follow this "creation" logic pattern. Actions, however, start with an idea of a destination or outcome. For example, when planning a vacation you start by choosing your destination (the who?). After which we determine *the what?* the type of transportation we will utilize (a car, bus, train); *the how?* the path we choose (various routes or highways, departure times); *the why?* is fine-tuning our journey such as adapting to delays, taking breaks, sightseeing (all things affecting the trip which have to do with our personal needs); and finally *the who?* is realized in our arriving at our destination.   In other words we start with *a who?* (an idea or goal) and conclude with a who? (i.e., *the who or the doer's* completed action).

One more example. When cooking we start with a recipe. The recipe is the plan or idea of what we are to realize such as a pizza. In order to accomplish this we need the ingredients: cheese, sauce, spices, olives, pizza dough and cooking utensils. Then we need to combine them and place them in the oven. Next we check the pizza to see if it is to our liking: crispy. And finally, when all is well, our idea/plan is realized and we can eat:

What? the ingredients

How? combining and baking

Why? checking the baking process

Who? the recipe is finished and ready to eat

Philosophers have talked about an "organic-living" thinking[2], but have never clearly illustrated what that is. They have offered plant analogies, created categories, and developed schema of levels, but have never succeeded at expanding upon the old logic of Aristotle. There is already a trend in today's society toward considering problems from multiple perspectives rather than simply accepting accepted methods or materialistic dogma. This pre-existing movement opens the door to the introduction (or re-introduction) of creation logic, which inherently incorporates this activity systematically. We realize that only a new logic of perspectives can address the questions of our present age.

The benefits of this perspectivism are clearly visible in the various strategies people are using in treating individuals with ADD. Some practitioners approach ADD as a physiological and neuro-

[2] There are many philosophers who have touched on aspects of organic living thinking. Hegel, Heidegger, Schopenhauer, Novalis, and Schiller. Often they describe its attributes but never made an attempt to apply it.

chemical imbalance; others argue it is a question of diet, family habits, and over-stimulation. Some psychologists claim it is childhood depression arising from a lack of a father-figure in the house, a divorce, or "boring schooling." Jeffrey Freed suggests that some children may be partakers in the evolving of a new form of thinking ('right-brained learner in a left-brained world') thereby suggesting that they are right-brained people (non-linear thinkers) suffering in solely left-brained (linear thinking) educational system. Regardless, these various perspectives outline a variety of treatment plans to consider:

> What? **Physical** cause: neurochemical imbalance "treated" with Ritalin
> How? **Diet, social, media** cause: change the diet and social habits
> Why? **Depression** as cause: treat the child for depression by counseling
> Who? **Evolution** of thinking as cause: schools are used to teach linear thinkers, and now the teaching methods need to change.

(Can anyone say that one perspective is more correct than the other? Who can honestly claim that the others are completely wrong? True living thinking encourages us to have many perspectives and to see the strengths and weaknesses of each without being too personally attached to one single perspective.)

Congruently, Steiner elucidated these same four general perspectives as they exist within the university disciplines. On the physical- or What?- level we have chemistry and physics; and for the how?-perspective, we have life or biology. The astral- or why?- perspective corresponds to the study of sociology and psychology (study of generic human thoughts and feelings) and the who? or ego level perspective, history, with its focus on individual ideas and contributions. Thus the four main university perspectives are:

> Physical level: physics, chemistry
> Etheric/life level: biology
> Astral/feeling level: psychology, sociology,
> Ego level: history

Humanity itself can benefit from the application of these perspectives to the core concerns that threaten its very existence in the present day. These perspectives are more than justified in their own domains and many arguments would be solved if people were simply able to view issues and arguments from a variety of perspectives, each considered with equal respect - even in their limitations. The four points of view of creation logic aid in developing a systematic perspectivism necessary for a new way of thinking.

*

Who is using living form or creation logic in the real world? Individuals who can perceive an archetypal pattern with in their areas of expertise are utilizing creation logic in their work. They see a logical flow of as they view their work from the perspectives of the four levels. After having studied this thinking for years, I am always pleasantly surprised when I find it being used in mainstream books.

Byron Katie, the best-selling author of <u>Loving What Is</u>: *four questions that can change your life* and <u>I Need Your Love – Is That True?</u>, has created a whole self-help movement based on four comparable, *familiar* questions. These questions are designed to change the way we perceive and think about people and situations in our lives which cause us pain. By following her four-question sequence, one is able to free oneself from thoughts which are at the source of one's suffering. For example, if I think "my wife doesn't care about me because she prefers to go out with her friends," then I ask myself, according to Katie, these four questions in order to get to the bottom of my incorrect perception so I can halt my suffering. (The bold font sentences are Katie's and the others are my interpretation according to living form as well as her elaborations from her book.)

1. **Is it** (the thought of my wife not caring about me) **true?**
The What? The situation as I think it to be.
2. **Can I absolutely know that it is true?**
The How? The questioning of how my thought processes work such as: do I know for sure what is in her best interest? And how I judge her? If she preferred to go out with me, would I be happier?
3. **How do I react when I believe that thought?**
The Why? Where do the feelings hit me? How do I treat myself when I have these thoughts?
4. **Who would I be without the thought?**
The Who? How would I treat others differently without this thought?

To put the four levels into really clear and simple terms:
the what? the situation;
the how? my thought processes;
the why? my feelings and reaction;
the who? *who I am* in a pure state of being therefore without my upsetting thought.

It is amazing that an entire self-help method can arise out of the four levels/questions. However, it seems justified since these questions unfold so naturally and explain the actual steps which are required in the evolving of a thought-process. Notice how things flow from the concrete to the abstract. Creation logic is an excellent pedagogical tool.

A conscious application of living form is Otto Scharmer's U-Theory, a method of accessing new ideas for solving problems in business.** Management theorists have been trying to express new ways of approaching solutions to problems in business. Otto Scharmer argues that "we know a great deal about what leaders do and how they do it. But we know very little about the inner place, the source from which they operate. And it is this source that "Theory U" attempts to explore." Scharmer, an MIT professor, recommends a process of accessing "the source" – also called "presencing," a quasi-meditative state in which individuals divine the future direction of their business. Theory U is nothing other than using the process of creation logic for the purpose of working out problems in business through collective leadership. To access the "source," there are five steps: two steps for gaining information, one for inspiration, and two final steps for exploring the future and acting from a perspective of the whole.

** Scharmer was familiar with Rudolf Steiner's and Florin Lowndes' work before developing it into his U-Theory. This is quite an achievement since Steiner and Lowndes gave so few indications concerning the applicability of the model.

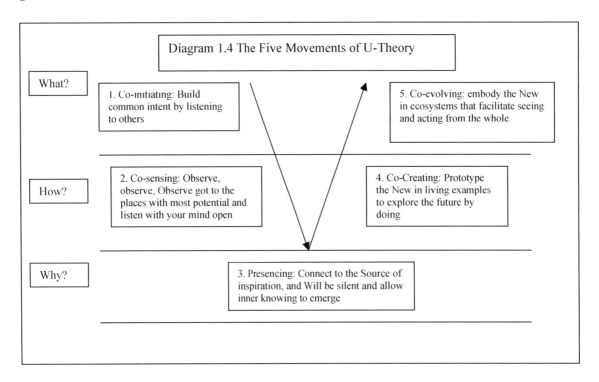

Diagram 1.4 The Five Movements of U-Theory

What?

1. Co-initiating: Build common intent by listening to others

5. Co-evolving: embody the New in ecosystems that facilitate seeing and acting from the whole

How?

2. Co-sensing: Observe, observe, Observe got to the places with most potential and listen with your mind open

4. Co-Creating: Prototype the New in living examples to explore the future by doing

Why?

3. Presencing: Connect to the Source of inspiration, and Will be silent and allow inner knowing to emerge

U-theory is living form turned upside-down. The four questions - albeit in a slightly truncated form resulting in only three levels and five steps - are evident:

    what? building;
    how? by observing with an open mind;
    why/who? connecting to your inner knowing/self;
    how? explore the future by doing;
    what? embody the new and do from the whole.

There is a clear movement from the concrete (building a common intent) to the abstract (presencing and inner knowing), and back to the concrete (co-evolving and embodying the new). I have heard that his seminars to heads of corporations are informative, clear, and inspiring. I wonder if Scharmer's present success with this model simply has to do with the fact that he uses an archetype of living form. The pedagogical values of living form may reform not only business management but our educational systems in the future.

All teachers know Ralph Tyler's <u>Basic Principles of Curriculum and Instruction</u>. Tyler's book has been in print since 1947 and one hears a lot of criticism about its limitations. But it is nevertheless still used. Is it possible that so little has changed in the educational field that this book is still a classic? Its staying-power in my opinion is due to the fact that Tyler has set up a nice archetypal structure akin to Byron Katie's. The schemas (of what? how? why? who?) seem to be as natural as the stages of the plant: seed, leaves, bud, and flower. Tyler breaks down the curriculum study into four domains which can easily be correlated to the archetypal four questions:

The foundation (what?): the purpose and main philosophy of the school
The activities (how?): teaching strategies in harmony with the purpose
The design of the program (why?): skills, sequence, integration, coherence according to the purpose
The evaluation of results (who?): Were the objectives and purposes realized?

Tyler has answered the four questions quite nicely in his explanation of the four domains: What? the foundation of ideas that the teachers work from; how? the scholastic activities used to make these ideas alive; why? the design of the program so the learning experience is coherent; who? the evaluation of whether the school's philosophy is realized! Can one find four better questions when considering the curriculum of a school? Many inconsistencies in a school's curriculum could be cleaned up by wrestling with these questions.

*

We have covered the basics of the seven-fold and four-fold living form thought-structures. In the next chapter we will delve further into various aspects of living with the intention of presenting this material over and over again from different perspectives. In chapter three, I present examples of living form as it appears in the *Book of Job*, *Matthew Gospel*, *The Lord's Prayer*, the original *Credo*, Plato's <u>Republic</u> and <u>Symposium</u>, two Blake poems, and a Robert Frost's "The Road Less Traveled," Lincoln's *The Gettysburg Address*, Neale Donald Walsch's <u>Conversations With God</u> (volume one), and R. W. Emerson's <u>Nature</u>.

Chapter Two, Methods of Living Form

In the last chapter living form manifests itself as the logic of all actions and as way of organizing our ideas. In this chapter it is important to give some foundational examples with which the reader may be familiar such as Aristotle and the five-paragraph essay before we cover the dynamic and imagination-stretching forms in work of Rudolf Steiner's the Philosophy of Freehood.

1. Goethe Once More: When practicing Goethe's method of thinking and researching, one studies *an object or process from the whole-to-the-parts*. In order to arrive at his model, or living idea of the archetypal plant, Goethe sketched the stages of growth in minute detail. He eventually arrived at two results. The first result was that he had developed a diagram of plant growth and the multiple laws and inter-relationships between the various stages of this growth. The second result was more subtle: Goethe stated that he had developed a capacity to think in these new laws and could behold the Idea behind all plants. Goethe claimed a new metamorphic thinking, one which he learned through years of study.

Goethe's metamorphic model can be studied and incorporated into our own thought-patterns. Follow, for example, a process which underlies the growth of a living being. Use Goethe's perspectives to see if patterns of living forms emerge. Goethe's archetypal plant form has four main movements: rhythm, climb and descent, polarity, and inversion. By acquiring an understanding of these four movements, we can begin to transform our thought patterns into a new metamorphic thinking; or in other words we can make our thoughts imitate living processes.

Rhythm is seen in the contraction and expansion of the seed, leaf, bud etc. Climb and descent follow the movement of the plant's growth up to the sun and back to the earth. Polarity is detectable in the mirroring of the rhythm as well as the inner aspects (function) of the leaf and fruit, both of which are responsible for the nourishment of the plant. Inversion occurs with the flower and signals a change from the more outward life processes of the leaf and bud to the more hidden processes of the pistil and fruit.

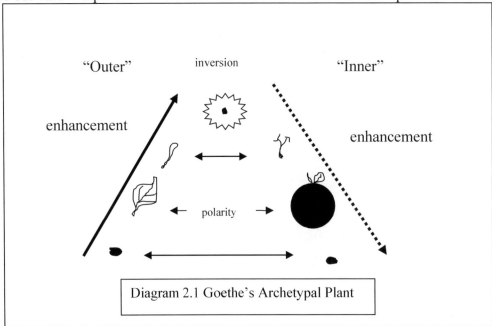

Diagram 2.1 Goethe's Archetypal Plant

Goethe viewed the flower as a highly differentiated leaf, and the seed as a crumpled, dry leaf, but both are leaves in different forms. These *subtle repetitions* at various levels create the philosophical basis behind living form in that one need not say something new, just recast the same idea from different perspectives. In writing or thinking with Goethe's model as our guide, we can organically grow successive ideas. Or, as Plato puts it as quoted by Orsini:

> "Every discourse must be composed in the likeness of a *living being* with a body of its own as it were so as not to be headless or feetless, but to have a middle and members arranged in fitting relation to each other and to the whole." It may be noted that what is generally considered an essential point of organic unity is not mentioned here: i.e., that an alteration of a part, whether by addition or removal, involves the alteration of the whole. [3]

Ideally speaking, our writing would imitate the rhythm, enhancement, and polarity of a living organism.

Goethe's model should not be seen simply as an abstraction because it shows the actual inter-relationships of life and growth. Goethe said that behind each phenomenon is an idea that always remains unchanging. We want to feel that our work has an inner coherence. Authors, in order to make their writing organic and living, would write with polarity and climb and descent in mind. These laws of life abstracted from the plant become the laws of logik of the heart as we shall see in some canonical writings in chapter three.

2. Another Look at the Four-Levels of Creation Logic: Let's take another look at of the four levels: what? how? why? and who? In chapter one, we covered several applications of creation logic by other authors. We focus now in on the various qualities of these levels.

Keep in mind that creation logic has two aspects: 1) it is the logic of all actions in that all actions follow the four-leveled sequence; and 2) creation logic can be used to analyze or categorize four points of view of an object or an idea. It should be emphasized that the first aspect of creation logic is fixed since actions require a certain sequence of events to occur while the second aspect is *malleable* (flexible applications) because the analysis of an object can be adapted to the point of view(s) being emphasized. In the university example in the first chapter, one could easily change one's perspective and make a new four-leveled schema with the professors on the Who? level, and results of the research on the what? level. It all depends on what is being emphasized.

Pizza making was used before for the 1st definition because it follows the sequence of what? how? why? who? while the second definition was used to define the various aspects of a university: name of the university (who?), professors (why?), graduate students/researchers (how?), and buildings/labs (what?). In the pizza making example no changes can be made because there is a certain sequence of events that comes naturally with all our actions.

In the diagram below it is important to consider the various themes of each of the four levels. Let's go over the qualities of four levels of creation logic:

> the what-level has a physical or static quality;
> the how-level a dynamic or living quality;
> the why-level a feeling or intentional aspect;
> the who-level a thinking or identifying or self-conscious aspect.

The perspectives create a movement from the concrete-formal (what?) to the abstract essential (who?).

---

[3] Orsini, <u>Organic Unity in Ancient and Later Poetics</u>, page 35. Orsini is expanding on Plato's quote from *Phaedrus*.

12

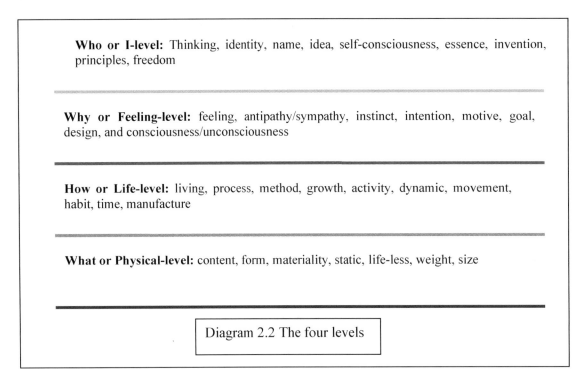

Who or I-level: Thinking, identity, name, idea, self-consciousness, essence, invention, principles, freedom

Why or Feeling-level: feeling, antipathy/sympathy, instinct, intention, motive, goal, design, and consciousness/unconsciousness

How or Life-level: living, process, method, growth, activity, dynamic, movement, habit, time, manufacture

What or Physical-level: content, form, materiality, static, life-less, weight, size

Diagram 2.2 The four levels

Now, the cycle of a new idea follows a broader sequence of creation logic. The main idea flows from the I-level down to the physical level (materials), and goes back again up to the "realized idea," which is at the I-level. Nearly everything we do can be broken down into these creative archetypes. It is a process of how an idea becomes incarnate.

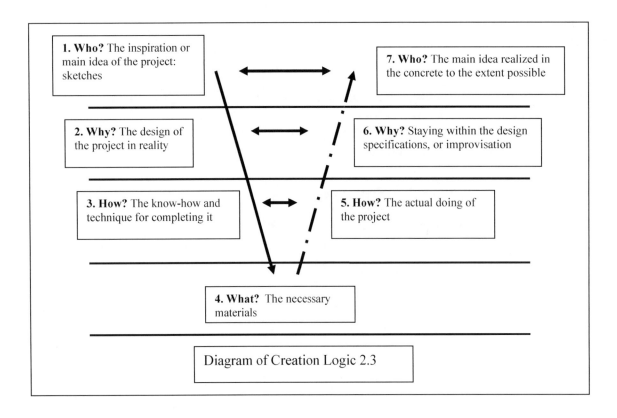

1. Who? The inspiration or main idea of the project: sketches

7. Who? The main idea realized in the concrete to the extent possible

2. Why? The design of the project in reality

6. Why? Staying within the design specifications, or improvisation

3. How? The know-how and technique for completing it

5. How? The actual doing of the project

4. What? The necessary materials

Diagram of Creation Logic 2.3

This diagram is the expanded version of the creation logic process. The left side shows that, in order for an idea to become manifest, we need four levels to be realized. Leonardo Da Vinci's helicopter was just an idea (sketch) which required the why? (a realistic design), and the how? (the engineering competence and technique), and the what? (the proper materials), before we can start to ascend to the process of making it. Leonardo's model had a corkscrew for a propeller which wouldn't have worked, and the materials available in those days would not have served the situation much better. This diagram aids in understanding what is needed in order for something to be materialized.

The important notion to take away from this section is that the creation process is often the reverse of natural process (archetypal plant starts on the physical level). In summary the creation process begins with an Idea, becomes a specific design, a method of construction is devised and materials are chosen. Then the materials are assembled, the object is constructed, the product is used for the purpose for which it was intended, so a goal is achieved.

3. Systematizers of Living Form – Lowndes and O'Neil: Let us now focus in on the pioneers and background information of living form. After learning about this method I wanted to know why there were no books or articles concerning this topic. Let us just say as most things in life, even the simplest of things can be clouded by personalities, historical circumstance, and conflicts.

Rudolf Steiner (1861-1925) started researching the importance of a spiritual method of thinking and writing in his late teens according to Florin Lowndes. After being a researcher of Goethe's scientific works, he went on to write books and give lectures on a multitude of topics. There was evidently an occult rule (that very advance spiritual adepts must follow) which forbade Steiner to speak openly about what he knows unless asked or invited. Instead he used examples from the Bible and other disciplines to illustrate and hint at this new living form. He never disclosed the details of the living form in his own work, but challenged his followers to discover it.

George O'Neil (1906-88) had been given a unique education in Europe and America. George traveled to Europe with his wealthy family, who were close friends with, and on occasion patrons to, the expatriate writers, Hemingway, Ezra Pound, and other artistic luminaries such as G. Antheil. (The O'Neil siblings included George's sister Barbara who was the grandmother in the movie, Gone with the Wind, and his brother Horton who was a Hollywood set designer.) George later went on a spiritual quest in which he studied Rudolf Steiner's work in Switzerland. Over decades of study, he made his first discoveries of living form in Steiner's books. Evidently George was confident enough to teach courses on lecturing in living form, reading in living form, and meditating, but he never wrote a book or discourse on the actual technique and its importance. Holding study groups for decades in the United States, he had to stop public teaching after he realized Anthroposophists of the 1960s and 70s were not ready to internalize this new thinking.

Florin Lowndes (1935 b.), a monumental artist by profession, had studied with George in the mid-1970s. He also kept up the tradition of trying to teach Steiner's living form in small study groups and in college classes. Lowndes eventually published Das Erwecken des Herz-denkens in 1998, the first book on living form, written unfortunately in the obscure verbiage of the Anthroposophical Society, a crusty organization committed to preserving Steiner's heritage in Basel, Switzerland - a kind of Sturbridge Village of Theosophy. Since George's discovery of Steiner's use of the living form method in the early 1950's till Lowndes' book, nearly half a century went by. Lowndes has made available George's research, which otherwise would have fallen into complete obscurity. I still have the sense that the few knowers of living form, both here and in Europe, feel a need to maintain the occult mood around what should, by now, be a well-publicized method.

George's written presentations of living form were done on mimeographed sheets which he handed out to his friends and study partners. They were more than adequate for the times they were printed, but appear now to be simplistic sketchings of Steiner's work. With modern technology coming to the rescue, Lowndes has republished Steiner's original German texts with colorful and pedagogical diagrams in the margins, which aid study and meditation while reading. Similar editions are destined to come out in English eventually.

Despite lacking materials for teaching living form, I experimented with what I learned from Lowndes and O'Neil about living form by giving assignments in high school and college settings. I believe that living form can bring a new playfulness to the way we think about our own work and the work of others. I have seen in my classroom that living form invigorates students' writing, and allows for very deep levels of discussion of content, form, and of course, living-form. In my experience living form is not a rigid set of rules for reading and writing. Rigid rules have existed since time immemorial and we certainly don't need more. Living form gives the art of writing new compositional options. The main attribute of living form is its flexibility; it gives authors a whole plethora of ideas for shaping the compositional element of their work. In this sense, writing becomes like painting, that is, a true art of organizing ideas with proportion and color.

When Rudolf Steiner set out to write a book, he had all the chapters, paragraphs and sentences in his mind's eye before he put pen to paper. If he wrote, for example, an essay consisting of seven paragraphs, he constructed it so that each paragraph would stand in polarity to the others: thus the 1st is polar to the 7th paragraph; the 2nd to the 6th ; and 3rd to the 5th; with the 4th standing alone in the middle. The principles of this compositional method are fairly simple; however, each author is attempting to bring elements of their work into a uniquely meaningful organic unity. After bringing these simple principles to students, I was amazed how quickly they felt a kinship to this idea-art. It speaks to something deep inside our psyche as the human-being's seven-fold form becomes the measure of all things.

4. Aristotle's Gift: Aristotle contributed much to Western thought: logic, rhetoric, the form of plays and arguments, scientific thinking, categories and so on. There should be no surprise that aspects of his teachings are at the foundation of living form. On occasion I find scholars who describe aspects of living form but of course don't realize it. According to Aristotle scholar T. A. Robinson, Aristotle used a five-fold living form for scientific treatises.[4]

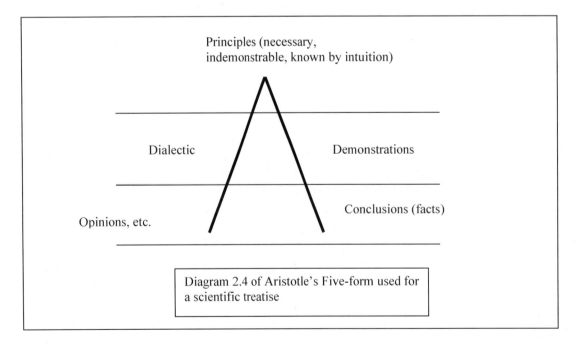

Principles (necessary, indemonstrable, known by intuition)

Dialectic   Demonstrations

Opinions, etc.   Conclusions (facts)

Diagram 2.4 of Aristotle's Five-form used for a scientific treatise

---

[4] <u>Aristotle in Outline</u>, (Hackett Publishing Company: 1995) p.41

Aristotle's model moves from the concrete to the abstract (Principles) back down to the concrete. This method follows a kind of archetypal pattern with certain necessary steps. This model trickled down into American schooling as a format for essays and debates. Some educators have modified the traditional format and theme of the five paragraphs. The only constant is that teachers still require their students to use a five paragraph essay to address questions in social studies courses.

The five paragraph essay follows a nearly identical form to the one Aristotle recommended for scientific treatises. Here is an outline of the rules for the five-paragraph essay so commonly found in school to this very day:

1. Introduction: a thematic overview of the topic, and introduction of the thesis;

2. Narration: a review of the background literature to orient the reader to the topic; also, a structural overview of the essay;

3. Affirmation: the evidence and arguments in favor of the thesis;

4. Negation: the evidence and arguments against the thesis; these also require either "refutation" or "concession";

5. Conclusion: summary of the argument, and association of the thesis and argument with larger, connected issues. Reworded thesis

There must be some attraction that people have to the five paragraph essay. Once we know to look for form it is easy to see. By comparing each element of the whole book or play, we come to some idea of its form or in our case living-form. In our quest for understanding ever more complicated examples of living form, it helps to consider first, places where it is already common place in our culture.

The five act play has an archetypal structure which allows for an easy analysis of its form: 1) exposition, 2) rising action, 3) climax, 4) falling action, 5) denouement. There is nothing more organic than these simple structures which follow the qualities of creation logic and the polarities of living form.

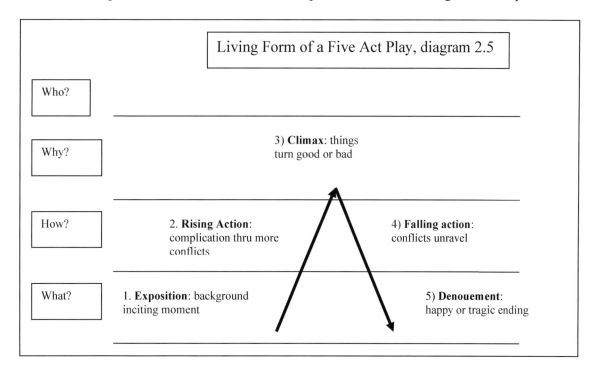

Living Form of a Five Act Play, diagram 2.5

Who?

Why?

How?

What?

3) **Climax**: things turn good or bad

2. **Rising Action**: complication thru more conflicts

4) **Falling action**: conflicts unravel

1. **Exposition**: background inciting moment

5) **Denouement**: happy or tragic ending

Important inherited forms were evidently created according to the inversion, polarity and intensification of organic thinking. What is truly amazing is that so much of Shakespeare, Greek tragedies, and early drama lived in this wave-like process as if unconsciously keeping us linked to a life-bringing archetypal form until the 1700s.

5. The Director's Consciousness: What is the value of knowing such structures? According to Michael Chekov[5], the famous acting coach, each act presents a change in the psychological state of the characters. The first act demands a different inner gesture than the final act. Chekov writes that these fine differences (metamorphoses) in psychological states of, for example, Hamlet and other characters must be first understood, and then communicated by the actors to the audience. Actors communicate this experience of metamorphosis, if they themselves are able to see and compare the inner nature of each act of the play. Thus, the actors have to know how the first act relates to the fifth, the second to the fourth, and how the third act presents an "inversion" of the plot.

Chekov, in his approach, is consciously highlighting the *living form* of the play, where other directors, who are less conscious of the form, may be limited to executing a more linear understanding of the play. Living form is a state of comparative consciousness; it is active; it seeks the archetype and lives in a state of playfulness.

Seeing form requires us to think like a director. By sketching out the individual elements and comparing them, we begin to understand otherwise hidden aspects of great works of literature. The director or author of a play tries to see the content (what is said) and the form (how it said and in what context) so that the inner, living dynamic can be communicated to the actors. A good director is someone who sees and understands the significance of the *form of the whole play.*

Michael Chekov spoke about how polarity is the foundation of theater:

> In any true piece of art, the beginning and the end are, or should be, *polar in principle*. All of the main qualities of the first section should *transform* themselves into their opposites in the last section. It is obvious, of course, that the beginning and the end of a play cannot be defined merely as the first and last scenes; beginning and end in themselves usually embrace a series of scenes.[6]

The study of dramatic works allows us to enter into the inner shifts and dramatic moods of the play. Build up, suspense, transformation of character, resolution, unfolding of the plot, are all part of theatrical process. In the diagrams of living form it is easy to see how the first half is polar to the second half; how the mid-point announces a transformation in the plot.

The structure, as Chekov said, means nothing without the attention of the writer. By adding the transformative or polar quality to the essay we can achieve, according to Chekov, the art of transformation.

Living form presupposes three inter-relationships: 1) the logical unfolding of the plot or argument, 2) the turning point, and 3) polarity. Chekov notes on how the director must use his intuition in order to sense these gestures and principles in the play and in this living frame of mind actors are able to communicate the inner transformations of the characters over the course of the play.

6. Writing in Form: The new aspect comes with this new awareness of polarity. We could, therefore, *tweak* the five-paragraph essay so that the polarity and transformation were more intentional. The accepted format above could be expanded into more general gestures, e.g., instead of narration and affirmation, we could try to see how paragraphs #2 and #4 could mirror each other. Steiner gave a series of questions which capture the gesture and polarity. In the example below, the inner gesture of the five-paragraph essay is now represented by a more living form:

---

[5] The famous acting coach was also nephew of the Russian playwright Anton as well as one of the first theorists of living form. In his To the Actor Chekov outlines his technique. Throughout the book he quotes Steiner and Goethe, the two mothers of living form.

[6] To The Actor, (Routlege: 2003) Chapter 8, The Composition of the Performance; p. 94.

Paragraph 1. What?
Paragraph 2. How?
Paragraph 3. Why?
Paragraph 4. How?
Paragraph 5. What?

By recasting the old form in terms of the new form, we can bring a new aesthetic consciousness of living form to our work. There are already some good suggestions in place such as the transformation of the thesis statement in the first paragraph into the reworded thesis in the 5th paragraph. The third paragraph needs to fulfill the function of turning the argument inward! If paragraph two develops the theme, then in order to create the proper mood for paragraph three, the author might state his own *personal* opinion. This would create a transition in paragraphs one and two, which are the general aspects of the essay, to a more specific or personal perspective in paragraphs three through five!

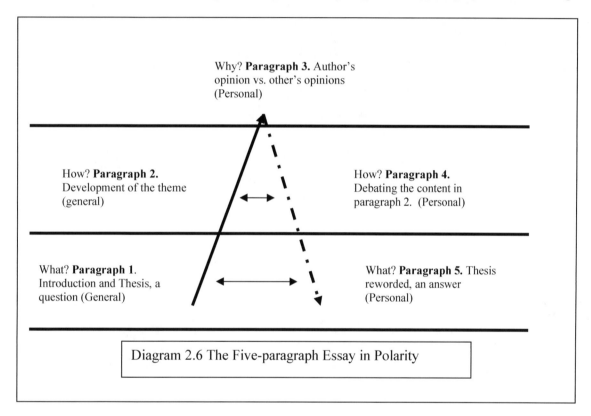

Why? **Paragraph 3.** Author's opinion vs. other's opinions (Personal)

How? **Paragraph 2.** Development of the theme (general)

How? **Paragraph 4.** Debating the content in paragraph 2. (Personal)

What? **Paragraph 1.** Introduction and Thesis, a question (General)

What? **Paragraph 5.** Thesis reworded, an answer (Personal)

Diagram 2.6 The Five-paragraph Essay in Polarity

Here we have a possible alternative to the linear way most writing is done. By keeping the inter-relations of the paragraphs in our mind, we can tweak the form of our essays without substantially altering the accepted formats. The questions (what? how? etc.) serve to help us be aware of polarity. The "climb and descent" diagram gives our work a picture out of which we can write and make adjustments to the inner dynamic of our work. As we become more proficient in this diagramming method, students and teachers alike can start to critique each other's work in terms of content and form. By expanding our awareness of polarity by starting with the simplest of writing exercises, we can work toward a renewal of dead inherited forms by returning the archetypal principles which brought them into being in the first place.

Below is a list of the basic living forms. So far we have covered examples of a five-form and six-form. We saw a sketch of the <u>Philosophy of Freehood</u> and its lengthy thought-forms (chapter one was sketched in some detail). The reader may find this section a little overwhelming in its complexities and should simply try to glean from the overall concept of living form that it exists in variety of works.

18

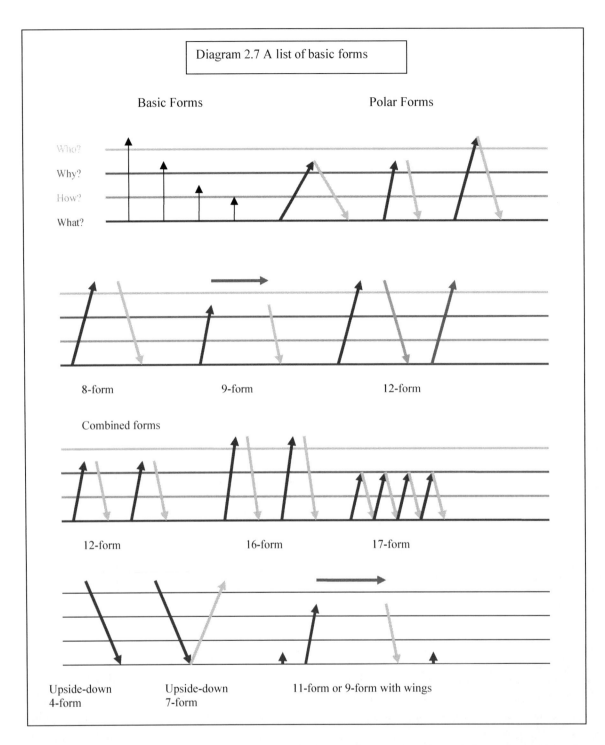

Diagram 2.7 A list of basic forms

Basic Forms   Polar Forms

Who?
Why?
How?
What?

8-form   9-form   12-form

Combined forms

12-form   16-form   17-form

Upside-down   Upside-down   11-form or 9-form with wings
4-form   7-form

7. The Training Manual of Living Form: Rudolf Steiner wrote <u>The Philosophy of Freehood</u>*** in 1893. He had several intentions in writing it. Steiner's loftiest intention was to write a training manual for thinking in the levels of creation logic; the chapters and paragraphs and sentences were to flow through

---

*** <u>The Philosophy of Freehood</u> is the most recent title of my translation of Steiner's <u>Die Philosophy der Freiheit</u> (GA 4). There are numerous translations since the turn of the century most of them available online at www.Philosophyoffreedom.com Steiner's book has other titles such as <u>The Philosophy of Spiritual Activity</u>, <u>Intuitive Thinking as A Spiritual Path</u>: *a philosophy of freedom*, and simply <u>The Philosophy of Freedom</u>. None of these translation attempt to grasp the living form.

the four levels of creation logic and thereby serve as a model for the new type of thinking. Steiner's secondary intention was to present a sound freedom-philosophy which argues that:
1) our human thinking is adequate to the task of knowing everything, since everything consists of thought (against Kantianism or dualism)
2) we are able to act freely out of intuition and create new ethical ideas in spite of the fact our being is conditioned by society, religion, family, and gender (against determinism).

Steiner's four-level method of writing was discovered long after his death, since during his lifetime none of his students asked him about his special method of writing. George O'Neil worked out the basic scales of living form, immersing himself in Goethean botanical studies and in Steiner's own books and claims of an "organic-living" method.[7]

What did George do? He put Steiner's philosophical style into a color-filled musical score. The colors represent the movement from concrete to abstract as well as the levels of polarity. George put the living form into a workable four-perspective system which allows authors and readers to scan written work and inter-relate their inner dynamic!

Rudolf Steiner composed his Philosophy of Freehood in a grand German style reminiscent of a great Beethoven symphony. Some chapters have about fifty paragraphs, which climb and descend in colored lines like the waves on a cardiogram. In contrast to his other books, which are quite short, the Philosophy of Freedom has long thought-waves which the reader can study and use/apply in their own work. One should not be intimidated by such long forms. Each chapter is designed to expand our limits of what living form can be. They are profound exercises in creation logic of the new thinking.

The book was written in three parts. The first two parts have seven chapters each making up the main thought-picture of the book. The third part is one chapter called the *Consequences of Monism*. The chapters of the book answer the questions: what? how? why? who? why? how? what? - if not literally, at least in gesture.

---

[7] Anyone searching for literature about the subject will be disappointed. Outside of Lowndes' Das Erwecken des Herzdenkens not one Steiner scholar carried the torch of living form. Lowndes has never made the entire corpus of George O'Neil's research available.

20

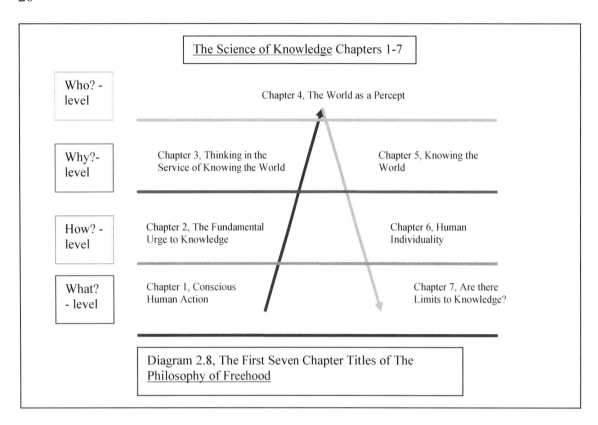

The Science of Knowledge Chapters 1-7

Who? - level

Chapter 4, The World as a Percept

Why?- level

Chapter 3, Thinking in the Service of Knowing the World

Chapter 5, Knowing the World

How? - level

Chapter 2, The Fundamental Urge to Knowledge

Chapter 6, Human Individuality

What? - level

Chapter 1, Conscious Human Action

Chapter 7, Are there Limits to Knowledge?

Diagram 2.8, The First Seven Chapter Titles of The Philosophy of Freehood

Each chapter has a different form. The living-form scales usually move up and down the four levels, although some only reach up to three levels such as chapter 2, 7, 13. There are no chapters which have asymmetrical or two-level forms. Steiner designed the Philosophy of Freehood so that individuals would borrow these forms for their own writings. One can see the larger forms consist of smaller ones sometime connected, other times not. There is a science of thought-forms that was extracted from Steiner's work.

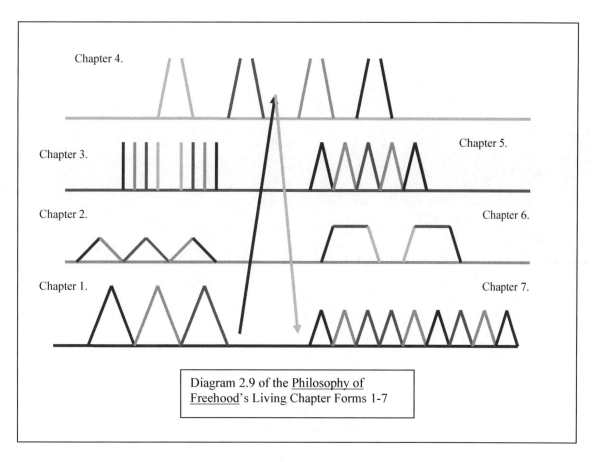

Diagram 2.9 of the Philosophy of Freehood's Living Chapter Forms 1-7

Steiner made the living forms (polarities and all) within his book challenging to decipher in that some familiarity with the forms is necessary to decode them. In contrast, I endeavored to present my synopses and catchwords of chapter one (diagram below) in a reader friendly manner. Each wave has been assigned a color representing the theme of the chapter. We have the three main parts of chapter one: 1. 2. 3.

The reader should also make note that the questions of the levels of creation logic (what? how? why? and who?) are given new designations. The pattern of creation logic for chapter one consists of "question" (what?), "answer" (how?), "reasoning" (why?), and "conclusion" (who?).* All these elements lend themselves to a deeper understanding of the content, form, and significance of Steiner's work, but for now I just want the reader to consider the colors and polarity.

---

* See the Study Guide.

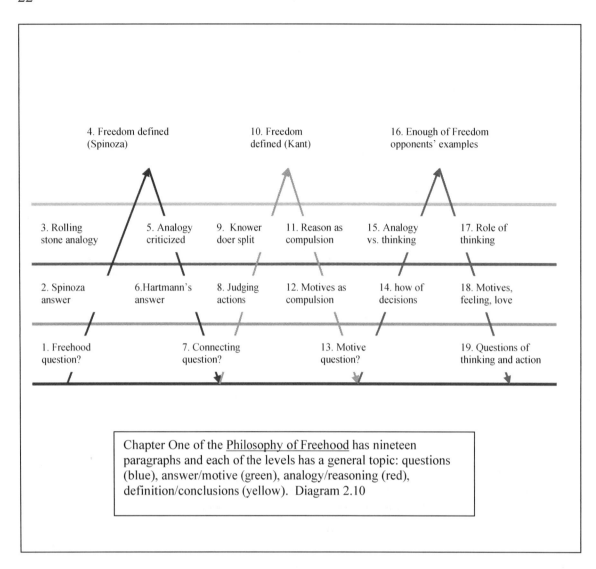

4. Freedom defined (Spinoza) 10. Freedom defined (Kant) 16. Enough of Freedom opponents' examples

3. Rolling stone analogy 5. Analogy criticized 9. Knower doer split 11. Reason as compulsion 15. Analogy vs. thinking 17. Role of thinking

2. Spinoza answer 6. Hartmann's answer 8. Judging actions 12. Motives as compulsion 14. how of decisions 18. Motives, feeling, love

1. Freehood question? 7. Connecting question? 13. Motive question? 19. Questions of thinking and action

Chapter One of the Philosophy of Freehood has nineteen paragraphs and each of the levels has a general topic: questions (blue), answer/motive (green), analogy/reasoning (red), definition/conclusions (yellow). Diagram 2.10

8. How to Read for Living Form: How do we now experience this living form? The first step is learning how to read the work of others with the precepts of living form. In deciphering living form, we always start with viewing the whole work and then delving into its component parts, just as a musician does when learning to play a new piece. They will initially attempt to play it in its entirety, and then focus their attention on particularly difficult sections.

Condensing and distilling are essential activities of making living form visible. By distilling the concepts in each paragraph or chapter, the reader is able to master the content and, in turn, is able to recognize the form more easily. Finding and creating skeletons of a text give the reader (and writer) greater ownership and insight, since they are able to scan how the parts relate to each other and to the whole. To know a great work of literature, it helps to take it apart and put it back together. The condensing of Steiner's Philosophy of Freehood will give us models for living form's thought-scales. It may not be a "great work" of literature, but it is a book designed for training us to think in living form. ♥

♥ It is interesting to see that Steiner's first six books cover identical themes. Some of the books even have identical chapter titles. This gives credence to the idea that his was trying to educate people in a new thinking since the significant difference between his books is the ordering of the ideas not their contents.

The best way to grasp living form is to sketch it out in pictures. I will introduce the method I learned, and hope that it will inspire others to come up with new and unique ways of presenting living form. In the analysis of the *Preface to the new revised 1918 edition* of the Philosophy of Freehood, we will cover the organic structure at the paragraph level, as was done with chapter one. Keep in mind that Steiner's living form can either be really obvious, or is so subtle one doubts its existence. We will begin by looking at the text, making synopses, and placing them into living form.

I have numbered the paragraphs and sentences of the *Preface*. The notation 1/9 refers to the first paragraph which contains nine sentences. There are six paragraphs altogether. Each paragraph is followed by my own synopsis and I recommend that the reader makes their own synopses in order to gain a fluid understanding of the process.

PREFACE TO THE REVISED 1918 EDITION of the Philosophy of Freehood by Rudolf Steiner

1/9
1. There are two root-questions of the human soul-life toward which everything is directed that will be discussed in this book.
2. The first question is whether there is a possibility to view the human being in such a way that this view proves itself to be the support for everything else which comes to meet the human being through experience or science and which gives him the feeling that it could not support itself.
3. Thereby one could easily be driven by doubt and critical judgment into the realm of uncertainty.
4. The other question is this: can the human being, as a creature of will, claim free will for himself, or is such freehood a mere illusion, which arises in him because he is not aware of the workings of necessity on which, as any other natural event, his will depends?
5. No artificial spinning of thoughts calls this question forth.
6. It comes to the soul quite naturally in a particular state of the soul.
7. And one can feel that something in the soul would decline, from what it should be, if it did not for once confront with the mightiest possible earnest questioning the two possibilities: freehood or necessity of will.
8. In this book it will be shown that the soul-experiences, which the human being must discover through the second question, depend upon which point of view he is able to take toward the first.
9. The attempt is made to prove that there is a certain view of the human being which can support his other knowledge; and furthermore, to point out that with this view a justification is won for the idea of freehood of will, if only that soul-region is first found in which free will can unfold itself.

SYNOPSIS 1/9: there are two questions (view question and freehood question), and the freehood question depends on point of view toward the first question.

2/5
1. The view, which is under discussion here in reference to these two questions, presents itself as one that, once attained, can be integrated as a member of the truly living soul life.
2. There is no theoretical answer given that, once acquired, can be carried about as a conviction merely preserved in the memory.
3. This kind of answer would be only an illusory one for the type of thinking, which is the foundation of this book.
4. Not such a finished, fixed answer is given, rather a definite region of soul-experience is referred to, in which one may, through the inner activity of the soul itself, answer the question livingly anew at any moment he requires.
5. The true view of this region will give the one who eventually finds the soul-sphere where these questions unfold that which he needs for these two riddles of life, so that he may, so empowered, enter further into the widths and depths of this enigmatic human life, into which need and destiny impel him to wander.

24

SYNOPSIS 2/5: The view can be integrated, not memorized, in a living manner through a living soul activity.

3/1
1. - A kind of knowledge seems thereby to be pointed to which, through its own inner life and by the connectedness of this inner life to the whole life of the human soul, proves its validity and usefulness.

SYNOPSIS 3/1: This knowledge seems to have validity for soul life.

4/10
1. This is what I thought about the content of the book when I wrote it down twenty-five years ago.
2. Today, too, I have to write down such sentences if I want to characterize the purpose of the thoughts of this book.
3. At the original writing I limited myself to say no more than that, which in the utmost closest sense is connected with the two basic questions, referred to here.
4. If someone should be amazed that he finds in the book no reference to that region of the world of spiritual experience which came to expression in my later writings, he should bear in mind that in those days I did not, however, want to give a description of results of spiritual research, but I wanted to build first the foundation on which such results could rest.
5. This Philosophy of Freehood does not contain any such specific spiritual results any more than it contains specific results of other fields of knowledge; but he who strives to attain certainty for such cognition cannot, in my view, ignore that which it does indeed contain.
6. What is said in the book can be acceptable to anyone who, for whatever reasons of his own, does not want anything to do with the results of my spiritual scientific research.
7. To the one, however, who can regard these spiritual scientific results, as something toward which he is attracted, what has been attempted here will also be important.
8. It is this: to prove how an open-minded consideration of these two questions which are fundamental for all knowing, leads to the view that the human being lives in a true spiritual world.
9. In this book the attempt is made to justify cognition of the spiritual world before entering into actual spiritual experience.
10. And this justification is so undertaken that in these chapters one need not look at my later valid experiences in order to find acceptable what is said here, if one is able or wants to enter into the particular style of the writing itself.

SYNOPSIS 4/10: The book contains no results of either spiritual or scientific research, but it gives the foundation for results and proves the human being lives in a spiritual world, if the reader enters into the writing style.

5/5
1. Thus it seems to me that this book on the one hand assumes a position completely independent of my actual spiritual scientific writings; yet, on the other hand, it also stands in the closest possible connection to them.
2. These considerations brought me now, after twenty-five years, to republish the content of the text almost completely unchanged in all essentials.
3. I have only made somewhat longer additions to a number of sections.
4. The experiences I made with the incorrect interpretations of what I said caused me to publish comprehensive commentaries.
5. I changed only those places where what I said a quarter of a century ago seemed to me inappropriately formulated for the present time.
(Only a person wanting to discredit me could find occasion on the basis of the changes made *in this way*, to say that I have changed my fundamental conviction.)

SYNOPSIS 5/5:   The author republished the book with additions and commentaries because it was misunderstood.

6/6
1. The book has been sold out for many years.
2. I nevertheless hesitated for a long time with the completion of this new edition and it seems to me, in following the line of thought in the previous section, that today the same should be expressed which I asserted twenty-five years ago in reference to these questions.
3. I have asked myself again and again whether I might not discuss several topics of the numerous contemporary philosophical views put forward since the publication of the first edition.
4. To do this in a way acceptable to me was impossible in recent times because of the demands of my pure spiritual scientific research.
5. Yet I have convinced myself now after a most intense review of present day philosophical work, that as tempting as such a discussion in itself would be, it is for what should be said through my book, not to be included in the same.
6. What seemed to me necessary to say, from the point of view of the Philosophy of Freehood about the most recent philosophical directions can be found in the second volume of my Riddles of Philosophy.

SYNOPSIS 6/6: The new edition included no recent philosophical work, work which can be found in Riddles of Philosophy.

Below is a diagram of the six paragraphs of the *Preface* in their living form. First one sees the movement of creation logic from what? to the how? to the why? Second, we see the polarities in the synopses of paragraphs 1/9 and 6/6 (Content of the book); 2/5 and 5/5/ (methods: reading and changing the book); 3/1 and 4/10 (the value of the book). Rudolf Steiner composed all of his chapters in this fashion.

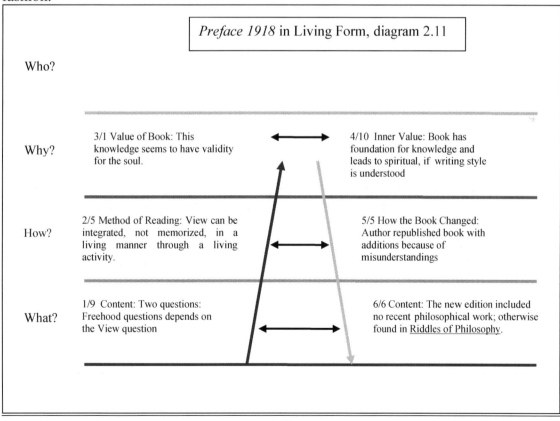

Let us review the process again. Read, take notes, and distil the essence of each paragraph. From this point it is possible to compare the elements and see how they relate to each other. Don't force relationships, let the content speak for itself.

In Chapter 3, I cover famous books, chapters and poems which were not consciously written in living form. Nevertheless, books such as Plato's <u>Republic</u> and the *Gospel of Matthew* contain living forms which have been discovered by scholars who studied them carefully.

9. A Goethean Approach to Literature?: The forms of the <u>Philosophy of Freehood</u> resemble a kind of platonic perfection and a new science of thinking. But for the average person what is the value of this method of condensing? In my experience, it makes difficult thought easy. Even if an author's form is not particularly living, it is an incredible pedagogical tool to condense (summarize) and analyze books or essays.

Can we use the method of living form to enter into the inner essence of someone else's work? In working with students, I found that we all have an unconscious and primal need to know that life and creativity correspond to some archetypal patterns in the universe. O'Neil found these patterns in many writers and in different forms. Were these patterns reflections of creative, universal rhythms? Recall the ribbons of Renaissance painting as an example that humanity has known about these wave-thoughts of creation logic on an unconscious level for centuries.

At university, we view literature from several critical perspectives such as Freudian or Marxist. Living form provides a new 'essentialist' approach to viewing the creations of others. The goal of the living form approach is not to apply rigidly the categories of creation logic. For example, in considering Madame Bovary one would normally study its plot, theme, development, the author's innovations and symbolism. However, Goethe's method would additionally ask the student to visualize the more fluid movement between these elements as is seen in the chapter intervals themselves as Goethe himself did in his scientific works. The Goethean task has to do with viewing the thoughts, phenomena, and art of authors, poets, playwrights, and musicians as they are.

If teachers would view books, plays, and poems through of living form's techniques and diagrams, students would learn to feel and see the interval quality of literature, nonfiction, and poetry. Goethe's method asks the reader *to survey, compare, and contrast in order to find the underlying method of composition of an author.*

There are many existing methods of analyzing literature. Marxist, Freudian, feminist and all contribute something important to our grasp of the work of great authors. However, Mortimer Adler's method outlined in <u>How to Read a Book</u> contains the first steps of a Goethean method: first read the book quickly through and grasp the main thesis, then read and take notes and see to what extent the thesis is supported in the book. The method of living form should take Adler's method one step further by researching the archetypal patterns in literature, patterns which help us understand the content and form in such a way they become inspiration for our own work.[8] Goethe's method of studying literature is purist approach to finding living-forms within what is written an approach which allows the forms to speak for themselves.

*

---

[8] Adler argues that instead of becoming experts or memorizers of the content, reading and discussion of great books should lead us to be creative. Adler complained about the methods of education in which students are taught fixed conclusions about the works of great authors (he pointed out Catholic Colleges and Leo Strauss's method as the culprits). Adler pointed out that philosophy grad schools usually don't produce philosophers but passive thinkers, and biology programs produce lab techs instead of natural scientific thinkers. To avoid the slave-mind-set of fixed conclusions, students should have a purist approach to reading and discussing, which I believe Adler delivers.

In the next chapter, there are examples of Goethe's method applied to the reading of great works of literature. The question remains whether great works also have great form. I covered great works which have canonical staying power in Western culture. I have my doubts on many levels whether certain works are truly organic as to whether I bent their form to fit Goethean Laws of Polarity and Enhancement. Some examples may only follow the organic logic in parts and aspects, but completely fail as living form as a whole. Some of the examples may be questionable especially since the chapters of Plato's <u>Republic</u> were decided by scholars centuries later and not by Plato himself. Readers will have to bring their own experience into this process of working with living form.

Chapter Three, Reading for Living Form

We have seen Steiner's quasi-mathematical approach to creating "perfect" living form. Now it is a question of whether such livingness has inspired the work of others. Hegel said that those who look for *Reason* in the world will eventually find *Reason* in the world. In grad school while reading great books I often wondered if a certain book had a living form similar to Steiner's. I analyzed chapters, paragraphs, and sentences in novels, poems, and philosophy books a process I found overwhelming. However, instead of giving up I kept in mind that it was Steiner's conscious intention to write in living form and I have been surprised by their discovery in scores of books and poems. Even where there is complete doubt about the structure of a text at the chapter or paragraph level, or where there are divisions of a text which the original author never intended (Bible or Plato's Republic), one can still find that later divisions were done with some innate sense of living form.

The highlighting of the living forms has three sources: my own reading and diagramming, hints given by friends, and scholarly summaries and discussions. I have read the selections many times in preparation for the diagrams. I have been particularly blessed in being able to find scholarly material which supports the structure of living form in the chosen texts. It is important that the living form is *not imposed upon* great books, but instead can be experienced as a reality within the structure of a book. A close and honest reading and charting of the chapters and thoughts of a text should suffice in the discernment of a structure of living form. I have done my best to accomplish this and have left open the possibility that some texts contain living form only *in part*, or that certain texts allow several workable if not contradictory forms.

Could it be that a portion of the pivotal works of Western Culture has a living form? Lowndes has mused that since the necessary invention of dead, logical thinking (Aristotle) which aided humankind's conquering the physical world, humankind has, at the same time, been seeking a living thinking* that will enable us to regain a unity to the world and each other. A unity we've practically destroyed through logical thinking. This seeking of a new thinking has expressed itself in an unconscious human need to express ideas in an archetypal thought-wave. We can never know for sure whether authors envisioned their works as whole, living documents; or, whether the inspirations in the form of the universal archetypes of creation logic simply streamed into their consciousness.

This method of reading highlights the climb and descent, polarity, and inversion of philosophic, religious, poetic, theatric, and non-fiction writing. The diagrams serve as models for picturing any text; however, not all will reveal a living form. Parts of books may have living forms. Some examples are certainly not as convincing as others. Living form can be experienced more as a "living feeling," since the inter-relationships are so subtle that they are almost vibrational in quality. The ultimate value of living form is for your own personal use. When we view the living form as it lives in the work of others, we have the opportunity to recognize it in ourselves *in potentia*.

---

* Living Thinking has been represented by the double-helix wave of genetics, by Eros or heart-thinking - symbolized as the Heart of Jesus - the divine proportions of art, and by fractals theory of the new ontology, and our transcendence of religious formalism into truly gentle, loving human beings.

Religious Texts:

> This is where the subjects are repeated, not in alternation, but in introversion; i.e. from opposite ends. In this case there will be as many subjects as there are pairs of introverted members. Suppose we have an example of four subjects. This will give us eight members, in which the 1st will correspond with the 8th; the 2nd with the 7th; the 3rd with the 6th; and the 4th with the 5th.[9]
> E. W. Bullinger

> Make the *heart* of this people fat,
> And make their *ears* heavy,
> And shut their *eyes*:
> Lest they see with their *eyes*,
> And hear with their *ears*
> And understand with their *heart*.
> —Isaiah 6:10

One would expect that the Bible must have some special form, after all it is God's Word. Cabbalists, the bible code folks, and the prophecy people find various secrets in our sacred text. My search has been for living form. Since I am only looking at the general *shifting* of topics, and not perfect sentence-for-sentence living forms, I have trusted that some attributes would appear. It is only natural to follow a living archetype in nearly all fairy tales, stories, or histories.

The work of E. W. Bullinger supports our notion of living form. Bullinger worked out of a tradition of biblical scholarship, which believed structure was essential to understanding the Bible at all levels. Where Steiner and his followers used Goethe's terms such as rhythm (Rhythmus), climb and descent (Steigerung), polarity (Polaritaet), and inversion (Umstuelpung), Bullinger wrote about *gradational, antithetic, constructed, introverted* structure of biblical writings. Bullinger's "introverted" is Steiner's inversion and polarity combined; and Bullinger's gradational and constructed laws of writing function more or less as Steiner's climb of creation logic. The only difference is the structure and quality of the levels (what?, how?, why?, who?), and that Bullinger did not find Goethean 'rhythm' in the biblical writings.

In this section several chapters of the <u>Bible</u>, and some prayers are covered. The Bible forms are drawn from the synopses of the unique <u>Bullinger Bible</u>. This particular Bible has very detailed breakdowns of the Bible chapters, which are singly supportive of the idea of living form. In fact, Bullinger completely ignored the traditional bible numbers and verses, which themselves were created only for convention and theological debates. By attempting to read the pure content of the bible, Bullinger came up with some challenging patterns.

Rudolf Steiner pointed to the living forms of the *Lord's Prayer*. His living form differs from the one used here. To his credit, he did give several competing versions of the organic form. Steiner often referred to living form in various religious terms: "Michaelic thinking," "Christ thinking," organic-living thinking. Steiner believed that a new form of thinking could unify the religions of the world because at some level all religious ideas discuss the same living forms whether they are in the worship service or in their understanding of the human being's ascension journey.

In any case, let us proceed to some biblical forms as they relate to Steiner's.

---

[9] <u>How to Enjoy the Bible</u> (Kregel Classics: Grand Rapids, MI, 1990) p. 203-204. E.W. Bullinger. In this book, Bullinger discusses his predecessors. Ancient Hebrew and Christian scholars such as Josephus and Origen said that they "discovered metres in the Hebrew original." Then follows a series of Jewish and protestant scholars.

The Old Testament Book of Job: The Bible is a long book. One could argue that I have chosen sections to fit Steiner's manner of thinking and composing with the intent of canonizing him. I use Bullinger because his work is so thorough and counters any of my own arbitrary notions of living form. His general summaries are easy to follow, and the more I read and compare his work to my own studies, the more I agree with him.

To my disappointment, the first five books of Moses, according to Bullinger, have next to no fully developed living forms in the Steinerian sense. Biblical forms come in *alternation* of theme in which a topic is simply repeated: A B C, A B C. Or as an introversion of a theme, A B C C B A, as would be the case with a fully developed living form. In order for a form to be living it must have the laws of inversion and polarity, otherwise it is a climb without a descent!

The *Book of Job* has an outstanding form. Let us first consider what a normal version of the Bible has to say. The Tyndale Bible[10] summarizes the *Book of Job* in seven sections:

1. The onset of Job's misery, 1:1 – 2:13
2. First set of speeches, 3:1 – 14:22
3. Second set of speeches, 15:1 – 21:34
4. Third set of speeches, 22:1 – 31:40
5. Elihu's speech, 32:1 – 37:24
6. The Lord's response to Job, 38:1 – 41: 34
7. The restoration of Job, 42:1 – 17

This summary given in the Tyndale Bible is straightforward. It is however, without any noticeable pattern. Bullinger's assessment disregards the typical Bible chapters. Bullinger looked for slight changes in tone and theme. For example, he breaks Job chapter 1 and 2 into several parts: 1:1–1:5 and 1:6 – 2:10 and again 2:11 – 2:13. Compare Bullinger's summary of the *Book of Job* to the Tyndale one:

1:1 – 1:5	Introduction. Historical
1:6 – 2:10	Satan's assault. Job stripped of all.
2:11 – 2:13	The three friends. Their arrival.
3:1 – 31:40	Job and his friends
32:1 – 37:24	The Ministry of Elihu
38:1 – 42:6	Job and Jehovah
42:7 – 42:9	The Three Friends. Their Departure.
42:10 – 42:13	Satan's Defeat. Job Blessed with Double.
42:14 – 42:17	Conclusion. Historical

One could argue that there is no reason for Bullinger to separate what Tyndale sees as a whole, "The onset of Job's misery" 1:1 – 2:13. Bullinger places his thematic breaks in places in which there is a change in theme. So it seems that Bullinger is placing the chapters in places where they actually belong; not because they evenly and mathematically divide up the books in a reader friendly manner.

The *Book of Job* stands as one of the few books of the Old Testament which has what Bullinger calls an *introverted* form. The majority of the Old Testament books have *alternation* as their organizing principle which has the climb aspect of living form, but not polarity. We see below how the *Book of Job* is a nice seven-form with wings.

---

[10] Holy Bible, Authorized King James Version, (Tyndale House Publishers, Wheaton Illinois: 1979)

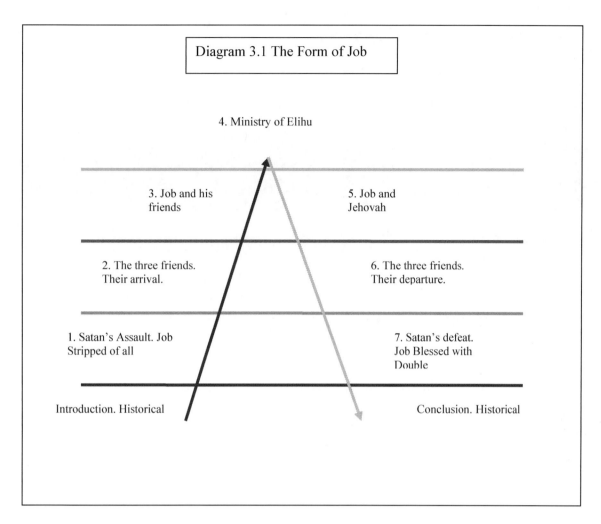

Diagram 3.1 The Form of Job

4. Ministry of Elihu

3. Job and his friends

5. Job and Jehovah

2. The three friends. Their arrival.

6. The three friends. Their departure.

1. Satan's Assault. Job Stripped of all

7. Satan's defeat. Job Blessed with Double

Introduction. Historical

Conclusion. Historical

The book starts with Satan's assault and ends with his defeat. On the how?-level we have the friends coming and going. On the why? or astral level, Job is in a discussion with his friends and Jehovah. In the mid-point, the Ministry of Elihu, Elihu is the mediator of the discussion with Job and friends, while he also introduces Jehovah in what Bullinger calls a "grand introversion." The Ministry of Elihu stands on its own at the ego or who? level. Those who are familiar with the *Book of Job* can feel the balance of the living form.

The *Book of Job* has quite a few "introverted" forms at the sentence or clause level. Bullinger gives this example which without further discussion one can surmise the basic laws:

Book of Job 1:1 – 5.

1 A man came to be in the land of Uz, whose name *was* Job; and this man came to be inoffensive and upright, and one that feared God, and eschewed evil.

2 And there were born unto him seven sons and three daughters.

3 His substance also was seven thousand sheep, and three thousand camels, and five hundred yoke of oxen, and five hundred she asses, and a very great house hold; so that this man was the greatest of all the men of the east.

4 And his sons went and feasted in their houses, every man his day; and sent and called for their three sisters to eat and to drink with them.

5 And it was so, when the days of their feasting came round about, that Job sent and sanctified them and rose up early in the morning, and offered up burnt offerings according to the number of them all: for Job said, "It may be that my sons have sinned and cursed God in their hearts." Thus did Job continually.

Bullinger's synopsis presents this six-form with polarities:
1. Job's character.
2. His sons and daughters. Their number.
3-. His possessions. Great.
-3. His position. Great.
4. His sons and daughters. Their unanimity.
5. Job's conduct.

The polarities are clear:

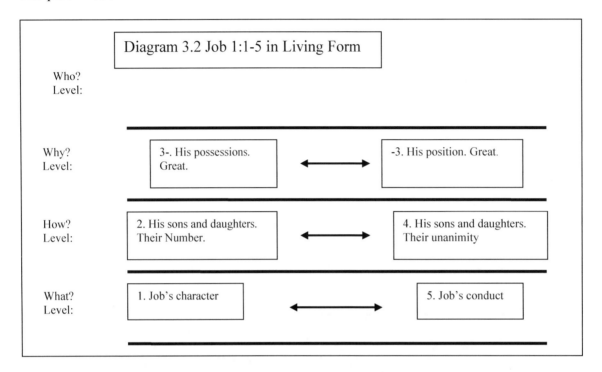

Bullinger breaks down line 3. into two parts: "his possessions" and "his position." Whether this contradicts his own methods, I can't say. Nevertheless, Bullinger has found the principle of polarity even on the sentence level of the Bible.

There may be some problems for the modern reader who doesn't see the significance of living form in the Bible. Is the Bible what it is, because of its form as well as its content? The *Book of Job* is considered a really important section in the OT, and possibly its living form has unconsciously drawn readers for centuries.

The Matthew Gospel: Bullinger gives outlines of the whole New Testament. What is striking is how the four canonical gospels have nearly the same form. It is hard to believe that no one noticed this before Bullinger. Let's look at *Mathew Gospels* as representative.

The *Gospel of Matthew* has twenty-eight chapters. Bullinger has divided it into eight distinct parts with two prefaces and conclusions: Preministerial, Post-ministerial, The Forerunners, and Successors. The main story is couched in prehistory and post history of Jesus. The main body of the Gospel has eight sections which mirror each other clearly:

Pre Ministerial 1: 1 – 2:23. Genealogy, Nativity, magi, Flight into Egypt and Herod

The Forerunner 3: 1 – 4. John the Baptist

The Baptism: with water 3: 5 – 17. John's Baptizing and speech to Pharisees, Jesus Baptized, God's voice and the dove

The Temptation: in the wilderness 4: 1 – 11.

The Kingdom 4: 12 – 7: 29. Jesus departs to Capernaum, "Kingdom of Heaven is at Hand", Sermon on the mount

The King   Proclaimed 8:1 – 16:20. Healing a leper, centurion, rebuke the winds, two possessions, Palsy, Mathew recruited, Fasting discussed, woman and his garment, ruler's daughter, etc.

The King   Rejected   16:21 – 20:34. Mainly discussions with his disciples: Jesus tells of his future death, disciples exorcism fails, and betrayal, little children blessed, etc.

The Kingdom 21: 1 – 26: 35. Enter Jerusalem interacts with people: temple incident, fig tree, criticizes Pharisees in front of crowd, Judgment Day, Ten Virgins, Plot to kill Jesus, anointing, Last Supper, Peter's denial

The Agony: in the garden 26: 36 – 46

The Baptism: of suffering (Death, Burial, and Resurrection) 26: 47 – 28: 15 Told to go to Galilee.

The Successors 28: 16- 18 Eleven disciples went to Galilee and Jesus spoke to them.

Post Ministerial 28: 19, 20 Go forth and Baptize all nations

Diagram 3.3 The Gospel of Matthew

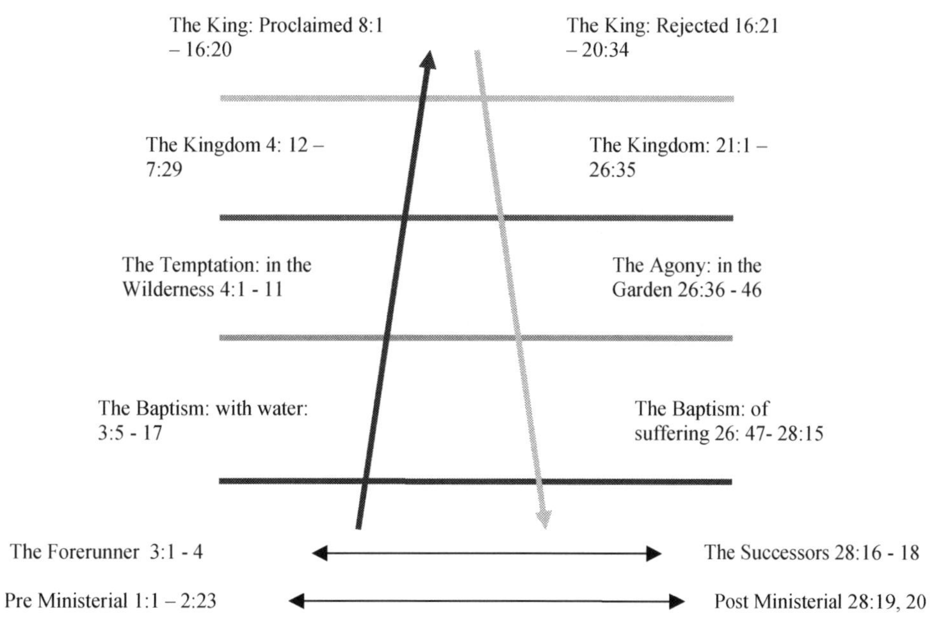

The two 'baptisms' start and conclude this *Gospel*. The polarity one finds in the contrast between outer and inner baptism, or preparation and completion. The temptation in the wilderness stands over against the garden agony. In the Wilderness section, he answers the devil three times and avoids temptation while in the Garden he prays three times in the company of his disciples. And in similar fashion to Plato's <u>Republic</u>, Jesus' teaching takes the central position in the Kingdom and King sections in the Gospel and from there slowly winds down.

The "King Rejected" section was at first difficult to figure out in the terms of the law of inversion. Is there a stark contrast or movement from the first half of Matthew to the second half to the extent that one can claim a true living form? Matthew 16: 21 starts:

> from that time forth began Jesus to shew his disciples, how that he must go unto Jerusalem, and suffer many things of the elders and chief priests and scribes, and be killed, and be raised again the third day.

It seems that Bullinger in dividing the book here, has touched on a point of inversion in that now Jesus foresees things to come i.e., the goal of the second half of the Gospel.

The *Gospel of Matthew* contains both the law of climb and descent, polarity, and inversion. Bullinger, of course, believes that such forms are God's method of communicating. Even if there have been slight alterations to the content over the centuries, the form itself has survived humanity's tampering with the Holy Writ.

Credo and Lord's Prayer, or reverse living forms:

> All formulas for meditation in the world's great religious societies throughout history have had their origins in "spiritual science." Analyze every true prayer that exists - word for word - and you will find it to be no arbitrary stringing together of words. Never has a mere blind impulse been followed to string together so many beautiful words. Not at all; rather, the great wise men have adopted these prayer forms from the wisdom teaching that is now called "spiritual science." Every true form of prayer was born of this great knowledge; and the great Initiate who founded Christianity - Christ Jesus - had in mind the seven principles of human nature when he taught His prayer, expressing in it the seven-principled nature of man.
> – Rudolf Steiner

There are many versions of the *Credo* and the *Lord's Prayer* in print. My first alternate version was Rudolf Steiner's rewrite of the *Lord's Prayer* which has nine lines instead of the traditional seven. Each line he expanded in order to explicate what he thought was its deeper meaning. The *Credo* seems to have gone through many changes and debates and today we have as many versions as there are churches.

I limit my discussion to the original version of the Nicene Creed of 325 A.D. This version had seven main clauses with an anathema added at the end. The anathema is quite un-organic and distracting so I left it out for purpose of living form analysis.

The *Credo* is a succinct statement of Christian faith with many versions depending on the current debate and emphasis of the theology of the time.* I am personally unaffected by the content, and have sought the form to the extent that it is living. It seems this earliest of version has "a purity" to it, when excluding its anathema.**

---

* A Wikipedia Article on the creed has the following to say: "The Nicene Creed of 325 explicitly affirms the <u>divinity of Jesus,</u> applying to him the term "God". The 381 version speaks of the Holy Spirit as worshiped and glorified with the Father and the Son. The <u>Athanasian Creed</u> describes in much greater detail the relationship between Father, Son and Holy Spirit. The <u>Apostles' Creed,</u> not formulated in reaction to Arianism, makes no explicit statements about the divinity of the Son and the Holy Spirit, but, in the view of many who use it, the doctrine is implicit in it."

** The anathema had these words, obviously not part of the body of the Credo: "But those who say: 'There was a time when he was not;' and 'He was not before he was made;' and 'He was made out of nothing,' or 'He is of another substance' or 'essence,' or 'The Son of God is created,' or 'changeable,' or 'alterable' - they are condemned by the holy catholic and apostolic Church."

There are seven clauses which can be divided into two halves. The first half presents God, His creation, and descent into the world as the incarnation; the second half is the ascent to heaven (from where he judges us). It concludes with the third member of the trinity, the Holy Ghost:

1. We believe in one God, the Father Almighty, Maker of all things visible and invisible.

2. And in one Lord Jesus Christ, the Son of God, begotten of the Father the only-begotten that is of the essence of the Father, God of God, Light of Light, very God of very God, begotten, not made, being of one substance with the Father;

3. By whom all things were made both in heaven and on earth;

4. Who for us men and for our salvation, came down and was incarnate and was made man;

5. He suffered, and the third day he rose again, ascended into heaven;

6. From thence he shall come to judge the quick and the dead.

7. And [believe] in the Holy Ghost.

The polarities are clear: sentences 1 and 7 are God and the Holy Ghost i.e., the un-incarnated aspects of the trinity. Sentences 2 and 6 describe Christ and his role as judge. Sentences 3 and 5 present the activities of creation and the crucifixion. Sentence 4 is the mid-point of Christ's process on earth as he became incarnate.

The form is upside-down! (Spirit into matter, and matter into spirit!) The polarities are subtle with the activities taking place in the central sentences (3 through 5) and the beliefs (creed part) in sentences 1, 2, 6, and 7. In microcosm the form of the Creed mirrors the incarnation aspect of the Christ!

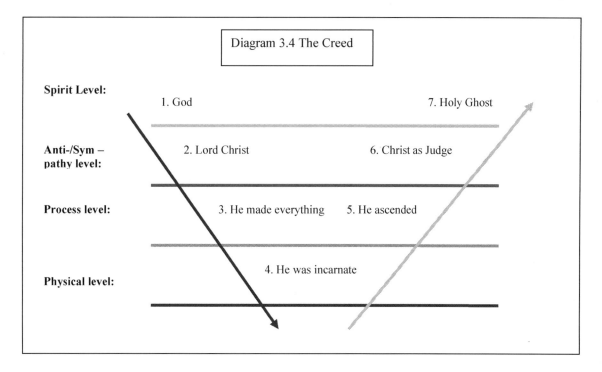

Diagram 3.4 The Creed

What about the current *Apostle's Creed*? It has twelve sentences; each Apostle dictated one line as the legends goes.✦ On a quick glance, one sees that the first half covers Christ's life; and the second

36

half our beliefs in preparation for his judgment. Living form is not limited to finding forms where they don't exists, but more importantly how to read and understand the meaning of the construction of written works. My own experience in college was that when a student or teacher found some pattern no one thought much of it. Now we can explore whether there are in fact symmetry and polarity which are reflective of a higher organizing principle.

*

The *Lord's Prayer* is a central to Christian spirituality. The prayer has seven petitions, a title, and a doxology. For our purposes, we will leave out the doxology and title in approaching the living form of the prayer.[11]

The prayer goes as follows:

[Title: Our Father in heaven]

1. Hallowed be your name,
2. Your kingdom come,
3. Your will be done, on earth as in heaven.
4. Give us this day our daily bread.
5. Forgive us our trespasses as we forgive those who trespass against us.
6. Lead us not into Temptation
7. And deliver us from evil.

[Doxology: For the kingdom, the power, and the glory are yours now and forever. Amen.]

In a similar fashion to the *Creed*, the *Lord's Prayer* begins on the who?-level and descends to the what?-level and then climbs back to the who?-level. The first line "hallowed be they name" is the most abstract and line four "give us this day our daily bread" is the most earthly. Without too much analysis, let's let the form speak for itself:

♣ Apostle's Creed in twelve lines:
1. I believe in God, the Father almighty, creator of heaven and earth.
2. I believe in Jesus Christ, his only Son, our Lord.
3. He was conceived by the power of the Holy Spirit and born of the Virgin Mary.
4. He suffered under Pontius Pilate, was crucified, died, and was buried.
5. He descended into hell. On the third day he rose again.
6. He ascended into heaven and is seated at the right hand of God the Father Almighty.
----
7. He will come again to judge the living and the dead.
8. I believe in the Holy Spirit,
9. the holy catholic Church, the communion of saints,
10. the forgiveness of sins,
11. the resurrection of the body,
12. and the life everlasting.

[11] The breakdown of the Lord's Prayer was first worked out by Steiner. The version and form I used here is from Florin Lowndes.

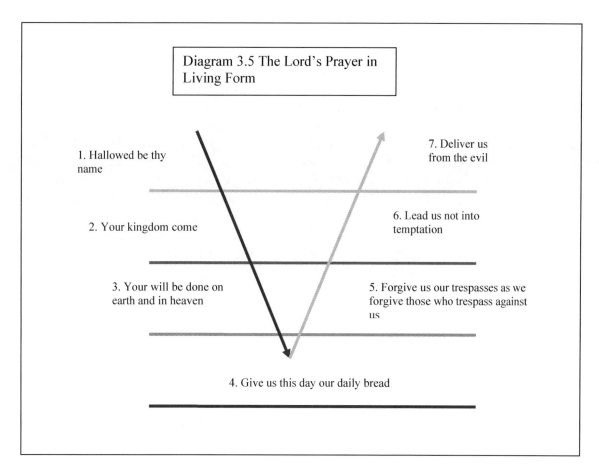

It is interesting to me that these central Christian prayers seem to have a reverse or bathtub forms when compared to other forms of writing. As mentioned already prayers and their form have in microcosm a picture of the process of the prayer; that is they bring down the spirit from above. The polarities are more subtle than in the previously presented works. They are qualitative polarities, which differ from the simple repetition of words on the same level. For example line 3 "your will be done" and line 5 "Forgive us our trespasses" both have quite a bit of movement or interaction between heaven and earth or between people. Line 2 and 6 both fit the goal-orientation of the why? level: "your kingdom come" and "lead us not into temptation."

The first half of the *Lord's Prayer* petitions and celebrates God; the second half petitions for inner development and strength. Thus we have a contrast of the outer and inner in the flow of the prayer. Rudolf Steiner had only the highest praises for this prayer and its form. It is a dynamic prayer which, when meditated daily, keeps our mind living in the levels of God's living form.

(Rudolf Steiner had expressed this living form in various ways often using the spiritual, religious, and philosophical terminology popular at end of the 19th Century. He applied creation logic to various disciplines such as education, architecture, dance (Eurythmy), politics (Three-fold Social Order), and to a renewed form of sacramental Christianity (The Movement for Religious Renewal). Steiner did not clearly explain his special creation logic and living form to his followers, and to this day they do not recognize his method as real or important to his work. A great opportunity for understanding and researching living form is available in all of Steiner's endeavors.♠)

♠ Those readers who want to deepen their studies of living form will have a difficult time finding related literature. I need to emphasize the fact that although Rudolf Steiner can be seen as father of the scales of living form, and George O'Neil as the re-discoverer of living form, Steiner's followers do not recognize the living form aspect of their founder's work. In fact, all organizations related to Steiner's work deny the existence or value of his living form such as: the Anthroposophical Society

Plato, or the Philosopher

The Living Form of the Republic: When analyzing a work for organic forms, it is helpful to look at the introduction, conclusion, and mathematical middle of the essay or book. In other words one tries to sketch the book and feel out its various contours. This process of discovering a thought form of an author takes time and patience. George O'Neil supposedly once banged his head out of frustration because he could not grasp a living form of a Steiner book. I didn't need to bang my head, but instead gave a modest account of the tricky living form of the <u>Republic</u> of Plato.

The <u>Republic</u> is an ancient text. It has been given ten chapters historically, although no one knows for sure if they are from the author or scholarly convention. In my analysis, and in spite of the numerous thematic overlaps of the chapters, I believe the ten chapters to be a valid way of dividing the book. Just as valid (and marvelously in harmony with living form) is F. M. Cornford's breakdown and translation of the <u>Republic</u>. Cornford has arranged the <u>Republic</u> according to where new themes begin and end. For him the book has seven major sections:

1. Prologue (chapter 1),
2. Introduction (chapter 2),
3. Genesis of Polis (chapter 2-4),
4. Embodiment of the Idea (chapter 5-7),
5. Decline of the Polis (chapter 8-9),
6. Conclusion (chapter 9),
7. Epilogue (chapter 10).

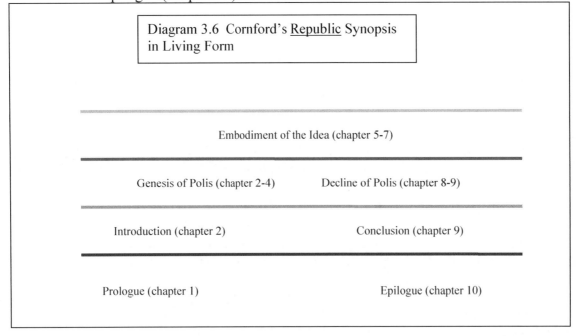

Diagram 3.6 Cornford's <u>Republic</u> Synopsis in Living Form

Embodiment of the Idea (chapter 5-7)

Genesis of Polis (chapter 2-4)   Decline of Polis (chapter 8-9)

Introduction (chapter 2)   Conclusion (chapter 9)

Prologue (chapter 1)   Epilogue (chapter 10)

---

and Das Goetheanum (its main office in Switzerland); the Waldorf schools and their Teacher Training institutions such as Rudolf Steiner College in California; and the "Steiner Church," the Christian Community. Without getting into too much speculation of why this strange situation is the case, I can only say that no Anthroposophical publications will help the curious reader in their studies of Steiner's living forms. Except for Florin Lowndes and George O'Neil's work, there is no research available on this groundbreaking new method of reading and writing.

Anthroposophical work is really good and very talented individuals work within the various anthroposophical endeavors. I like the Anthroposophists because they are kind people; however, I am *completely* dumbfounded as to why they are so dismissive of Steiner's living form.

What a wonderful skeleton! The chapters in Cornford's schema mirror each other nicely. He defied the traditional ten chapters of the <u>Republic</u> and came up with his own grasp of the form (living) of the book. Eva Brann, in her <u>Music of the Republic</u>, has the <u>Republic</u> spelled out in a series of concentric circles. Living form can manifest itself in many ways.

One of the problems with charting the <u>Republic</u> is its overlapping themes. This is why Cornford possibly moved away from the traditional chapters. I see the overlap as an aspect of living form that resembles quasi-musical recapitulations in each of the chapters, as if Plato sometimes builds the main theme up from the beginning. Plato did not simply make a linear argument, but reworked a theme like a composer a motif. Between chapter 2 and 3 the education of the guardians is interrupted and taken up in the next chapter; the three parts of society is started in chapter 3, but developed further in chapter 4. Do we call this organicism or sloppiness? Do modern philosophers have a need for a theme to be limited to a chapter? The <u>Republic</u> makes sense to me in the subtle building of the levels, not in the sense of building blocks, but a slow and "fuzzy" movement from the concrete to the abstract, and back to the concrete again.

The <u>Republic</u> in its ten-fold living form has an eight-form with "wings." The first half of the book is the building of the state through early education, and the regulation of the life style and mind set of the ruling class; the second half answers the question as to whether the philosopher is fit to rule, and what would happen if philosophers ruled. Nearly all the chapters, except chapters one and ten, discuss these themes: Guardians, education and higher knowledge, and the harmony of virtues of people and classes.

Let us look at the same themes of each chapter and see if a living schema emerges:

Chapter 2, What?: question of justice, emergence of a state and its needs, and education

Chapter 3, How?: Education to age 20, rulers selected from the three soul-metals (bronze, silver, gold), brotherhood of governance.

Chapter 4, Why?: Balance in riches, unity, education to prevent lawlessness, each class has a virtue: rulers have wisdom; soldiers courage; and common people temperance. Justice means keeping these classes distinct!

Chapter 5, Who?: The ruler's both male and female, their social laws, the Philosopher king who loves the Whole!

Chapter 6, Who?: Philosophers fit to Rule? The knowledge of the good, the four stages of knowledge.

Chapter 7, Why?: 50 years of Virtue Training: the cave, math, astronomy, dialectic

Chapter 8, How?: The Fall of the State: breeding guardians out of season: Timocracy (property), Oligarchy (wealth), Democracy (the poor rob the degenerate rich), Despotism (individual and private army enslave the people).

Chapter 9, What?: Answers the question of Justice

(Chapter 1 presents the problem of what comes in the afterlife which provokes the question of a just life. Chapter 10 gives account of the afterlife, the Myth of Er.)

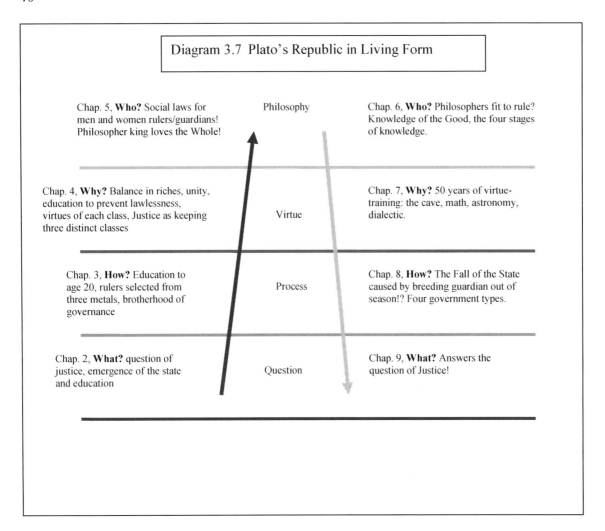

Diagram 3.7 Plato's Republic in Living Form

Chap. 5, **Who?** Social laws for men and women rulers/guardians! Philosopher king loves the Whole!

Philosophy

Chap. 6, **Who?** Philosophers fit to rule? Knowledge of the Good, the four stages of knowledge.

Chap. 4, **Why?** Balance in riches, unity, education to prevent lawlessness, virtues of each class, Justice as keeping three distinct classes

Virtue

Chap. 7, **Why?** 50 years of virtue-training: the cave, math, astronomy, dialectic.

Chap. 3, **How?** Education to age 20, rulers selected from three metals, brotherhood of governance

Process

Chap. 8, **How?** The Fall of the State caused by breeding guardian out of season!? Four government types.

Chap. 2, **What?** question of justice, emergence of the state and education

Question

Chap. 9, **What?** Answers the question of Justice!

Are the central chapters a living form? I see a clear focus in chapters 5 and 6 on the guardian and philosopher kings and their special mind-set. In chapters 2, 3, 8, and 9 the topics cover less lofty themes than chapter 5 and 6, such as physical needs of a state, the building block of society (3 metals), the fall of the state and so on. The central chapters (4, 5, 6, and 7,) deal with virtue and higher philosophical training, while the others are more concerned with troubles and doubts about human nature and justice.

In the diagram, we see in the curve how the central chapters form the crest of the wave and swoop down into "reality" of the green and blue levels. One must test for oneself whether the polarities between the chapters are reality. We can see that the How? chapters are about the "rise and fall of the state." (Typically one might expect the How? chapters to be concerned with an education process etc.) The who? chapter definitely captures the question by limiting itself to a lengthy discussion of the guardians' laws and lifestyle. The why? level of chapter four is answered pretty well by the topic of "virtue."

Other forms have crossed my mind such as two five-forms. These things must be tested from different perspectives. I am comfortable with mine and Cornford's versions; however, I see Cornford's diagram as a five-form with two wings, and not a pure seven form, because of the parenthetical quality of chapter one and ten.

I conclude this discussion with some examples from the Republic of Plato's creation logic. I read the Republic after having worked with Steiner's forms and creation logic. I was so amazed at the levels in Plato's thinking. I wondered whether the ancients naturally thought in creation logic. Here is a list of some the terms from the Republic:

Topic: Justice — Temperance, Courage, Wisdom
Topic: Soul types — Appetitive, Spirited, Reason
Topic: Human types — Bronze, Silver, Gold

Topic: Cognition — Images, Visible things, Mathematical objects, Forms
Topic: Cave — Shadows, Fire, light into the cave, gazing at the sun
Topic: Education — 1-17 liberal arts, 17-20 military, 20-30 select few have math, 30-35 dialectics
Topic: Society — Common people, Warriors, Guardians under 50, Philosopher kings

Topic:
Four governments — Despotism, Oligarchy, Democracy, Timocracy

Topics:	Justice	Soul Types	Human types	Society	4 Gov'ts
Who?				4. Philosopher kings	4. Timocracy
Why?	3. Wisdom	3. Reason	3. Gold	3. Guardians	3. Democracy
How?	2. Courage	2. Spirited	2. Silver	2. Warriors	2. Oligarchy
What?	1. Temperance	1. Appetitive	1. Bronze	1. Common People	1. Despotism

Diagram 3.8 The Creation Logic of Plato's Republic

The platonic world-view is a series of steps as one idea builds upon the other. In the same fashion as creation logic, Plato's logic starts with an idea and then builds up to it. Therefore, justice is attained by first having temperance, then courage, and finally wisdom in balance. Plato then inter-relates the human types, to the soul types to the professions, and to the education. The entire book was conceived with an eye on the inner workings of living form.

The Living Form of Plato's Symposium: The *Symposium* is Plato's work concerning the true nature of love. Seven speakers give their opinions on the subject, each from a distinct point of view. If we treat the symposium not as a dialogue, but as Plato presenting seven distinct points of view, something "living" seems to arise. The first observation is that the seven opinions become gradually more sophisticated or esoteric.*

Phaedrus, the first speaker, starts with a general description of Love as one of the original gods who inspires honor and greatness, and Alcibiades, the seventh and final speaker, concludes with a description of a god-man (atman) Socrates ("inside Socrates …so divine, golden, so utterly beautiful and amazing" 217a).

The first three speakers present love as having two parts: 1st speaker about Earth and Love came after Chaos; 2nd speaker about common and higher Love; and 3rd speaker about Love as antagonistic elements. Aristophanes then speaks of Love as restoring us back to wholeness that is bringing together/healing the two parts! Finally the last three descriptions are higher or more conceptual descriptions: Agathon says Love is harmonizing and Goodness; Socrates, birthing virtue; and Alcibiades tells of the archetypal human. By limiting our focus to finding the unique elements and essences of their speeches, it seems some living schema is discernible.

---

*My Synopses of the seven speeches of the Symposium:

1) Phaedrus: (Love's origin and a source of honor) Love was regarded as a great god who came after Chaos with Earth. Commitment and courage, honor, a source of greatness comes from love. A lover is divinely inspired.

2) Pausanias: (Love as Common and Higher) Two types of love heavenly and common Aphrodite. No activity is inherently right or wrong but dependent on the way it is done. Common love is for inferior people. Higher love is attracted to what is naturally more intelligent (boys) because Aphrodite has mostly maleness. A boy is admirable if he does something for someone in order to gain virtue i.e., gratify a lover.

3) Eryximachus: (Love is the balance of antagonistic elements) Love is expressed in bodily responses of every kind of animal, in plants growing in the earth, in virtually everything that exists, and medicine. Pausanias said that it is right to gratify good people but wrong to gratify self-indulgent ones and it is right to gratify the good parts and not the diseased parts. The doctor brings about changes so that the body acquires one type of love instead of another. Create friendship between antagonistic elements. Divination is directed at maintaining one kind of love and curing the other. The seasons are controlled hot and cold are well-tempered than there is a temperate mixture.

4) Aristophanes: (Love restores our wholeness and power) Original human being Androgynous: human beings used to be so powerful so Zeus cut them into two. Love is our desire for wholeness. Reverence for the gods will restore us to our true nature, healing us. We have to find our loved one and restore us to our original nature.

5) Agathon: (Love is young, gentle, composer of all things, harmonizing) Love is the god and we must praise his nature first: Love (god) is the happiest, beautiful and best, and youngest of the gods. Love hates old age. God had they had Love would not have battled each other in the past. He settles in the soft characters. Love doesn't use force but mutual consent. Moderation, pleasure, masters desire, bravest, wisdom, composer of everything, after the Birth of Love all good things came to man and gods through the love of beauty. Love fills us with familiarity not estrangement. Every man should follow him singing praise!

6) Socrates: (Love is the staircase to birthing virtue) Love is not good or beautiful or ugly either, but in between. They carry messages from humans to gods enabling the universe to be whole. Love is in between mortal and immortal. The child of resource and Poverty and Love is the follower of Aphrodite and therefore lover of beauty. He is tough and has hardened skinned. He schemes to get hold of beautiful and good things, brave and intense, a hunter weaving tricks, uses magic and sophistry. Dies and comes back to life. Mortal creatures achieve immortality thru intercourse and giving birth. The object of love is reproduction and birth in beauty.
The object of love is immortality

Great men leave behind children of virtue for society such as Solon. The mystery training: To be strengthened to the resolve of seeing the beauty of the mind and see beauty in the law. The higher beauty appears as beauty in and of itself in single form, unchangeable. The staircase reaching the beautiful: from two to all beautiful bodies, and then to beautiful practices, and to beautiful forms of learning, to beauty itself. A birth giver of true virtue!

7) Alcibiades: (Love represented by the archetypal man) Socrates is a god-like man who presence makes others better. Open yourself up and look inside and you will understand Socrates.

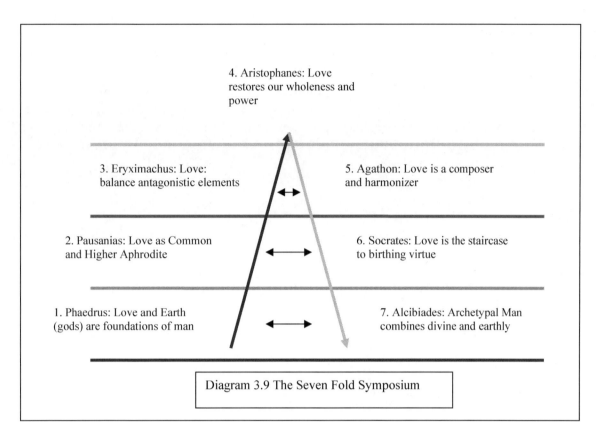

4. Aristophanes: Love restores our wholeness and power

3. Eryximachus: Love: balance antagonistic elements

5. Agathon: Love is a composer and harmonizer

2. Pausanias: Love as Common and Higher Aphrodite

6. Socrates: Love is the staircase to birthing virtue

1. Phaedrus: Love and Earth (gods) are foundations of man

7. Alcibiades: Archetypal Man combines divine and earthly

Diagram 3.9 The Seven Fold Symposium

The first polarity is between 1 and 7, between Phaedrus and Alcibiades. Phaedrus says that Love and Earth were born together. Human beings require of course both Earth, in order to live, and Love, in order to live in a godly manner. Alcibiades presents the archetypal human being who lives in this divine combination in that inside of his earthly veneer he has incorporated the divine, so "utterly beautiful." Thus the archetypal man can incorporate the heavenly in the physical earth existence.

Speeches 2 and 6 or Pausanias and Socrates are polar in that they cover the difference between higher and lower love. What appears as a simple idea in 2 becomes part of a mystery training in 6 whose goal is to view Love itself. Similar to 1 and 7, the ideas in 2 find their elaboration in 6.

Speeches 3 and 5 have their contrast in that 3 presents the antagonism of love from a scientific and external point of view; and 5 explains the harmonizing effect of love from a philosophic, inward perspectives. As was said before, the first three speeches present love as a duality and the last three address the unity of love. The mid-point or the fourth speech states: we seek to heal the split in our human nature through love to our other half, and a cultivation of connection to the divine! Thus the fourth speech puts the inversion or turning-inside-out into motion.

In contrast to the Republic, there are no chapters or sections in the Symposium. I have only looked at the inner content of the speeches. Other interesting observations are: the central speech of Aristophanes is the most abstract and unusual, similar to the central chapters of the Republic, which cover the levels of knowledge. I have never experienced the Republic or the Symposium solely as a dialogue or debate, but as a collection of archetypal points of view which bring the readers awareness into a consciousness of point-of-viewism.

Some final remarks: Reading philosophy in this way makes the content a little more accessible. Even where living form is not present, it is easy to detect and follow the main argument using this method of making synopsis and comparing the parts. The philosopher Schelling once said that having overviews in manifold subjects turned him almost into a genius. I could imagine that students and teachers will want to look for their own forms of various essays and books. The depth and quality of the work may dispel notions that this work is a rigid schema, imposed onto great books.

Plato can be seen in a certain sense as the founder of living form in the Occident. Although his other dialogues may not have such clear forms, there is, at least thematically, a devotion to Eros and Form in all of his writing. Rudolf Steiner himself pointed to several philosophical works, Johann Gottlieb Fichte's <u>Wissenschaftslehre</u> and Hegel's <u>Logic</u>, as being written in living form. These questions always have to do with levels. It may be the chapters are in living form but not the paragraphs, or sentences.

(**Interlude** *The Nine-fold, Seven-fold, Four-fold, and Three-fold Human Being*: In order to practice the living form, it can be helpful to know its origin. Rudolf Steiner called this living form "the human being systematic" because the four levels are a microcosm of the human being. According to tradition, there are four kingdoms of nature: the mineral, plant, animal, and man. And accordingly there are four aspects of every human being: the physical body, the life or etheric body, the astral or feeling body, and the I (ego). Our four levels of what? how? why? and who? then become humanized through the four aspect of physical, etheric, astral, and ego. These four members of man make up the four fold human being.

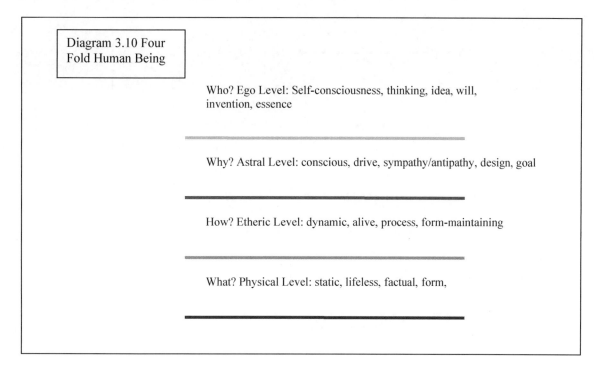

Diagram 3.10 Four Fold Human Being

Who? Ego Level: Self-consciousness, thinking, idea, will, invention, essence

Why? Astral Level: conscious, drive, sympathy/antipathy, design, goal

How? Etheric Level: dynamic, alive, process, form-maintaining

What? Physical Level: static, lifeless, factual, form,

The Ego or I is the human being's true being and identity. The astral body gives us feelings, the etheric body our life-forces and life rhythms, and the physical body is the mineral aspect of our being. As we grow, the I learns new things and begins to refine the other bodies. We surround ourselves with beautiful things, we prefer certain foods, we learn a certain kind of manners, we learn to express ourselves, and thereby shape our astral body. Religion and music shape our etheric body and habit life. The physical body is conditioned by what we eat, exercise, and posture. Our four bodies are shaped by our culture and family from one side, and from our I on the other.

It is the job of the ego to learn, love and keep us balanced in our three bodies by refining them through wise and loving choices. A strong ego can exert itself, and therefore can bring marvelous changes and growth into a person's life. The ego purifies the sloth of the physical body by getting to be active. The ego purifies the etheric body by getting it to break old rigid habits and resistances. The ego purifies the self-indulgence of the astral body by ennobling it through higher ideas and loving choices. The ego's work builds the soul- and spirit-bodies.

Steiner also divided the human energetic form into three members: the body, soul, and spirit. The soul is the mediator of information from the spirit into the body. Each of these three members has three parts, thus making the four fold human being into a nine-fold human being:

The Body consists of the physical body, etheric body, and the sentient body.
The Soul consists of the sentient soul, intellectual soul, and the consciousness soul.
The Spirit consists of the spirit self, life spirit, and spirit man.

46

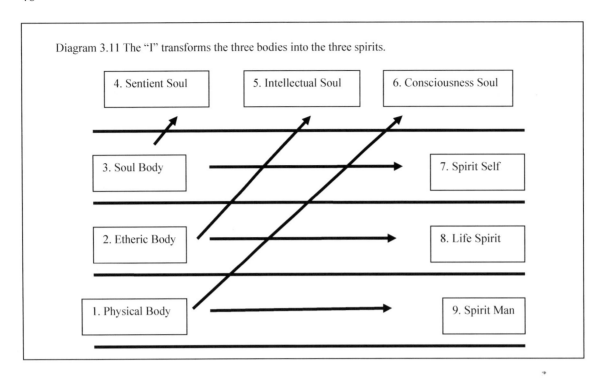

Diagram 3.11 The "I" transforms the three bodies into the three spirits.

The nine-fold human being is the human being in full plumage. The first mention of the nine-fold human, Steiner said, comes from the Ancient Hindu culture. The four-fold human being is the nine-fold human being which is condensed (the soul body and sentient soul become the astral body, the intellectual soul, consciousness, and the three spirit bodies become the ego). Thus the four fold human being does not consist of different members, but is the nine-fold human being seen from a truncated perspective.

Another simplified version of the nine-fold human being is the seven-fold human being. The seven-fold human being is the four-fold human being with the three spirit bodies, thus forming polarities. The seven-fold and the four-fold are most common. We all know the importance in history of the number seven (seven notes of the scale etc.).

The four main bodies – the physical, etheric, astral, and ego – are called are "God-given" bodies while the three higher spirit bodies – spirit self, life spirit, and spirit man – we must create ourselves. In various traditions this has been known and expressed in various symbols.

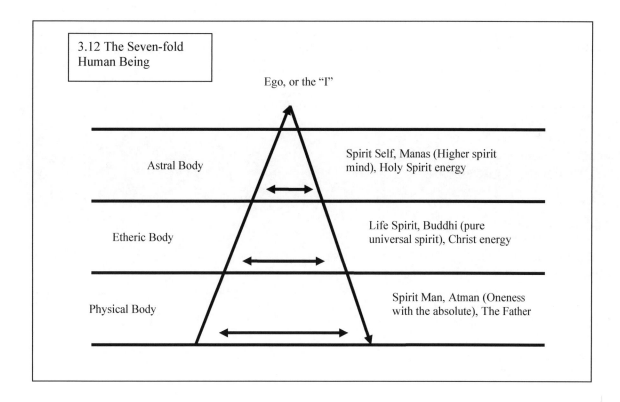

3.12 The Seven-fold Human Being

Ego, or the "I"

Astral Body — Spirit Self, Manas (Higher spirit mind), Holy Spirit energy

Etheric Body — Life Spirit, Buddhi (pure universal spirit), Christ energy

Physical Body — Spirit Man, Atman (Oneness with the absolute), The Father

In Judaism, the Star of David has the six bodies connected with the ego in the middle regulating the process. It is nothing other than the diagram of the seven fold human being reconfigured into overlapping triangles. In *Genesis*, God created foundation of four members: the earth (physical), plants (etheric), animal (astral), and human being (ego); and Christianity, for example, requires us to connect to our higher members: Holy Spirit (spirit self), Christ (life spirit), and The Father (spirit man). In the Hindu tradition the three spirit bodies are called: Manas, (the higher spirit mind/ego); Buddhi, (vehicle of pure universal spirit, which differentiates truth from falsehood); and Atman (one's true spirit self, oneness with the Absolute). The seven-fold human being is a picture of our attaining connection to our higher principles and thereby completing our spiritual evolution.

The seven-fold human being is the main model for creation logic. It is from this point of view that it is easy to understand why famous prayers and creeds often have the number seven: the seven sacraments, seven words of Christ, the seven I AM statements in the *Gospel of John*. The mystery of the number seven is often an archetype of the mystery of human growth and potential.)

Poetry:

Poetry and plays present a problem similar to the ancient texts of Plato and the Bible. How does one find living form in texts where there are sometimes no clear punctuation or divisions? Does poetry even lend itself to living form, or is its medium meant for dynamic passionate swings, evading capture in rigid levels of living form?

It is important to point out that living form is also a method of reading. By applying it to various texts, even when unsuccessful in finding perfect living forms, it helps comprehension by providing a whole-to-the-parts understanding. Let's keep in mind my two-fold intention of looking for form as well as applying the method itself for the purposes of text clarification.

I have chosen famous poems so that there is no argument as to whether or no they are representative of poetry. William Blake's *The Tyger* has had quite a bit of staying power over the years. Hundreds of critics have voiced their opinions about what this poem means. It is supposedly the most anthologized poem of the English Language. Blake is not your average poet and his work has a large following of spiritually oriented admirers. There is no question that it is central poem in our history, and, could it be because of its form, at least in part?

Stanza 1.
Tyger! Tyger! burning bright
In the forests of the night,
What immortal hand or eye
Could frame thy fearful symmetry?

Stanza 2.
In what distant deeps or skies
Burnt the fire of thine eyes?
On what wings dare he aspire?
What the hand, dare seize the fire?

Stanza 3.
And what shoulder, & what art,
Could twist the sinews of thy heart?
And when thy heart began to beat,
What dread hand? & what dread feet?

Stanza 4.
What the hammer? what the chain?
In what furnace was thy brain?
What the anvil? what dread grasp
Dare its deadly terrors clasp?

Stanza 5.
When the stars threw down their spears
And water'd heaven with their tears,
Did he smile his work to see?
Did he who made the Lamb make thee?

Stanza 6.
Tyger! Tyger! burning bright
In the forests of the night,
What immortal hand or eye
Dare frame thy fearful symmetry?

The poem has a stark symmetry reminiscent of the New Testament chapters. The poem begins and ends with the same stanza with the question of the Tyger's framer.

The second and fifth stanzas take place in the skies and heavens. Also they both describe airy broad movement using such words as "skies," "heaven" "aspire," "threw," "spears," watered." Also the most common sound is "ee" reinforcing the notion of airiness of these stanzas: skies, deeps, eyes, seize, see, thee, he, tears, and spears.

The third and fourth stanzas mirror each other perfectly. Both stanzas are concerned with the blacksmith and creation. In stanzas three and four the heart and brain are created, and the dominant vowel is "a." The "dread hand" of stanza three and "dread grasp" of stanza four are the essence of the conflict between heart and brain with the violence or the astral aspects of the tiger. Qualitatively each stanza is so radically different and wonderfully polar!

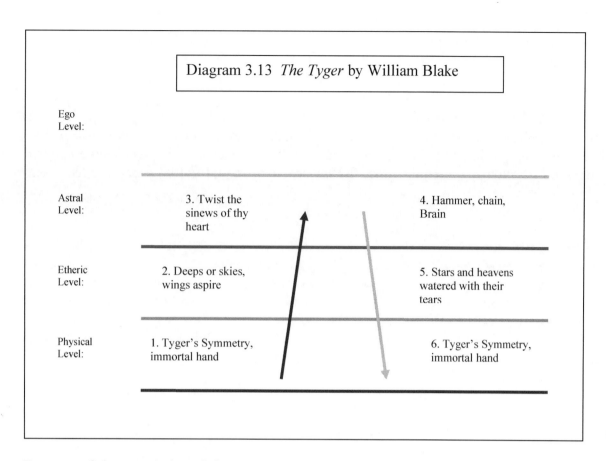

Diagram 3.13 *The Tyger* by William Blake

Ego
Level:

Astral
Level:

3. Twist the
sinews of thy
heart

4. Hammer, chain,
Brain

Etheric
Level:

2. Deeps or skies,
wings aspire

5. Stars and heavens
watered with their
tears

Physical
Level:

1. Tyger's Symmetry,
immortal hand

6. Tyger's Symmetry,
immortal hand

Because of the popularity of the poem and the fact that no one claims to fully understand what Blake was trying to say, it is allowable to claim that Blake's living form may have something to do with its unutterable greatness.

*

In *The Angel* by William Blake we have a poem without polarity. It seems to have the climb of creation logic: What? (static); How? (dynamic); Why? (feeling, goal); and Who? (identity, essence). Blake was fond of four-line stanzas in his poems, and nearly every line has a subject, verb, and object.

Stanza 1. What? Static
I Dreamt a Dream! what can it mean?
And that I was a maiden Queen:
Guarded by an Angel mild;
Witless woe, was ne'er beguil'd!

Stanza 2. How? dynamic
And I wept both night and day
And he wip'd my tears away
And I wept both day and night
And hid from him my hearts delight.

Stanza 3. Why? Feeling, consciousness
So he took his wings and fled:
Then the morn blush'd rosy red:
I dried my tears & arm'd my fears,
With ten thousand shields and spears.

Stanza 4. Who? Identity, Self-consciousness
Soon my Angel came again;
I was arm'd, he came in vain:
For the time of youth was fled
And grey hairs were on my head

It is plain to see that stanza four has a reflective quality; stanza three, an emotional quality; stanza two is concerned with time and action; and stanza one sets the scene of his protected youth and his life as a dream. Creation logic requires that the theme build up and unfold according to several qualitative points of view.

*

One of the most famous American poems is *The Road Not Taken* by Robert Frost. Like Blake before him, Frost was born with a developed sixth-sense. It should not be a surprise that their poems have been so much staying power in anthologies - a possible result of their incredible spiritual prowess. Where Blake seems to have living form in the themes and qualities at the level of the stanzas, Frost in this example has living form within the very lines of the stanzas.

When discovering living forms in poems it is helpful to read them aloud. The first stanza seems to have a very strong living form and answers the questions: what? how? why? how? what? The themes of the four stanzas have a particularly clear living form.

I have named the levels of the poem: static, dynamic, and conscious. In living form the usual names physical, etheric, astral are not always very helpful. It is important to figure out what type of unique living form is present within the composition. I have tried my best with this one.

The Road Not Taken

Two roads diverged in a yellow wood,
And sorry I could not travel both
And be one traveler, long I stood
And looked down one as far as I could
To where it bent in the undergrowth;

Then took the other, as just as fair,
And having perhaps the better claim,
Because it was grassy and wanted wear;
Though as for that the passing there
Had worn them really about the same,

And both that morning equally lay
In leaves no step had trodden black.
Oh, I kept the first for another day!
Yet knowing how way leads on to way,
I doubted if I should ever come back.

I shall be telling this with a sigh
Somewhere ages and ages hence:
Two roads diverged in a wood, and I –
I took the ones less traveled by,
And that has made all the difference.

Poem with synopses:

The Road Not Taken

Synopsis, Stanza 1. (What?): Choice: I stood before the roads: the first one

Static	1. Two roads diverged in a yellow wood,
Dynamic	2. And sorry I could not travel both
Conscious	3. And be one traveler, long I stood
Dynamic	4. And looked down one as far as I could
Static	5. To where it bent in the undergrowth;

Synopsis, Stanza 2. (How?): Path: took the second road, grassy

Static	1. Then took the other, as just as fair,
Dynamic	2. And having perhaps the better claim,
Conscious	3. Because it was grassy and wanted wear;
Dynamic	4. Though as for that the passing there
Static	5. Had worn them really about the same,

Synopsis, Stanza 3. (Why?): doubt of going back: contrast the first and second

Static	1. And both that morning equally lay
Dynamic	2. In leaves no step had trodden black.
Conscious	3. Oh, I kept the first for another day!
Dynamic	4. Yet knowing how way leads on to way,
Static	5. I doubted if I should ever come back.

Synopsis, Stanza 4. (Who?): Self-analysis: choice makes the difference

Static	1. I shall be telling this with a sigh
Dynamic	2. Somewhere ages and ages hence:
Conscious	3. Two roads diverged in a wood, and I –
Dynamic	4. I took the ones less traveled by,
Static	5. And that has made all the difference.

The synopses work at the stanza level:
> in stanza 1. (what?) he stands;
> in stanza 2. (how?) he takes a path;
> in stanza 3. (why?) considers both;
> and in stanza 4. (who?) he analyzes his choice.

The lines on the conscious level seem to have a slight pause (in stanza 1. line 3. "long I stood," Stanza 2. line 3. "Oh, I kept," in Stanza 4. line 3. "and I-"). In stanza 2. line 3. the use of "Because it was grassy" in particular "because" is often used as a device to create an astral or why?- level mood. The dynamic level sentences have actions predominantly supported by the use of gerunds, active verbs, and the certain key words. The static sentences, well, generally have a static quality with a few exceptions. In context nearly every line seems to fit in the organic whole. Simply perfect!

The Gettysburg Address:

George O'Neil searched the forms of great books and other literary works. Early in his career he analyzed the *Gettysburg Address* and its form. In this speech Lincoln re-founded the American nation. There is no shortage of commentary on the centrality and uniqueness of this speech.

Although the original speech was divided into three sections, O'Neil puts them into a unity of ten sentences. The first half of the address talks about dedicating a resting place to the fallen soldiers. The second half says that we cannot consecrate, but, at best, continue the work of freedom that the soldiers sacrificed for.

In the first half sentences 1 and 2 discuss our engagement in a war of liberty. And sentences 4 and 5 cover the dedication. Sentence three is a turning point in that the speech now becomes more specific to Gettysburg: "we are met on a great battlefield." Thus the first two sentences cover the outer aspect of the topic (war) while the last three the inner aspect (dedication).

In the second half of the address sentences 6 and 7 talk about the past and bravery, while sentences 8, 9, and 10 cover the future. Sentence 8 announces that Gettysburg will not be forgotten! Sentences 9 and 10 cover the task ahead. The *Address* is one of the most challenging examples of organic form.

When analyzing the sentences of the *Address*, it is difficult to establish the polarities and other living form perspectives. George felt that there were very delicate transitions between sentences, which certainly did not scream living form like some of the other examples given in Chapter 3.

What? 1. Four score and seven years ago our fathers brought forth on this continent a new nation, conceived in Liberty, and dedicated to the proposition that all men are created equal.

How? 2. Now we are engaged in a great civil war, testing whether that nation, or any nation, so conceived and so dedicated, can long endure.

Why? 3. We are met on a great battle-field of that war.

How? 4. We have come to dedicate a portion of that field, as a final resting place for those who here gave their lives that that nation might live.

What? 5. It is altogether fitting and proper that we should do this.

What? 6. But, in a larger sense, we can not dedicate... we can not consecrate... we can not hallow this ground.

How? 7. The brave men, living and dead, who struggled here, have consecrated it, far above our poor power to add or detract.

Why? 8. The world will little note, nor long remember what we say here, but it can never forget what they did here.

How? 9. It is for us the living, rather, to be dedicated here to the unfinished work which they who fought here have thus far so nobly advanced.

What? 10. It is rather for us to be here dedicated to the great task remaining before us - that from these honored dead we take increased devotion to that cause for which they gave the last full measure of devotion - that we here highly resolve that these dead shall not have died in vain - that this nation, under God, shall have a new birth of freedom - and that government: of the people, by the people, for the people, shall not perish from the earth.

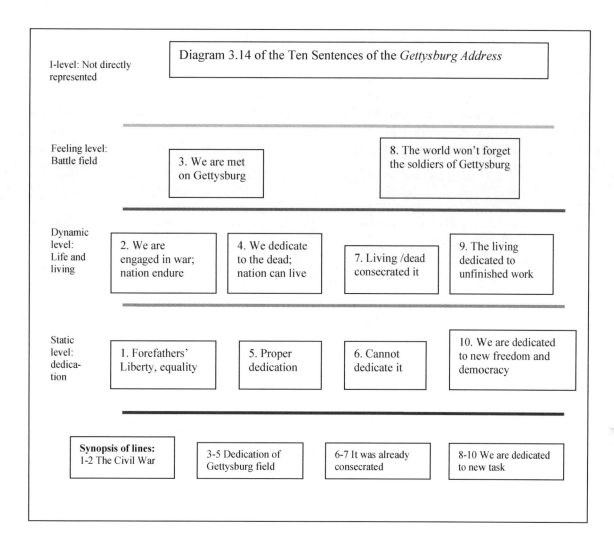

Essays:

Conversations With God: An Uncommon Dialogue: Neale Donald Walsch wrote a series of books called Conversations With God. They became instant bestsellers. The books were so inspiring that several initiatives have sprung up in which people incorporate the principles and new ways of thinking about the vocation of being a human on the way to Godhood. The direct and plain style of the books is wonderful, especially after having read other more esoteric authors.

The first volume of Walsch's trilogy is called Conversations with God: *an uncommon dialogue, Book 1*. The book starts off with Walsch asking God questions. God surprised Walsch by answering in an audible voice! And so it begins.

I had heard from friends that CWG had a living form. When making synopses I was really curious as to whether this book would add up to an organic structure. There were some questions I had: did Walsch arbitrarily divide the chapters? How did he punctuate God's words i.e., did God tell Walsch where to put the commas, colon, and indentations? I settled these questions by only considering the dominant themes of each chapter.

One of the great difficulties in finding living forms is the fact that each written work has its own inner dynamic. Therefore, applying the question of creation logic (what? how? why? and who?) may not serve the discovery of the form. Nevertheless, CWG has a clear and unique form; each level has its own themes and qualities which don't resemble other texts I have read. For example, the how-level usually has a method or activity aspect but in his book the level has to do with problematic behaviors something one would expect on the astral level.

The book has fourteen chapters which can be further subdivided into two themes: the first half of the book (chapters 1 through 7) cover the individual and basic principles; the second half, the application of the principles with others and the world. The themes of each of the fourteen chapters seem to climb and descend within the four levels of: God's what? the basics; how? problematic behaviors; why? the soul; and who? self-transformation. Below are some thematic synopses of the book's fourteen chapters:

Chapters Synopses:
1. **God's basic principles**: Sponsoring Thoughts: love or fear; Life is a creation; Reality is dyad or triad; Each soul is a master; Jesus and healing the world

2. **Changing our inherited judgments:** God doesn't judge Good and Evil: How God appears to us; Money and sex; Gospel writers and worthiness

3. **The soul's purpose**: The three-fold reality; We forgot who we are; Watch your words

4. **Discipline your mind:** 10 points of self-transformation; New Reality

5. **Ten signs of success**: True path: pure being-ness; Heaven and renunciation

6. **Path of suffering?:** Pain is a reaction; a master is quiet; Suffering means we still have something to learn

7. **God Consciousness**: Life is scary? No attachment to results; Cause and effect, family and survival,; God's pay, difficult events become blessings or tests! Choosing and self-responsibility.

Chapters 8-14
8. **Smooth relationships?** Relationship purpose: to challenge you to create the higher you; Salvation is in your reaction; The highest good for you is good for the other too! What would love do? See the higher in yourself and partner.

9. **Life, killing, and pain:** Life is challenging! Acting on authority instead of experience means trouble! Killing: Pain, love and wisdom

10. **I love you**:

11. **Change sponsoring thought**: List of questions; Reverse the process: deed, word, thought; Gratitude vs. worldly success

12. **Fun and making a living:** Insistence on being happy vs. being grumpy; Soul mechanics

13. **Health Problems**: Self-created illness and negative thoughts; Healer's absolute faith; Mental lepers; Care of the body and living forever; Creation and evolution

14. **Karma and reincarnation**: God's closing words; The three volumes; Listen to your soul!

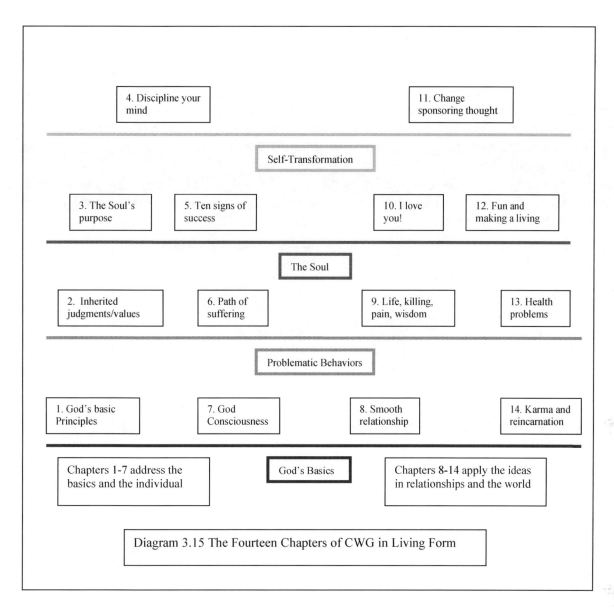

Diagram 3.15 The Fourteen Chapters of CWG in Living Form

The otherwise esoteric structure, which comes naturally from a flowing conversation, seems to have streamed out in organic-living qualities. The blue level presents the basic principles; the green level, pain and suffering; the red level, the soul, joy and success; the yellow level is completely devoted to self-transformation. Whether God himself spoke to Neale, or some other angelic being, I won't debate. We read in the dialogue that God has determined where the books begin and end. It matters not if Neale broke the chapters down arbitrarily, because in his choice, he chose a living form. In one of his later books, God tells Neale to count the sentences of a passage, possibly hinting to the form in which God expresses his thoughts!

Emerson's Nature: Text analysis is challenging. In researching for this project, I often consulted the work of friends and scholars. In the case of Plato, the secondary literature on his philosophy and style is so enormous that time prevents me from looking into it. But what validity would there be to living form if only pedantic scholars could locate it?

I trusted that Emerson, the founder of an American transcendental spirituality, laid out in living form, the basic tenets of his thought in his essay *Nature* (1836). In spite of many scholarly synopses available, I found that they had a difficult time grasping the essence. I was not able to use the work of others and although somewhat confident of my reading of *Nature*, I would like to keep this organic sketch "experimental" at best.

I have stated before that only Steiner sought scientific and mathematical precision in his living form. In Steiner's work we can count on living form as it appears on the chapter-, paragraph-, and sentence-level (and even clause level!) – that is, when publishers and translators didn't alter the structure of his work after his death. One can appreciate an author's work even more when one discovers in it some semblance of a living thought-wave. In Emerson's *Nature* it is the skeleton of the essay that has living form, not the details.

The dynamism and flexibility of the living thinking helped me to survey this essays from multiple perspectives. The first element I looked for was a change in the quality of the writing. Was there a transition from the first half to the second half? It seems so to me.

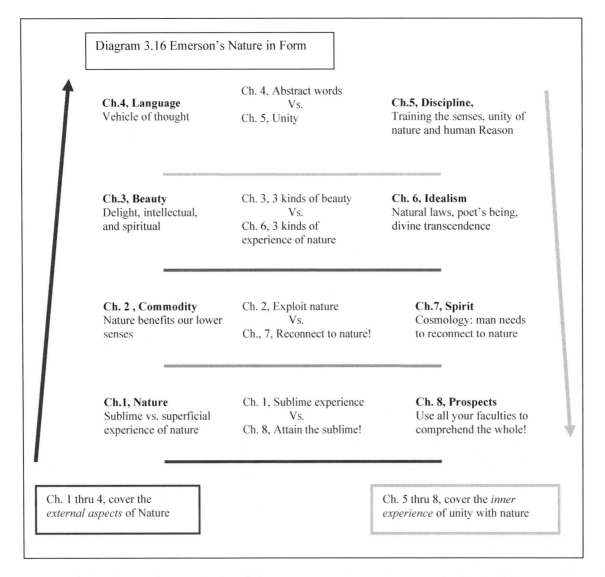

Diagram 3.16 Emerson's Nature in Form

Ch.4, Language
Vehicle of thought

Ch. 4, Abstract words
Vs.
Ch. 5, Unity

Ch.5, Discipline,
Training the senses, unity of nature and human Reason

Ch.3, Beauty
Delight, intellectual, and spiritual

Ch. 3, 3 kinds of beauty
Vs.
Ch. 6, 3 kinds of experience of nature

Ch. 6, Idealism
Natural laws, poet's being, divine transcendence

Ch. 2 , Commodity
Nature benefits our lower senses

Ch. 2, Exploit nature
Vs.
Ch., 7, Reconnect to nature!

Ch.7, Spirit
Cosmology: man needs to reconnect to nature

Ch.1, Nature
Sublime vs. superficial experience of nature

Ch. 1, Sublime experience
Vs.
Ch. 8, Attain the sublime!

Ch. 8, Prospects
Use all your faculties to comprehend the whole!

Ch. 1 thru 4, cover the *external aspects* of Nature

Ch. 5 thru 8, cover the *inner experience* of unity with nature

The first half, chapters 1 through 4, presents the basic facts and the external aspects of nature: commodity, beauty, and language. Chapter 5, *Discipline*, is completely opaque in meaning. The entire form of the essay becomes abstract and obtuse. It presents the role of Reason. In other words, the discussion turns to an inward perspective. I have considered the strong possibility that Chapter 6, *Idealism* might have been a better choice for the introversion of the living form in that it clearly deals with pure thinking - thus better fitting the who-level.

Each living form has its own inner dynamic. Emerson clearly placed his chapters in polarity. As is seen in the diagram, each 'potential' mentioned in the first half of the essay is realized or solved in the second half e.g. in chapter 1, the sublime experience of nature is realized in chapter 8 where Emerson instructs us to use all our faculties. The three qualities of beauty in chapter 3 become the three ways of relating to nature in chapter 6. The weakest link is of course the polarity of chapters 4 and 5.

Is living-form really real? Where living form cannot be attained in mathematical perfection, I guarantee that by looking for it - via synopses, diagramming, and comparing ideas -students will, nevertheless, come to a more intimate knowledge of the author's original meaning and its validity for us today.

Significance of these Living Forms: Did Plato and others write this way on purpose or naturally? Don't all good stories have a climb and swoop as Chekov pointed out? It is fair to say that Plato <u>Republic</u> is more widely read and popular than his other books, because its form is so living?

Bullinger made his discoveries in the 1890's and his work is relatively obscure. His followers never thought of abstracting the method of alternating and introverted forms of writing and turning them into a modern system of composition. It could have been possible for Bullinger and his followers to approach Ancient Greek texts, Neo-Platonists, and Hebrew scholars to make a case for a universal-spiritual method of writing. Aquinas used a very formal method to dispute in various theological works, a method which follows very systematic steps and points of view.

Rudolf Steiner never revealed his method to his followers, supposedly tongue-tied as spiritual teachers are until their students ask them the eternal question. Steiner lectured about the living structure of famous poems, prayers, history, and architecture as if he were hinting or indirectly begging his followers to ask the question: "wow Rudi, if these prayers have forms based on the seven-fold human being, is it possible your books are based on them too?"

The significance of the form comes in Chapter Four as I attempt to teach strategies for writing in living form. Living form is a commitment to writing in a compositional style. Other pedagogical consideration and applications of living form can be found in the Chapter 5.

Chapter 4, Writing
Techniques of Living Form

I.   Your Character and the Writing Process

If the living forms presented in the last chapter made an impression on you, and by the subtle and blatant use of form in classic and time-tested works, the need may arise for you to compose your own organic forms. Whether you are taking old writing and checking their form, or using a form to inspire your writing, this chapter gives some pointers to help you in your process.

In my experience, living forms often stimulate individuals to enter into the writing process with a new confidence. By having a model such a seven-fold or five-fold form in front of them, the novice writer can gather their material around the four questions and their polarities. Thus living form serves as playful game in which one's ideas and paragraphs are organized. This chapter serves as kind of self-help program for writers' block.

Keep in mind that living form is created by the interval between the paragraphs and sections of your book or essay. Also, there is no fixed way to make your writing living. Sometimes when you are in the zone, living forms pour out from your pen. Honestly, good writing cannot be created by living form, but it can make you conscious of what you are writing and thereby give you a bird's eye view of how the parts relate to the whole.* In the future, I pray that these very introductory remarks will inspire writers to develop this foundling art further, well beyond what I have done here.

Two Approaches to Writing in Form: The question now is whether we can apply similar organic forms to our own work. In the examples in the last chapter we see many four leveled forms such as in the Bible and in Plato's Republic. Many writing guides for high school and college students recommend starting with the five-paragraph essay as was already mentioned in Chapter Two. Most of these guides recommend starting with a clear outline in which all of the paragraphs' details are worked out before the writing process begins.

Those attempting to write organically - but have little writing experience or expertise - may need to carefully construct an outline. The outline should have the questions and colors and fit the subtle laws of enhancement and polarity. Professional writers often do not need an outline because they have an *idea-picture-sequence*, which serves as a mental outline before they write. I recommend living in the levels, four questions, and sketches in order to get a feel and eye for organic structure.

But what if you are a relatively organized writer and you can write logically without making an elaborate outline? Is an outline really necessary? The answer should be obvious: write your essay first, and then fix the structure. One can always fine-tune it later - an activity that needs to be done eventually even if you had chosen a tight outline to begin with. Often writing out of your heart can produce some very inspired organic structures that sometimes require little tinkering.

It is hard to imagine that the authors of the Bible, Plato, and Emerson knew how to write in organic form. It is much more likely that the form came as an *inspiration* that they brought down to

---

* There is one central dilemma to teaching organic form to others. In trying to explain how to write organically, I have to give a structure with fixed questions that one answers rigidly. However, if you look at the many examples in chapter three from diverse authors, it seems there is no one best way of creating living forms. In other words, the only commonality in all of the examples in chapter 3 is seen in the fact that each example has a beginning and an end; and their sections - in the form of lines, stanzas, paragraphs, or chapters - relate internally in a way that a clearly discernible form is present.

earth from the world of ideas (the heavens). Thus, the question as to whether one should start with an outline is best answered by saying: **"use whatever gets you writing and do not get in the way of your inspiration."**

On the other hand, contemplating various forms and outlines may be fun for some people. For example, in writing graduate school essays, I tried to see what form works best in terms of presenting the history or philosophy of a famous educator. I would write down the questions What? How? Why? Who? and see how a philosopher's ideas and actions fit this model. Even when the four levels did not apply to the essay, the exercise in which I broke down the philosopher's ideas in terms of these questions gave me an unprecedented clarity in speaking on the essence of his ideas. I remember using this technique in a philosophy class presentation in which I really owned the material and even frightened the professor who typically was critical of his students, but this time had nothing to add. The four levels foster understanding and can aid in thinking about the structure of your essay.

The forms should serve as a way to make a paper stronger than it normally would be. They should increase possibilities of expression without seducing us to write wildly with absurd forms devoid of significance except to entertain our fancy. In other words, by using organic forms we are applying a sort of "healthy" architecture in our essays; and sometimes finding the "healthiest" architecture comes only through inspiration and playing with various possibilities of the form. Some may say: "I want to be inspired like Plato." Such a wish is fine but Plato lived in an age when pure inspiration was the *only* way to write, while today we are able to utilize a "science" of organic thought-forms.

Using Others as Models: It is normal practice that when learning to write, to copy the works or compositions of others. Imitation is not a bad method for learning a new skill. Great composers study and rewrite their predecessors' works. Some of my professional writer friends spent hours rewriting pages of their favorite authors before they developed their own style.

Rudolf Steiner's Philosophy of Freehood could be used as a writing-model and master-text for living thinking. His style may be unapproachable to the average student and his spiritual and philosophic topics do not always lend themselves as books that are easy to imitate especially if you are working on a typical essay or book. Another problem is that Steiner often uses very subtle forms difficult to model oneself after. The Philosophy also has very long forms consisting of 32 organically organized paragraphs, not something one would want to set out writing. Steiner was very playful and, at the same time, didactic; thus when reading through each of his 28 books one can see how every book in some way presents new forms, contradicts the old ones, and expands this nascent science of living forms.

It is possibly better for our American character to immediately apply and try out organic forms even with a minimal foundation in Steiner's work. As questions develop over time, one can study Steiner's Philosophy of Freehood in order to look for more techniques of creating polarity, enhancement, and turning-inside-out. A deep respect will arise for Steiner's unknown method of thinking. (Later in this chapter I will cover more examples from Steiner's Philosophy of Freehood.)

Taking Your Character into Account in Your Writing: My anthroposophical teacher, Frank Teichmann, once said that there are two types of people: Egyptologists and Orientalists. The Egyptologist approaches his research and scholarship in a completely different manner from the Orientalist. The bohemian Orientalist loves to travel, meet people, talk shop, explore, excavate; the Orientalist's scholarship has a lightness and sociability. In contrast, the pedantic Egyptologist, although doing similar kinds of research as the Orientalist, prefers being alone and reflecting on the perfection, impenetrable mystery, art, and order of Ancient Egypt. He takes meticulous notes and publishes unreadable books written in a deadly syntax. Sociability is not his forte - and neither was it the Egyptologist Teichmann.

You may also need to decide whether you fall into the Platonist or Aristotelian camp? Do you believe in sudden inspiration, or in knowledge that comes through systematic work and experience? Or are you a Raphael or a da Vinci, that is, are you easy to get along with or cantankerous at work? There are writers that like a good fight and others in the spirit of Raphael seek to make beauty and gentleness a priority in their art work. Self-knowledge is important to the writing process.

When utilizing living form, assess who you are. There are many ways to approach your work. For those individuals who dislike writing, possibly living form is the ideal tool of inspiration for you. I have met many great students who just did not have anything to say in their papers. So many said: "I loved my major, but I could not stand writing papers."

The point of this comparison is that some will feel a need to work out perfect, intricate organic forms as heavy as a pyramid, while others will employ them with a certain lightness. Personally, I want a perfect form before I write, I prefer inspiration to rewriting, and I am cantankerous. Living form is perfect for me because my soul needs to see the bigger picture in order for the writing to flow. It is a good idea to try to keep a balance between your inner Egyptologist and Orientalist instead of just giving in to the one persona.

II.   General Structure of the Paragraphs within an Essay or Chapter

Paragraph-Level Forms: Before you figure out whether you are a Platonist or Aristotelian, you might want to experiment with forms in order to overcome your discomfort with writing. Take a piece of paper and sketch out the topic. What is your main question you have to answer? How many topics and sub-topics are there?

Collect your information and see if your topics can be broken into what? how? why? and who? Use the living form method to sketch your ideas on a large piece of paper. E.A. Poe wrote that you should start with your conclusion and build up to it. By utilizing living form you have all the pieces to an interchangeable puzzle in front of you and now you have to bring them into a polar form.

The next step is to gather your ideas as you would with a normal essay and start to see if you can bring the ideas into a living order. If the essay has more than four paragraphs, then you need to consider the polarities. Most of the examples we covered in the last chapter were at the chapter level of a book or an essay (Plato, Emerson, and Walsch). That is: we did not cover many examples of structure at the paragraph level.

We want to avoid stringing together ideas that do not create an organic unity. Be brave and choose a seven-fold living form for your topic. It can be seven paragraphs or seven sections with several paragraphs in each section. An article on Michael Jordan's career might look like this:

1. What? Physical Level: General statements about Jordan and the theme/thesis of the article

2. How? Life Level: Jordan's biography, development, training

3. Why? Feeling Level: Jordan's interaction with the world, goals, achievements, passions, injuries, scandals

4. Who? I-Level: Jordan's contributions to basketball, original idea, his essence and uniqueness

5. Why? Feeling Level: Jordan's moral life, his life task, his inner dilemmas

6. How? Life Level: Jordan's overview of his life and his role in the history of basketball

7. What? Physical: His legacy(s) and final contribution

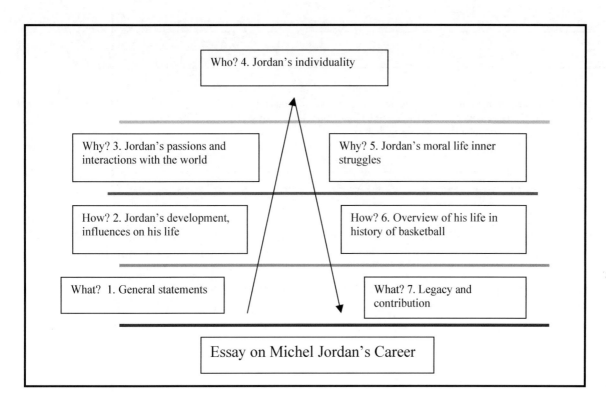

With this type of schema, the writer can cover these topics in many different ways. Regardless of one's choices of theme for each paragraph, one has the sense, after moving through the pattern of living form, that a full and multi-perspective picture arises. Notice at this point that the second half of the form (5. the why?, 6. how?, and 7. what?) has a more inward quality.

When starting your writing process, keep in front of you several forms and see which one works best. In the Michael Jordan example, one could remove one of the paragraphs and create a six-fold form.

62

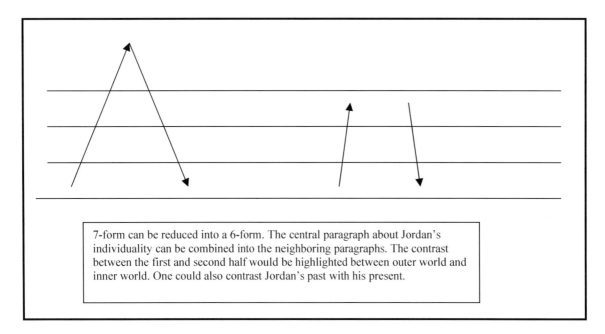

7-form can be reduced into a 6-form. The central paragraph about Jordan's individuality can be combined into the neighboring paragraphs. The contrast between the first and second half would be highlighted between outer world and inner world. One could also contrast Jordan's past with his present.

Start your paper by considering whether a seven-, six- or five-fold form fits your theme best. Fill out the outline with catchwords or section headings. If your paper has only seven paragraphs then there is no need to have section headings. If your paper has chapters, then you will need to number them, and eventually number/count the paragraphs.

Let's say your outline is very detailed with many sections or chapters and you organized your paragraphs according to living form. Chapter 1 may have five paragraphs; Chapter 2, thirteen paragraphs; Chapter 3, four paragraphs; Chapter 4, eight paragraphs; and Chapter 5 fifteen paragraphs.

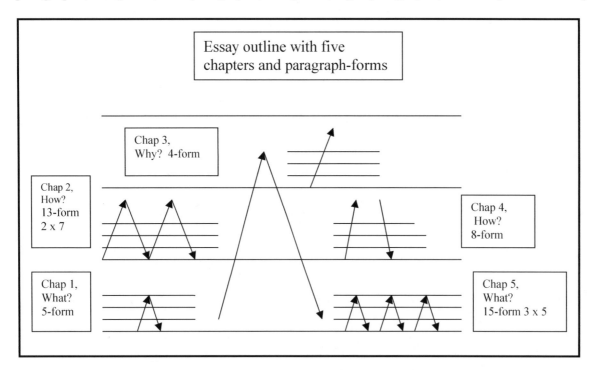

Essay outline with five chapters and paragraph-forms

This essay outline is missing the catchwords and themes of the chapters and paragraphs. The author would fill in the themes and color the diagrams like in the Michael Jordan essay above. Out of this tableau, one writes the paper, working out of this self-created picture. One can see aspects of musical form: in Chapter 2 there is a grand four-level monster form, while in Chapter 5 we have a more staccato, rhythmical form. Chapter 3 is subtle with its four paragraphs. These living forms give the author opportunity to compose an essay as if it were a musical composition!

III.   Feeling at the Sentence Level

This section needs to be read with a great deal of levity.

Writing in the Four Levels: Living form at the sentence level follows the same principles as the form on the chapter and paragraph level. One finds the main difference in the simple fact that a sentence is generally shorter than a paragraph. Therefore, the writer has less to work with in creating the mood of the levels and answering the four questions (what?, how?, why?, and who?). The qualities of organic sentences are light and subtle. Often one can barely detect a difference in mood when comparing several sentences in one of Steiner's paragraphs. Nevertheless, there is a way to detect and create organic structures at this level.

Letter writing is a good place to start. Choose a certain number of sentences and then write your letter. Then see to what extent the polarities match up. The central sentence in a paragraph with five sentences will turn the theme of the letter inside-out. For example:

Dear Alex,

1. Thank you for watching my dog for the week.
2. I am writing just to remind you about the dog's medicine
3. **Please don't forget to give it to him twice a day.**
4. Once in the morning and once before bed.
5. I will be back this weekend to get him.

See you Saturday,
Mark

The central sentence turns the form inside out by making an astral or emotional statement. The sentences also move from the general to the specific (1. Thank you, 2. a reminder, 3. DON'T FORGET, 4. Morning and evening, 5. The actual message). Here, the attempt was made also to have a static quality for the first sentence, action quality for the second, and an emotional quality for the third sentence and so on.

There are several techniques Steiner used to create the mood of each level:

The Physical or What? Level: Passive verbs and voice, intransitive, infinitives, objective voice, longish adverbial phrases

The Life or How? Level: Active voice, action verbs, describing the movement

The Feeling or Why? Level: Conditional verbs, wishes, problems, reasons for something

The Ego or Who? Level: Strong clear statements, definitions, insightful, declarative mood, judgmental

The Four Methods of Creating Organic Forms: In the examples that will follow, I want to emphasize the fact that living form is more of a feeling of proportions, than of a direct answering of questions. When analyzing Steiner, it can be difficult, if not impossible for us to find the levels. Living form seems like a like tapping on the levels, where even the rhythm of the sentences plays a role in addition to the content, word choice, grammar, and style.

Let us start by reviewing some examples from Steiner's work, starting with shorter paragraphs consisting of three- and four-sentences. Then we will cover longer paragraphs to look at the inversion of the theme. The goal is to learn a multi-perspectivism that will give you a plethora of tools for creating your own organic forms.

Living form can be analyzed from at least four perspectives. Typically, there are some tools one can use that predominate the four levels (passive voice for the physical, active verbs for the life level, conditional for the astral, and emphatic for the ego level). However, to limit ourselves to such dogmatic statements would foster a narrow-mindedness that is not to be found in Steiner, and categorically goes against the spirit of living form. Steiner had a flexible style that can be analyzed from these categories:

1. **Key words**: Steiner used key words or phrases in each sentence. Each sentence will have one word that may stand out. The key word whether it is a verb or noun or adjective will give the sentence a particular coloring.

2. **Sentence rhythm**: The varying rhythms of the sentences may create the levels of the organic thinking. By reading the sentences in a paragraph aloud, one hears immediately the movement from static to dynamic, from dynamic to emotional, from emotional to emphatic and so on. As is the case in poetry, sentence rhythm can be the basis of a living form in cases where verb, tense, and key words seem to shed no light on the levels.

3. **Grammar**: Grammar can be an essential part of the mood of living form. Infinitive verbs tend to be on the physical level while active verbs on the etheric. Physical level sentences often have several adverbial phrases (weighing them down), versus the tension of astral sentences, which contrast ideas or objects.

4. **Placement within paragraph**: No sentence in and of itself is physical, etheric, or astral. The levels and qualities of a sentence depend on what precede them and follow them. Therefore, in attempting to feel a quality of a sentence you must compare it to other sentences in the paragraph. Objectively speaking, the qualities of levels are relative. Thus there is no objectively blue sentence, there is only a blue sentence if a green sentence comes after it.

Living form, although based on certain general principles, is a type of *relativism* in the best sense of the word. It is a blending of objective laws of writing and organicism, and at the same time a highly personal process. For example, a true architect matches the design of the building to its geographical location, function, and the already existing buildings. The success of the project is dependent on subjective factors that are relative to each other. In finding an ideal design the architect looks at the whole and moves into the parts. In moving from the whole to the parts a living idea arises from living in the in-between-ness.

EXAMPLES USING KEY WORDS. From the *Second Appendix* of the <u>Philosophy of Freehood,</u> Paragraph 1/3. The key words are in **bold** and the verb phrases are in *italics*:

1. In what follows *will be reproduced* in all its essentials that which stood as a kind of "**preface**" in the first edition of this book.
2. *I placed it* here as an "**appendix**," since it reflects the type of thinking in which I wrote it twenty-five years ago, and not because it adds to the content of the book.

3. *I did not want* to leave it out completely for the simple reason, that time and again the opinion surfaces that I have something to suppress of my earlier **writings** because of my later spiritual **writings**.

Highlighted we see the key words of this paragraph. So here Steiner used the climb:
1. **Preface**,
2. **Appendix**, and
3. **Earlier/later writings**.

Also there is a very typical living form grammatical construction:
1. Passive verb (will be reproduced),
2. Active verb (I placed it), and
3. Conditional/wish verb (I did not want).

From Chapter One, paragraph 1/7 of the <u>Philosophy of Freehood</u>: The key words are in **Bold**:
1. This leads us directly to the **standpoint** from which the subject shall be considered here.
2. May the **question of the freehood** of will be posed at all by itself in a one sided way?
3. And if not: with what **other question** must it necessarily be connected?

The climb is clear. Steiner uses a series of words to create the sense of rising complexity:
Physical level: **standpoint**
Life Level: **question of freehood**
Astral Level: **other question?**

EXAMPLES USING SENTENCE RHYTHM. Sentence rhythm is based on the four levels. Physical level sentences tend to have clear, grounding statements, while etheric level sentences tend to have a staccato character.

From the Second Appendix, paragraph 3/3. The rhythm perspective is best detected when the sentences are read aloud over and over. In the example below, the first sentence must be read "calmly" because of its construction, the second sentence has a shortness resembling staccato, and the third sentence seems to have a rhythm of despair or concern.

Calmly 1. Only truth can bring us certainty in the development of our individual powers.
Quickly 2. Whoever is tormented by doubt his powers are lamed.
Concerned 3. In a world that is puzzling to him he can find no goal for his creativity.

An unusual example of creating rhythm is in paragraph 2/4 of the *Second Appendix*. Steiner inserts a part of a poem in the second sentence. Each of the four sentences has nearly identical subjects (truth and our age). What differentiates them are their rhythms and key words.

1. Our age can only want to draw *truth* out of the **depths** of man's being. [*]
2. Of Schiller's well-known two **paths**:

> "Truth seek we both, you in outer life, I within
> In the heart, and each will find it for sure.
> Is the eye healthy so it meets the Creator outside;
> Is the heart healthy then it reflects inwardly the World"

the present age will benefit more from the second.
3. A truth that comes to us from the outside always carries the stamp of **uncertainty**.
4. Only what appears as truth to each and every one of us, in one's own **inner being**, is what we want to believe.

Sentence one has a clear grounding quality. Sentence two literally has a poem, punctuated with many short phrases thus an airy rhythm. Sentence three contrasts outer with inner; and has particular feeling tone. Sentence four must be spoken with a slight awe or feeling of revelation. There are several tempos in which the sentence can be read: slow for the first sentence, light and quick for the second, conscious/cautious for the third, and clear and thoughtful for the fourth.

The key words follow the questions: what? **depths**; how? **paths**; why? **uncertainty**; and who? **inner being**.

EXAMPLES USING GRAMMAR. Steiner used grammar as a way of emphasizing the qualities of the levels of living form. The physical level presents a static quality best captured by the passive voice. Authors as a rule start a paragraph off with a general statement and often use the passive voice, or the verb "to be." Other techniques include the use of infinitive verbs and adverbial clauses, which 'weigh down' the sentence. Life-level sentences will have more active verbs unless their passive verbs are used in a more staccato style. Astral level sentences have to do with meaning, problem, wish, or imperative; thus they use modal verbs such as must, should, want, or have to.

Here, from Chapter One of the Philosophy of Freehood, in paragraph 11/3, is a fine example of climb/enhancement in grammatical construction: 1. passive, 2. active, 3. conditional.

1. Nothing is gained by assertions of this type.
2. For the question is just whether reason, purposes, and decisions exercise the same kind of compulsion over a human being as his animal passions.
3. If without my co-operation, a rational decision emerges in me with the same necessity with which hunger and thirst arise, then I must by necessity obey it, and my freehood is an illusion.

See how the key words do not have the same effectiveness for creating the levels, since there are so many prominent terms in each sentence: e.g., sentences two and three share many abstract terms making it difficult to claim a level. Read this paragraph aloud and test for yourself how the passive-active-conditional model works. And, here again another example from the same chapter, paragraph 8/3:

1. What does it mean to have **knowledge of the reasons** of one's actions?
2. One has paid too little attention to this question because, unfortunately, we have **torn into two** what is really an inseparable whole: the human being.
3. One has distinguished between the knower and the doer and has left out of account precisely the factor which comes before all other things: the **one who acts out of knowledge**.

The climb is created with a similar construction as in the example above. Sentence one is a question without a true subject (it) and has an infinitive verb which is typical of the physical level especially in scientific writings. Sentence two is an active formulation "pay attention" and "torn into two." Sentence three uses a more abstract or heady verb "distinguish."

EXAMPLES USING PLACEMENT WITHIN A PARAGRAPH. When key words, sentence rhythm, and grammar are indecisive, usually the placement of themes is essential. For example, a first sentence may have the characteristics of an astral level sentence such as key words that evoke feeling or verbs that express wishes. Or the rhythm of all the sentences in a paragraph are identical (Steiner tends to use three verbs in a well-balanced sentence) or seem to contradict the rhythms dictated by the levels (passive, active, wish-verb). In these cases, the placement of the sentence determines its level and quality, not the individual attributes.

1. We also do not want a form of knowing, which is fixed for all eternity in rigid academic rules and is kept in compendia valid for all time.
2. We hold that each of us is justified in starting from firsthand experiences, from immediate life conditions, and from there climbing to a knowledge of the whole universe.
3. We strive for certainty in knowing, but each in his own unique way.

A quick review of the verbs in each of the three sentences shows no typical pattern. If anything the verb "strive" in sentence three sounds like a how? level word, and in sentence one "want" normally fits the astral level. "We hold" with its static pose seems to fit the physical level best. The key words don't seem to shed much light on the living form dynamic. What to do?

There is a clear movement from the general (academic rules and compendia), to firsthand experience, to striving in a unique way. Sentence three is the most personal; sentence two a little less so; and sentence one, very impersonal and general in that academic knowledge is for everyone. Only through a careful comparison do we see the subtle climb upwards. (Steiner said that organic style should not slap the reader in the face and that is why his organicism can be very difficult to uncover. Steiner scholars who are opposed to idea that Steiner had an organic style, use this attribute to criticize O'Neil's great discovery. On a positive note, budding writers can take the quasi invisibility of their organic style as a boost to keep going in their work without worrying what other organic thinkers think.)

Polar Forms: So far we have covered four types of living form in three- and four-sentence paragraphs. At this point it might be helpful to consider other forms from Steiner and George O'Neil's work. Steiner wrote in German and thus all examples are translated into English. With George's work he searched for an American way of expressing living form. I have the feeling with Steiner's work that he was setting up models, some of which have an architectural quality in that his chapters and paragraphs tend to be long and parade like. George on the other hand kept things short and sweet.

The next examples illustrate the principle of inversion. My goal has been to open up possibilities of living form. By presenting examples, I sought to replace rules with a feeling of living form. I do not know of any other way to teach it. Not everyone can appreciate it in this life time, just as some of us cannot do math. There is no shortcut, and as in all things artistic there can be no true and final objective standard. In any case, let us proceed to the next example. Keep in mind the perspectives above, which help to decipher the living form structures.

In paragraph 8/6 of the *Second Appendix* to the <u>Philosophy of Freehood</u> we see how Steiner created the inversion by switching the perspective from sentence 1 through 3 to a new perspective in sentences 4 through 6. Sentences 1 through 3 cover the reading of the book, while sentence 4 through present the inner mind frame for accomplishing it. The pleasure of reading the book does not require a life change but moments of quiet contemplation. Sentence four is the inversion sentence in that we move from Steiner's book and opinion (sentences 1, 2, 3,) to the reader's inner life thereby inverting the form. Sentence 5 and 6 discuss the inner life of the East and West.

1. The book leads at first into more abstract spheres where thought must take on sharp contours in order to come to certain points.
2. However, the reader will be led out of these dry concepts and into concrete life.
3. I am certainly of the opinion that one must lift oneself into the ether world of concepts, if one wants to penetrate existence in all directions.
4. He who only knows how to have pleasure through his senses, doesn't know life's finest pleasures.
5. The eastern masters have their disciples spend years in a life of renunciation and asceticism before they disclose to them what they themselves know.

68

6. The West no longer requires pious practices and ascetic exercises for scientific knowledge, but what is needed instead is the good will that leads to withdrawing oneself for short periods of time from the firsthand impressions of life and entering into the spheres of the pure thought world.

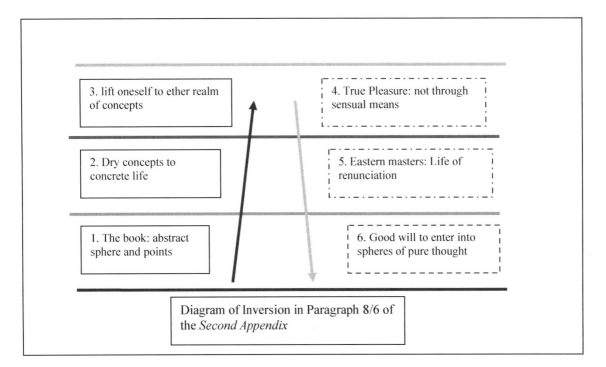

Another example of inversion or turning inside-out is paragraph 6/6 from the *Second Appendix*. In the mid-point, Steiner switches the topic from being compelled by academics to understand theories to an inner desire to form our own world view. Thus, the inversion is created by switching the perspective from outer compulsion to inner need.

1. Our scientific theories should also no longer take the position that our acceptance of them was a matter of absolute coercion.
2. None of us would give a title to an academic work such as Fichte once did: "A Crystal Clear Report to the Public at Large on the Actual Nature of Modern Philosophy.
3. *An Attempt to Compel Readers to Understand*."
4. Today nobody should be compelled to understand.
5. We are not asking for acceptance or agreement from anyone who is not driven by a specific need to form his own personal worldview.
6. Nowadays we also do not want to cram knowledge into the unripe human being, the child, instead we try to develop his faculties so that he will not have to be compelled to understand, but will want to understand.

Sentence four inverts the perspective by stating "nobody should be compelled." Sentence 1 through 3 presents the coercive nature of some philosophers. Sentences 4 through 6 seek a willingness from individuals to want to understand and develop from their own individual needs views. Also,

Steiner in the example switches from the past philosophy of Fichte (educate the same manner) to present day personal needs.

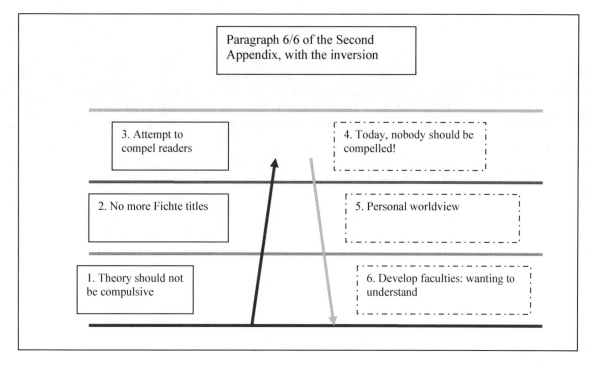

Here is an example from George O'Neil's <u>The Human Life</u>. Although George gleaned this organic style from Steiner, he seems to have made his own unique contribution by inventing a more American style of writing that is based on short and crisp sentences. In the example below, we have a clear inversion in sentence four, triggered with the use of such words as "now," which seems to turn the sentence perspective inward. In sentence four, the topic switches from the perspective of "man's organism" to "inner motivation," thus announcing the inversion from outer life to inner life.

1. By mid-life man is fully incarnated.
2. He and his organism are fully knit.
3. He realizes this all too well as weight replaces spontaneity.
4. It is **now** that the discovery of the inner motivation becomes the challenge.
5. Self-propulsion rather than being propelled by circumstance.
6. And this is felt as a life-necessity for the first time, as our susceptibility to external pressure lessens.

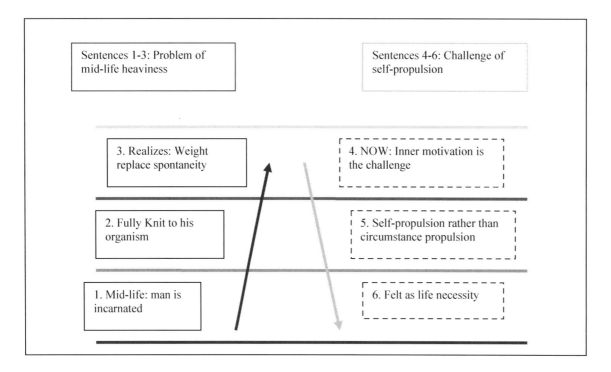

The seven-form has its turning point in the fourth sentence. In this six-sentence paragraphs, we see a clear movement thematically from left to right. In the seven-sentence paragraph, we have the inversion in the middle, thus not necessarily leaning to one side or the other. In the example from Steiner's book on Nietzsche, we see that sentence four turns the thought-organism inward by using negations: "**not** mislead", "**no** longer", "**not** overly concerned", and "**not** able to do". Sentences 1 through 3 are what Nietzsche does; sentences 4 through 7 are what Nietzsche doesn't do!

1. Nietzsche declares a thought or judgment to be valid when it finds agreement in the freedom loving life instincts.
2. Opinions which are decisive for life, he accepts without any logical doubt.
3. His thinking thereby gains a confident, free quality.
4. His thinking does not mislead him to such misgivings about: whether or not, a theory is "objectively" true, whether or not, a theory goes beyond the limits of the human capacity to know and so on.
5. When Nietzsche acknowledges the value of an opinion for life, then he no longer asks for further proof of its significance and validity.
6. And he is not overly concerned with the limitations of human knowing.
7. He is of the opinion that a healthy type of thinking creates what it can create and does not torture itself with useless questions such as: what I am *not* able to do?

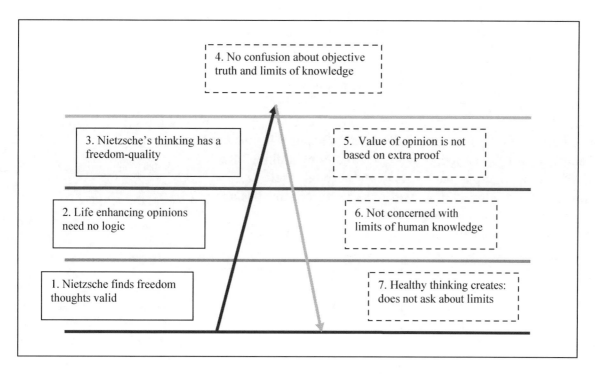

Another perspective: the first three sentences are concerned with what Nietzsche does in his personal philosophy i.e., accepts opinions that are free and life embracing. Starting in sentence four, he discusses the negatives: he dismisses terms such as "objectivity," limits, proof, and negative questions. The ascending blue arrow represents the life-enhancing aspects, while the yellow descending line Nietzsche's disregard for society's limitations.

In this seven-from taken from Steiner's complete edition #2 (p.24) we see a very straight forward inversion. In sentence four, Kant is mentioned by name and again in sentences 5 through 7. The first three sentences explain how Steiner's theory of knowledge differs from popular philosophy and the last four sentences talk about the limitation caused by Kant researchers in philosophy.

1. According to the accepted scientific terminology, our work must be called a theory of knowledge.
2. The questions that it answers are admittedly of a completely different nature to those which are generally posed by science nowadays.
3. We have seen why this is so.
4. Where similar research appears today it is based almost exclusively on Kant.
5. One has, in academic circles, totally overlooked the fact that in addition to the science of knowledge founded by the great Konigsberg thinker there are others schools of thought – at least the possibility of such schools – which are no less capable of objective philosophical discussion as Kant.
6. Otto Liebmann uttered at the beginning of the 1860s: If we want to have a world view without contradiction, then we must go back to Kant.
7. This is the very reason why today we have such an overabundance of literature on Kant.

In this example, from the third chapter of the Philosophy of Freehood there is a clear inversion in sentence four. The first three sentences present the idea of a self-supporting principle like Archimedes' lever. Starting in sentence four, Steiner has found this self-supporting principle in thinking itself. Sentences 5 through 7 support this by saying we grasp thinking only through itself. The turning point moves from a general principle in thinking to a principle which exists through itself and turns in on itself.

1. I believe I have given sufficient reasons for making thinking the starting point for my study of the world.
2. When Archimedes had discovered the lever, he thought that with its help he could lift the whole cosmos from its hinges, if only he could find a point of support for his instrument.
3. He needed something that was supported by itself and by nothing else.
4. In thinking we have a principle that exists in and through itself.
5. Let us try, therefore, to understand the world starting from this basis.
6. Thinking we can grasp through thinking itself.
7. The question is, whether we can also grasp anything else through it.

Just by reading the example aloud one can hear the inversion without much ado.

Eight-forms: Eight-forms follow the principle of inversion. Unlike the six and seven-forms, eight-forms have two ego level sentences. The fourth sentence however, does not mark the turn inward. In the example below, sentence five turns the form inward by stating "the situation is different." Normally, the central sentence judges the preceding sentences, or requires some reflection on the part of the reader.

1. There is a profound difference between the ways in which, for me, the parts of an event are related to one another before, and after, the discovery of the corresponding concepts.
2. Mere observation can trace the parts of a given event as they occur; but their connection remains obscure without the help of concepts.
3. I see the first billiard ball move towards the second in a certain direction and with a certain velocity; what will happen after the impact I must await, and again I can only follow it with my eyes.
4. Suppose someone, at the moment of impact, obstructs my view of the field where the event is taking place, then, as mere spectator, I remain ignorant of what happens afterwards.
5. The situation is different if prior to the obstruction of my view I have discovered the concepts corresponding to the pattern of events.
6. In that case I can say what will happen even when I am no longer able to observe it.
7. An event or an object which is merely observed, does not of itself reveal anything about its connection with other events or objects.
8. This connection becomes evident only when observation is combined with thinking.

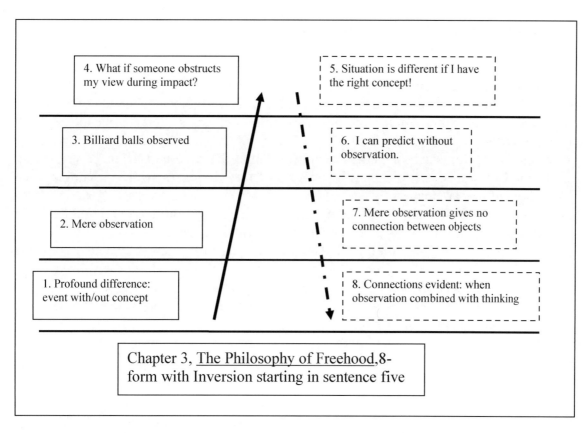

4. What if someone obstructs my view during impact?	5. Situation is different if I have the right concept!
3. Billiard balls observed	6. I can predict without observation.
2. Mere observation	7. Mere observation gives no connection between objects
1. Profound difference: event with/out concept	8. Connections evident: when observation combined with thinking

Chapter 3, The Philosophy of Freehood, 8-form with Inversion starting in sentence five

The first half deals with the mere observations of billiard balls. The second half tells how it is when one has the right concept for the situation. The polarities in this example also answer each other very nicely.

Nine-Forms: The nine-form can be seen as an eight-form with an extra sentence in the middle - or as three sets of three sentences. The nine-form has three sentences on the ego-level, which makes for an unorthodox form. The original model or archetype for the nine-form is the nine-fold human being that has three basic energy bodies, three levels of soul/mind, and three levels of spirit.

When working with a nine-fold form, we have two ways to look at the form. First, consider the two halves of the nine-form with its inversion point in sentence five. Second, change your perspective, and see the nine-form as three sets of three sentences – each set has its own theme.

In paragraph 3/9, the main topics are percept (object of observation), concept, thinking, metaphysics, and intuition. Steiner, in the first half of the paragraph, gives the problem: a dualistic theory of knowledge; and in the second half (sentence 5 thru 9) a solution in a monistic theory of knowledge. Sentences one through four discuss the results of having the percept and concept as foreign to one another, while sentences 5 through 9 present the concept and the percept as related via intuition. Sentence five turns the form inside-out by stating that our thinking is capable of grasping reality, thereby moving from a kind of dualistic metaphysics to a new non-dualistic metaphysics! Sentences 6 thru 9 simply continue this new line of thought.

If we consider the paragraph 3/9 from the second perspective we have sentences 1 through 3 tackle dualism's mistakes; sentences 4 through 6, dualism corrected; sentences 7 through 9, intuition!

Paragraph 3/9 of the 9th chapter of the <u>Philosophy of Freehood</u>

1. When we are contemplating thinking itself, two things coincide which otherwise *must* always appear apart, namely, concept and percept.
2. If we fail to see this, we shall be unable to regard the concepts which we have elaborated with respect to percepts as anything but shadowy copies of these percepts, and we shall take the percepts as presenting to us the true reality.
3. We shall, further, build up for ourselves a metaphysical world after the pattern of the perceived world; we shall call this a world of atoms, a world of will, a world of unconscious spirit, or whatever, each according to his own kind of mental imagery.
4. And we shall fail to notice that all the time we have been doing nothing but building up a metaphysical world hypothetically, after the pattern of *our own* world of percepts.
5. But if we recognize what is present in thinking, we shall realize that in the percept we have only one part of the reality and that the other part which belongs to it, and which first allows the full reality to appear, is *experienced* by us in the permeation of the percept by thinking.
6. We shall see in this element that appears in our consciousness as thinking, not a shadowy copy of some reality, but a self-sustaining spiritual essence.
7. And of this we shall be able to say that it is brought into consciousness for us through *intuition*.
8. *Intuition* is the conscious experience - in pure mind - of a purely spiritual content.
9. Only through an intuition can the essence of thinking be grasped.

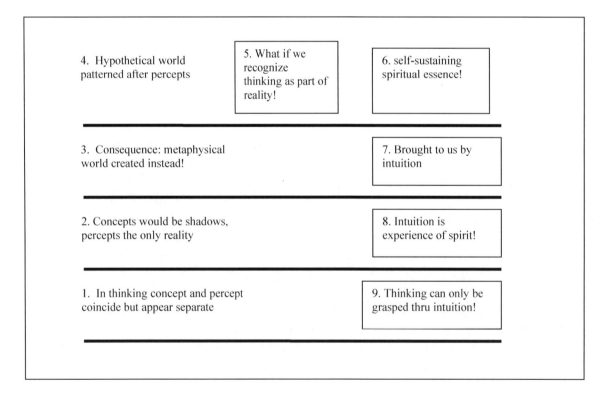

IV. Habits of the Mind Helpful to Writing Organically

Start with Your Conclusion: Steiner gave a lecture to workers at his center in Switzerland about spiritualizing thinking. He gave several examples in which he asked the audience to imagine that opposite is true. For example, the claim that "the shortest distance between two points is a straight line" should be doubted while the opposite should be considered true "the shortest distance between two points is a curved line." (In reality, airplanes fly in an arc, not in a straight line over the surface of the earth.) Similarly research projects often start with a conclusion or hunch and then the researcher looks for ways to prove what they already imagine to be true.

Edgar Allen Poe recommended starting with a conclusion.[12] It gives you a certain power and freedom to develop your form. Since you are not writing ahead of yourself, you have the time and consciousness to see and feel the proportions of your work. In school we learn to write linearly that is one paragraph after the next. However there are teachers who ask you to sketch out the whole essay before you embark on your project. See the whole, and the parts will have their significance.

Another advantage of emphasizing the importance of the conclusion is that your conclusion could have a more meaningful function. Normally, a conclusion simply ends a paper by reiterating your central theme. An organic living conclusion, however, seeks to connect to the next chapter, to leave the reader with a question, or seeks to answer to the original question posed in the first paragraph. Study Steiner's conclusions to each chapter to get an idea of this organic art.

Stick to One Theme and Grow One Paragraph Out of the Other: The process of organic writing has many similarities to the process of painting or of writing musical compositions. A painter has usually one main theme even when there are multiple elements to the composition. A symphony is mainly the repetition of one motif developed throughout a piece. Organic writing thus takes its time with one theme, and repeats the same topic from seven different perspectives: the what, the how, the why, the who, and so on.

Attention should be given to the first and last sentence of each paragraph. For example, does the first sentence of your second paragraph relate and connect to your first paragraph's last sentence? Is your second paragraph a variation on the theme of your first paragraph, but on a higher level? When you read it aloud, can you hear the growth from one paragraph to the next?

Although organic style calls for an inner coherence of organic logic, it also allows for a "jumping" or "collage style" of writing. A collage style means that each element may at first glance not fit smoothly into the bigger chapter or picture. The perplexed reader may ask: "why on earth did the author put that paragraph there? And how does this paragraph relate organically to the whole thought-organism of the chapter?" Often in the case of art, it may not be so easy to follow the creative "jumps" of others. In Rudolf Steiner's work (and in the work of many creative people), it is common to find unorthodox use of punctuation, upside-down organic forms of chapters/paragraphs/sentences, and a constant stream of contradictory innovations with each new book.

Moods, colors, and writing: Another helpful technique for organic writing is the use of moods or colors. Immerse yourself in a feeling of blue when writing the first paragraph; in a feeling of green, with the

---

[12] Poe wrote on his Philosophy of Composition: "It is only with the *dénouement* constantly in view that we can give a plot its indispensable air of consequence, or causation, by making the incidents, and especially the tone at all points, tend to the development of the intention."

second; red with the third. Let color, emotion, and energy of the level and content manifest itself in you! Spend some time meditating in the levels and colors before you sit yourself down to write.

A feeling of blue, static, grounding energy should enter into your mood. Then switch with the next paragraph, or sentence, into a dynamic green state. Go inward into a red state with a more subtle feeling of consciousness, conflict, and passion.

As you move downward in your form, enter into a feeling of inversion. Feel the inwardness, let polarity become a feeling beyond the mental construct of abstract polarity as an organic lawfulness; i.e. you are moving from the word polarity (which is in your head) into an actual feeling of polarity - a concrete feeling or soul gesture.

Success in organic writing seems to come out of a feeling state. It is important to enter into these states before you sit down to write, especially since higher understandings of living form ultimately must be derived out of a feeling for the whole organism of writing.

From Left to Right: Living form has several movements: enhancement, polarity, and inversion. A five-, six-, and seven-form will all have an inversion process in the middle paragraph where the author's perspective changes. Steiner often changed voices by using the third person (he/she, it, they, people) in the first half of the curve, and then the first person (I, we, my, myself) in the second half. The *preface* to the Philosophy of Freehood covered earlier is a good example of changing voices as a technique for inversion. But there is more to it.

A living form follows a pattern, but is, by no means, a fixed archetypal structure. Thus, one should interpret the example below as *one way* of characterizing the levels and inter-relationships of a living thought-form. The key to avoiding a rigid re-creation of this thought-form is to feel your way into the polarity and inversion. In this sense, the archetypal plant is safer as a model because it displays the inter-relations of organicism without taking a fixed standpoint of the four levels and their questions.

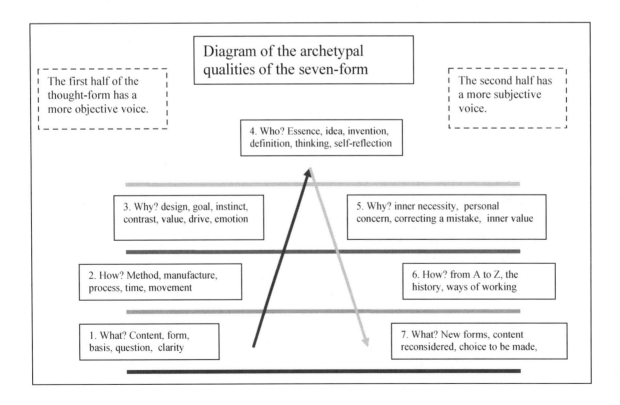

Diagram of the archetypal qualities of the seven-form

The first half of the thought-form has a more objective voice.

The second half has a more subjective voice.

4. Who? Essence, idea, invention, definition, thinking, self-reflection

3. Why? design, goal, instinct, contrast, value, drive, emotion

5. Why? inner necessity, personal concern, correcting a mistake, inner value

2. How? Method, manufacture, process, time, movement

6. How? from A to Z, the history, ways of working

1. What? Content, form, basis, question, clarity

7. What? New forms, content reconsidered, choice to be made,

This diagram shows both the linear progression of the seven-form (1. Content, 2. Method, 3. Purpose, 4. Essence, 5. Inner necessity, 6. History, 7. New Form) and the polar transition from left to right:

        1. and 7. Old Form and New Forms;
        2. and 6. Process and From A to Z;
        3. and 5. Outer Value and Inner Value.

This contrast of the left and right side of living form must arise out of an artistic playfulness. By considering some of Rudolf Steiner's gentle polarities, I believe the reader will feel a certain freedom to create their own thought-forms courageously. In Chapter One of the Philosophy of Freehood, *Conscious Human Action*, Rudolf Steiner gives what seems at first impenetrable examples of how to write in living form. Upon close inspection, his polarities are not aggressively prominent, but instead can be gently intuited. Steiner was against an aesthetic that "bombarded" his readers.[13] His polarities are subtle gestures that often go unnoticed because they are usually only detectable after they are placed in a living-form diagram.

Below are the first seven paragraphs of chapter one. I made synopses of each paragraph and placed them in their living form. I have tried to streamline them as much as possible so that beginners can follow easily. Those who have a natural affinity for living form will immediately recognize organic relationships.

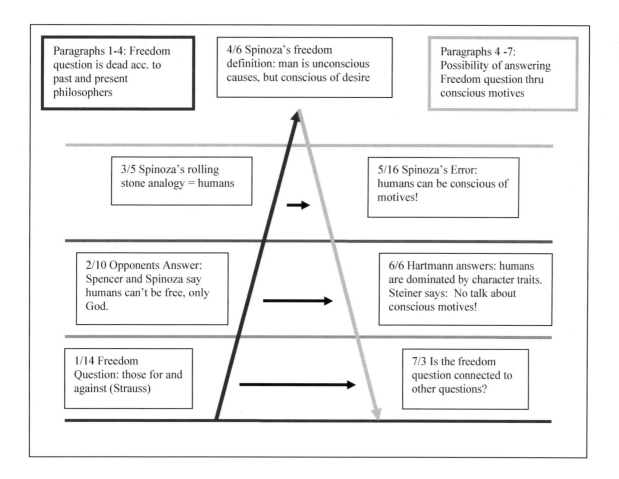

---

[13] This is the key reason why his followers have never understood what he was trying to do. They had tin-ears and could not believe that this thinking was his greatest contribution.

How did Steiner move from paragraph 3/5 to 5/16, 2/10 to 6/6, 1/14 to 7/3? If we compare these paragraphs to the diagram with the archetypal seven-form, we see there are several similarities. The first half (paragraphs 1-3) presents mainly the opponents of freedom (Strauss, Spencer, and Spinoza). The second half, starting in paragraph 4/6, turns the discussion inward by covering the idea of unconscious and conscious motives and causes.

Let us focus in on the polarities: paragraph 1/14 presents the freedom question and 7/3 the renewed freedom question; paragraph 2/10 covers the opponents Spencer and Spinoza (outer determinants) while paragraph 6/6 the inner determinants of Hartmann; and lastly, 3/5 discusses Spinoza's idea, while 5/16 reveals Spinoza's error. Steiner corrects the opponents' mistake in paragraphs 5, 6, and 7. These polarities would be hard to detect without having the diagram.

Our next consideration is how Steiner created his enhancement, or climb. We see that he starts with the question of freedom in paragraph one, and then concludes with an abstract definition in paragraph four. Thus the first enhancement follows this pattern of:

1. What? Question

2. How? Answer (negative)

3. Why? Analogy (humans are like stones, unfree)

4. Who? Freedom defined (unconscious of causes)

When we review the diagram of the archetypal seven-fold form, we see that the content of chapter one resembles the qualities of the levels. Thus, the "freedom question" is the what?/physical level; the "answer" fits the how?/life level; and the "analogy" answers the question Why?/astral level; and the who?/idea level is answered with a definition. No paragraph is by itself a why?- or how?- paragraph, because the content derives its organic significance from the position in the thought-composition. Thus paragraph three could easily be a how?-, or who?-paragraph, depending on what preceded it.

The descending curve, or enhancement, has as its main theme the correction of the freedom opponents: humans are not rolling stones but capable of consciousness of causes and motives (Spinoza's error) in their lives. The movement from right to left is completed by questioning Spinoza's analogy and adding a deeper, moral dimension which is important for everyone (knowing causes of why we act). The how?-level reflects the two ways freedom is negated: in paragraph two humans are determined by outer circumstance while in paragraph six Hartmann argues humans when not determined by outer causes are determined by their fixed characters! And finally the first question concerning freedom is given an additional question thus giving the descending enhancement the following schema:

5. Why? Humans can know causes, and are not stones (inner value)

6. How? Humans determined from external and internal causes (from A to Z)

7. What? Deeper question (new form)

The movement from the right side to the left side of the curve is possible with a little adjustment, depending of the perspective. The subtly of these relationships allows for more freedom for the writer because under circumstances, one could easily make paragraph six the polarity to paragraph three, instead of paragraph five. Keep in mind when we create a thought-form, it is *we* who determine how the thought-composition appears and what type of inner consistency exists.

*

Back to the drawing board. In addition to having a descending curve in the thought-form, we can also characterize the two sides in various ways. Some transitions Steiner used are for example:

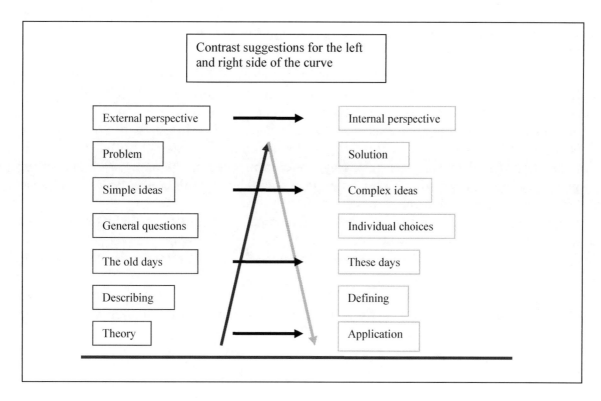

This diagram gives some possibilities for shaping your themes. In the first example there was more of a contrast between the "external and internal." Here we have elements of time, stylistic concerns, and knowing/doing. When setting out to write your form, choose a contrast between the right and left side.

Geometry and thought forms: One of the least explored aspects of organic thinking is Steiner's and George O'Neil's use of geometry in their writings. Behind the zigzag forms of the Philosophy of Freehood, George O'Neil found geometric shapes such as a five-pointed stars, mirroring curves, quasi architectural formations. In a chapter with many zigzagging seven-forms consisting of 35 five paragraphs, one could reshape the zigzags into straight or curved lines, which when rearranged create pentagons.

Is it helpful to explore such advanced geometry as regard our or Steiner's writings? I am not sure myself, especially since this area of artistic-spiritual understanding has not been further researched. But it is certainly worth looking at O'Neil's work to see if in some way our ultimate thoughts (reality) actually streams down from Platonic Solids glistening about the world of ideas.

It is well-known that Steiner had geometric forms in front of him when he gave a lecture.

V.   Parts of the Whole: How Do We Break Things Down?

Longer Outlines and their Structure: Living form is an artistic process. The first step is to move from the whole (the big theme) into the parts as a sketch-artist does. The next step is to ask yourself: how long is the paper going to be? Is it a 300-page book, a dissertation, or a twenty-page graduate school essay?

Also, how much time do you want to devote to your paper? The longer you live with your creation, the more time you will have with its formation and inner coherence. Steiner said that he would consider certain passages for days in order that they were formulated in harmony with the other paragraphs, chapters, and sentences. Always keep in mind it was Steiner's mission to be so exact, and there is no need to achieve such a high level of mastery.

When sitting down to write, immerse yourself in the theme, and feel the levels and colors. See where and how the theme can be arranged into a living form. Start with your conclusion and introduction and then use the questions of what?, how?, why? and who?, if they apply. Use an idea-sheet which has all the elements and themes of your paper.

Once you have your idea-sheet, start inter-relating the themes of your paper. If it is a twenty-page paper, start with section headings. For a two-page paper, chapter headings may not be necessary. Learning to "member" (divide) your paper into different sections and headings is essential for living form. Some questions you must answer, for example, for an essay longer than twenty pages:

- How many parts, chapters/subheads, subsections are there in total in the paper?

- Are the introduction and conclusion part of the living form, or separate wings?

- Are you using only chapter numbers or titles, or both?

- How many levels of subsections are there, and are they clear in your outline?

- Are you consistent in your usage of numbering and lettering of titles, sections, and subsections?

Written works naturally have various sections and ways of dividing the content into coherent parts. Living form requires that the author have a clear notion of how his work flows from part to part. One always keeps an eye on the title and theme when writing so that this organicism is transferred and the reader has the experience of moving through living perspectives. The outline of the paper should be carefully constructed so that the author is conscious of how the theme unfolds through the various parts.

*

Every writer has their preferences. Some will seek to write very structured essays with longish thought-waves and with perfect symmetry, while others will seek to be more accommodating to their content. In other words, some writers will get great joy from making their subject matter fit into elegant forms, possibly in an almost parade-like formation (let's call them our platonic-idealists). Others will keep their forms short, manageable, and multi-layered.

Living form has its life-force and heart-beat in the paragraph. Each paragraph communicates one main idea. We use headings, sub-heading and so on to divide the paragraphs into themes. Authors have to make personal choices as to how complicated or elaborate they want their forms to be.

Here are two examples of the different tendencies. The first example comes from Rudolf Steiner's Philosophy of Freehood. Steiner had a tendency to use elaborate forms with slight repetitions of certain key ideas, rephrased again in different parts of the chapters. A chapter consisting of 20 paragraphs has no printed subdivisions such as headings or subheadings. Although it is not unusual for a non-fiction author to have a chapter consisting of twenty or more pages without a heading, it is not advisable for those writing in living form, since forms consisting of forty paragraphs or more become difficult to manage.

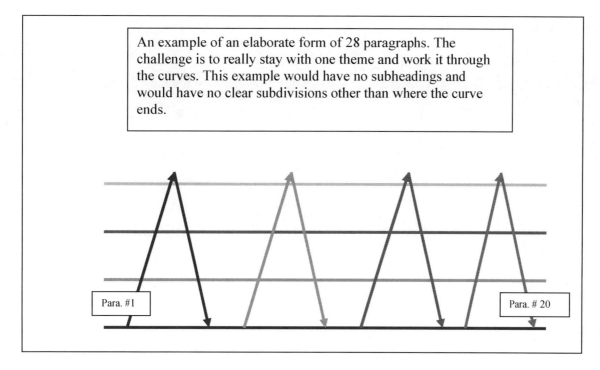

An example of an elaborate form of 28 paragraphs. The challenge is to really stay with one theme and work it through the curves. This example would have no subheadings and would have no clear subdivisions other than where the curve ends.

Para. #1

Para. # 20

Modern writers prefer 'short and sweet' chapters with plenty of breaks and headings. Dissertations and scholarly books usually have several parts. A book with two parts may have several chapters e.g., Part I contains chapters 1 through 6 and Part II chapter 7 through 11. In living form, it is important that when you are working with chapters not to separate them into parts, for it creates unseen difficulties with the living forms of the chapters. In other words, by numbering the chapters you should keep all 11 chapters together and not separate them into Part I and Part II.

In a paper or book with three parts, the chapters should be numbered according to the number of part:

Part I, chapter 1.1, 1.2, 1.3
Part II, chapters 2.1, 2.2, 2.3,
Part III, chapters 3.1, 3.2, 3.3, 3.4 and so on.

I make this point because if the chapter numbers continued through each of the parts – Part I, chapters 1, 2, 3, Part II chapters 4, 5, 6, Part III chapters 7, 8, 9, 10 – then *the book would have two forms*: one form based solely on the division of the parts and one based on the number of chapters! These at first glance contradict each other, but Steiner in his flexible thinking system makes them work. (This flexibility of Steiner's thinking is very difficult to grasp for most and needs to be taken up as an advanced study of his work.) How could two contradictory forms work? One form would be more content based, and the other more style based.

Example of the form with the chapter numbers 1-10 without parts:
Chapter 1 (what?)
Chapter 2 (how?)
Chapter 3 (why?)
Chapter 4 (how?)

Chapter 5 (what?)

Chapter 6 (what?)
Chapter 7 (how?
Chapter 8 (why?)
Chapter 9 (how?)
Chapter 10 (what?)

The same book however, seen from in a different form with the Parts! Notice the lack of symmetry compared to the example above.

Part I
Chapter 1 (what?)
Chapter 2 (how?)
Chapter 3 (why?)
Part II
Chapter 4 (what?)
Chapter 5 (how?)
Chapter 6 (why?)
Part III
Chapter 7 (what?)
Chapter 8 (how?)
Chapter 9 (why?)
Chapter 10 (who?)

The author would have to carefully incorporate and rework the content to fit both forms, however seemingly contradictory! By changing your perspective both possibilities can co-exist. In some of Steiner's books even three perspectives are evident!

Chicago Manual Works for Organic Writing: When writing a longer work, you'll want to have inner consistency. The Chicago Manual of Style offers a practical way to organize your papers or books. Here is the basic way to set up headings, and the important thing is to be consistent whether you follow the Chicago Manual or not.

Book Title
Parts of the book (Roman numerals)
Chapters (Arabic numerals)
Subheads (A-head) of a Chapter (Roman numerals)
B-head Italic Caps (no numbers or letters necessary)
C-head Italics followed by colon or period

It is obvious by now that there could be possibly several levels of depth in a book. The parts, the chapters, the subheads, b-heads, and c-heads. When sketching out your book, you would keep these levels of depth clear on your diagram by indenting each new heading.

In the example below is George O'Neil's the Human Life. This is the first book in English to be intentionally composed in living thinking. *I filled in the living form questions (what?, how?, why?) and numbered and lettered the headings and subheads for easy reference. Notice the different depths to the headings and subheadings starting with the chapters, then subheads, then B-heads, and finally C-heads.*

The Human Life
Ch. 1 THE MAP OF LIFE
Ch. 2 RIPENING OF THE SOUL FORCES
Ch. 3 THE BALANCE OF POLARITIES IN HUMAN LIFE
Ch. 4 THE LIFE OF THE COSMOS IN THE AGES OF MAN
Ch. 5 OUR KARMIC COMPANIONS
Ch. 6 HUMAN ENCOUNTERS IN THE LIGHT OF MOON AND SUN
Ch. 7 CRUCIAL YEARS IN HUMAN LIFE
Ch. 8 METAMORPHOSIS OF CREATIVE FORCES
Ch. 9 OUR SOURCES OF SPIRITUAL RENEWAL
Ch. 10 THE LIFE-CHART

The Human Life
WHAT? Ch. 1, THE MAP OF LIFE
HOW? Ch. 2, RIPENING OF THE SOUL FORCES
WHY? Ch. 3, THE BALANCE OF POLARITIES IN HUMAN LIFE
HOW? Ch. 4, THE LIFE OF THE COSMOS IN THE AGES OF MAN
WHAT? Ch. 5, OUR KARMIC COMPANIONS

WHAT? Ch. 6, HUMAN ENCOUNTERS IN THE LIGHT OF MOON AND SUN
HOW? Ch. 7, CRUCIAL YEARS IN HUMAN LIFE
WHY? Ch. 8, METAMORPHOSIS OF CREATIVE FORCES
HOW? Ch. 9, OUR SOURCES OF SPIRITUAL RENEWAL
WHAT? Ch. 10, THE LIFE-CHART

If you focus in on one chapter you see the various layers of depth. O'Neil only numbered the chapter titles and the main subsections (subheads A) of the chapter (I. An Affair of Everyman, II. The Years of Metamorphosis, III. Maturity: the Bridge at 35). O'Neil left the b- subheads without a numeral! Thus I gave subheads numbers and letters and added the questions of what? how? why? etc. The c-heads were denoted with lower case Roman numerals and have a 9-forms.

Chapter 1. The Map of Life
I. AN AFFAIR OF EVERYMAN
    A. **(What?)** *(INTRODUCTION, not given a title)*
    B. **(How?)** *WHAT THE WORLD IS SAYING*
    C. **(Why?)** *THE SCOPE*
    D. **(How?)** *SURVEY OF LIFE: ASPECTS OF BODY, SOUL, AND SPIRIT*
        i.   *[Introduction, not given a title]*

        ii. *Bodily maturity:*

        iii. *Maturity of the Personality:*

        iv. *The Personality Emerges:*

        v. *The Ego Comes To Itself in Rational-Feeling Soul (age 28-35):*

        vi. *The Ego Becomes Self-Aware in the Spiritual Soul (age 35-42):*

In the actual book, O'Neil numbered the subheadings, and he certainly did not put in the questions what?, how?, why?, who? It is easy to notice the basics of living form in the subheadings:

I. An Affair of Every Man (What?),
II. The Years of Metamorphosis (How?),
III. Maturity: The Bridge at 35 (Why?).

It seems O'Neil gave so many titles to subheadings as if he were trying to educate his public about what he was doing in his writing. The important thing here is that he organized his chapters and headings so carefully. The list of titles and headings is a good way to begin to see the form of your work in a way that each section and its subparts can be viewed with ease and grace.

The Value and Use of Punctuation: Punctuation in all its expressions helps to organize thoughts in useful segments. So far we have chapters and subheadings. There are several other accepted ways of dividing a chapter or paragraph.

We can divide a chapter further by using asterisks (or spacing) as is normally done in non-fiction books – instead of using headings. Thus instead of having new headings in the form of a title or numbers, we now have a simple asterisks. When one uses an asterisk to divide sections of a chapter, it means that the chapter has two parts: a what?-part, and how?-part; or an introduction and body. And following this line of thought, for example, three asterisks would mean the chapter has four parts, very subtly divided and without a heading.

Some uses of punctuation come and go with the age and culture. German language authors no longer use dashes in front of sentences. In Nietzsche and Steiner's times (pre-1920's German authors) the dash was used in front of a sentence often in the middle of a paragraph?! Steiner used the dash in the extreme, in that he used them in completely unique and contradictory ways. For example he separates parts (sentences) of a paragraph using the dash(es) to mark off a parenthetical sentences. On other occasions, Steiner placed dashes in the middle of a paragraph at the end of a sentence, thereby marking a new paragraph! Even stranger he would place a dash at the end of a chapter hinting that the form of a book could be varying according to the perspective. Steiner was consistent however enigmatic in his use of punctuation and grammar in a particular work.

In my opinion, the lesson for us is to use our punctuation creatively and in a consistent and meaningful manner.* When Rudolf Steiner used quotations from other authors, he often wove them into his text. For example, quotations can follow colons. Where possible, *quotations should be woven into the sentence-count of a paragraph*. Thus if your paragraph has five sentences, plus a block quotation consisting of three sentences, followed by four concluding sentences, your paragraph must have a form that includes all 12 sentences! The quotation has to fit the form, and Steiner himself often took liberties with various quotations he wove into his texts.

Dashes, Asterisks, and 'quote-weaving' are part of a bigger mission that Steiner set out to complete. Steiner, in nearly every field he worked, sought to re-enliven and improve upon accepted standards. He created a renewed kind of education, farming, speech training, spiritual-meditation, cosmology, and theory of government. A renewed form of organic writing does not mean a new form of dogmatic writing, syntax, and punctuation such as the APA or Chicago Manual of Style. Every generation must make societal form fits its creative needs and not slavishly imitate them. However, it is nice to appreciate this creative man's foray into a new world of avant-garde punctuation.

---

* Steiner did not leave a final statement on how to punctuate. It seems as long as you know what the significance of your own punctuation is, and others are able to experience it, then there is no limit to the choices we have.

VI.   Some Experimental Suggestions On Various Genre and Alternative Structures

Can you write a novel in organic form? Why not? George O'Neil reported that The Scarlet Letter had a clear organic form. Hawthorne's novel has long chapter titles which lend themselves to the discovery of possible organic forms.

After teaching some great books at a great books high school, I noticed how so very structured certain novels are such as A Tale of Two Cities, Frankenstein, and even Crime and Punishment. Each book has main parts which are further divided into Chapters (Chapters often have longer titles which help identify the theme, mood and color of a chapter's contents). Other not so great novels follow the typical manner of simply numbering the chapters and rarely have parts. It was as if these famous authors were pioneering a new organic thinking by giving their books such conscious and deliberate divisions and themes.

Whether these are perfect organic forms, or organic in part, is immaterial. *It would be simpleton's task to judge the greatness of a book because it chapters correspond to Goethe's Urpflanze.* On the other hand: what if a great book's "staying power," as Mortimer Adler called it, was connected not only to the authors' great writing and profound themes, but also to the fact that its form rang the bells of the seven-fold human being. It is not hard for me to imagine that Dickens, a man who constantly explored the most Christian of themes, was not on many levels close to the holiest of sources, sources which imbibed him with these types of godly forms.

The question may be: what is the source of inspiration and how do humans access it? For example, did the Gospel writers receive God's words in spite of the imperfection of language, or did they receive them in part because their listening skills were not up to par? Are some books dictated by God, others channeled from spiritual sources, and others created by connecting to spiritual archetypes? In my research, I have noticed that many popular channeled/dictated sources - Conversations with God, St. Germain Foundation books, and even lectures given by various spiritual luminaries - had noticeable organic forms. When other-worldly beings speak, they communicate their ideas in the coherent archetypes of living forms, the very opposite of our earthly human communication which is given in arbitrarily constructed sentences, sentence fragments, and at best logically connected ideas. Thus, 'uber-logical' or spiritual communication necessarily has an integrated organic form, while our brain-bound logical communication is, in the main, fragmented, dissociative, and atomistic.

In one of Walsch's books, "God" tells Walsch to count the number of sentences of "God's" own utterances. It is as if "God" wanted him to be conscious not only of his message but for him to be very conscious of the *form of his message* - in the same way that Bullinger was conscious of all of the forms and content of the Old and New Testaments!

Some skeptical reader might believe that all things are man-made and thus my reflections are irrelevant. What is relevant is that there is a race to use these form selfishly or in the service of others. Friends of mine researched the dark side of living form, having found that many ads in magazines and on TV are written in these godly forms. Florin Lowndes claimed that advertisers have figured out ad-writing formulae by empirically testing out ads on focus groups, and rewriting them and eventually abstracting these new patterns that best affect or "touch" human beings. This supports the thesis that godly form can be used for good or evil, or a combination.

Fiction and Form: I have really too little experience with modern novels or short story forms to say much of value to fiction authors. At most, I could say that novels are tough because they don't normally use chapter breaks in the same way that non-fiction or doctoral dissertations do. In spite of what I said about the living form of Hawthorne and Dickens, I don't believe their work should be slavishly imitated because their organic forms.

That said, novels do have scenes, conversations, descriptions of places and so on that may be used as a kind of organic-living punctuation which separate the parts of the development of the story. They would be used in place of an asterisk, subheading, and an extra space to mark a change of location or theme within a given novel's chapter. Here I am entering dangerous ground because to dictate how things ought to be would make living form into a new form of philistinism.

What if you still want to write fiction in living form? I recommend studying and meditating in living forms. Then see what arises out of your own soul experience and inspiration since you must be "free in heart and mind" to be an innovator. In holding onto my belief concerning the value of living form, I recommend that writers at least be conscious of the number of chapters and the content of each chapter or section of their novel; and most importantly see how each chapter relates to the other in terms of the totality of the book.

Inter-relating and comparing of the qualities of each chapter of your novel will give you a general feeling for the livingness of the chapters. Keep in mind that a collage style (where seemingly unrelated elements (chapters) allow organic connections to emerge) is just as valid as a story-line in which each chapter carefully grows out of the former. The polymath Rudolf Steiner never left a novel behind, probably knowing novel writing is a craft that should be carried only by those with a life-long dedication to the genre.

Plays and Living Form: Theater has stuck to the Aristotelian format from Ancient Greece thru Shakespeare to the French Playwrights. Modern structures deviated to three and four act plays and so on. Theater has all of the elements that can affect a complete organic living experience. It encompasses at least four levels of arts: 1) physical art in stage design, 2) acting/poetry/song, 3) lighting (special effects), and 4) Spiritually imbued actors ennoble their viewers by the high frequency of their performance.

Rudolf Steiner did some amazing work in theater. He applied living thinking to all four of these aspects of theater. Whether he was playwright worthy of his times or in fact a visionary still to be recognized, the guild will have to tell. Steiner incorporated innovative stage designs combining various back ground colors for their psychological effect on the audience, used lighting to enhance spiritual gestures of a scene, taught a newish type of speech exercises, and redefined theater's overall spiritual function and purpose.

Steiner wrote four Mystery Dramas. Since I have no theater background, it is hard for me to elucidate on the details of the form of his plays. But it is clear Steiner composed them in organic form, each scene containing an aspect of living form. I must emphasize that with such a complicated art, there is so much that is possible on the stage in terms of actor training, lighting, dialogue, and stage design, that any statement attempting to prescribe would be absurd. That said, Steiner's work, although possibly not worthy of copying, may provide insights into these four elements of theater and their archetypes.

Poems and Prayers: Poems and prayers vary in style, length, purpose, and language. I could imagine that many traditions have a storehouse of perfect organic prayers and similar texts that have stimulated the heart-chakra for centuries. Many ancient sources have no punctuation, no clear way of determining the parts from the whole. The bias here is: all inspired works must have at least some organic form elements.

In a certain sense modern poetry has also lost a sense of rhythm and structure. This point is important for those of us who believe in organic form 's power. Is poetry without stanzas, without structure still potentially living? Is the narrative prayer so popular in Protestant circles a true prayer of the heart, or merely a sentimental utterance devoid of a worthy spiritual form? Are those free verse poems, which drag on for pages, pure intellectualism? The validity of organic form comes only when it transcends genre.

Steiner left behind a *Calendar of the Soul,* a collection of 52 verses which reflect the inner changes the soul makes throughout the year. It may be of interest to poets and prayer writers because Steiner challenges accepted notions of syntax and poetic form.

Each line of a stanza represents a level. Some of the verses have one stanza; some lines contain only two words! (I guess he only needed few words to create the mood of the level!) Regardless of what one thinks of Steiner's art or spiritual achievement one has the feeling that he tried in his life-time to open up many modes of expression in this new art of composition.

A wonderful example of a challenging form is the Apostle's Creed with its twelve lines. These twelve lines can be rearranged to create several different forms. Some of these forms really challenge the imagination. I believe the very future of living form is contained in the fact that authors and readers can shift their perspective and see multiple possibilities within one poem. This is my wish for future prayers and poems.

My final recommendation is that whatever you write, keep in mind how the parts relate to the whole, and never let the form overwhelm the content. A poem or prayer must ultimately sound good to the ear and to the heart.

Chapter Five,
The Logik of the Heart

Chapter four may be a lot to digest for now, but don't lose hope. With time you will start teaching this living form, and slowly come to be expert in it. It is time for this thinking to become consciously applied. We will cover various ways to do it in this chapter, but first allow me to cover some points.

First, this new thinking has had a long and tricky history almost being eclipsed several times. In the Jewish and Christian tradition this thinking has been marginalized (or simply forgotten) to a curiosity of Biblical structures, rediscovered however in 1800s by Bullinger and his religious predecessors. Rudolf Steiner's own organization, The Anthroposophical Society, has absolutely no official interest in the structure of Steiner's writings or in George O'Neil's findings. The only people really using this new thinking are in the advertising industry with its four color ads and perfect organic scripts, which could have been written by Steiner himself.

Second, certain books seem to never go out of style. Plato's Republic is another important book with staying power. At so many colleges this book still seems to be required reading. I can't imagine its contents are terribly helpful to modern humanity. I had sober, science-minded professors profess the importance of The Republic in their own educational training, although they themselves didn't really believe a word of it - except maybe the idea that PhDs should run the world. Why don't these professors recommend studying a philosophical work more in line with modern, materialistic thinking like Spinoza's Theologico-Political Treatise, or Skinner's Walden Two? I really believe The Republic's staying power comes from our unconscious need for this organic thinking that Plato employed very clearly.

Third, the first and major aspect of this living form is this: when the reader immerses themselves deeply into this organic thinking, their heart chakra begins to open. This could be a major explanation of why people keep reading the Bible over and over again as it is one of the antiquated sources that continuously stimulates their heart chakra. Even if the content of the Bible is not grasped intellectually, it can be grasped at a feeling level as "good news," heart-chakra opening news!

Do you ever wonder why the Catholic Faith, in particular the Mass, is still so well attended? Practicing Catholics often say that they often ignore the priestly sermons, but attend Mass because they *feel its spiritual value*, a fact which can't be easily explained. Its organic structure must play a role in its attractiveness. Consider the main sections of the Catholic Mass:

1. Gospel reading—hearing the good news from the realm of the angels;
2. Offertory—offering ourselves in response;
3. Transubstantiation—the transformation of what is offered
4. Communion—receiving renewal in spiritual-physical form

At first glance, the four levels and questions may not be apparent, but this format has very organic roots. The Mass in fact is so organic, not only in its main sections, but also in its parts, that Rudolf Steiner simply reworded and modernized the Catholic Mass in the 1920's for a group of ministers who were founding a new church later to be called The Movement of Religious Renewal. He changed the vocabulary, but hardly touched the structure of the original Catholic Mass.

The Bible, The Republic, and The Catholic Mass, all popular foundation stones of Western Culture, still serve to keep our hearts open. The fact that so many people still engage in either reading or participating in these institutions must mean that they *continue* to have the capacity to open people's hearts as their organic form was designed to do. Of course, Rudolf Steiner had sought additional means to address the chakra of the heart such as all of his books, aspects of the Waldorf school plan, Eurythmy, and his own Christian Community. Steiner left enough information behind in order that a new generation to bring the power of the heart to bear on this great renewal project of human culture and evolution.

From The Tableau Consciousness to Inner Catharsis: Based on the examples in chapter three, we have several genres from which to study and practice this new heart logik. By meditating the *Our Father* prayer, by contemplating the chapter structures of Conversations with God, or by systematically reading certain Bible passages, we begin to start seeing the ideas in their living form. The contemplation of living-form brings our mind into a particular mental and chakral activity: firstly of seeing ideas on a tableau, and of scanning and comparing all the ideas at one glance; and secondly of bringing our thought-process into dynamic movement from one level into the next, and into polarity. This practice of heart-thinking is always done most successfully on large pieces of paper.

Our culture of "rush and cram" could also benefit from a good dose of heart-thinking. Scientific papers, business plans, and even financial reports could be artfully constructed in tableau heart-thinking form. What's the point you may ask? Heart-thinking makes inter-level thinking easy to grasp. Following the what? how? why? who? gives people new clarity in terms of understanding the bigger picture. The details of how to teach, organize, and write have to be worked out by the various academic disciplines.

There are many excellent beginnings in the various initiatives set into motion by Rudolf Steiner and his followers. Steiner produced a new church and school whose very foundation rests on the new thinking both of which include a modern spiritual view of the world. Sadly enough, heart-thinking in all its applications has never been used as a pedagogical tool in the very Waldorf School Steiner created! Worse is the fact that the heart-thinking could be an effective spiritual path for scientists to open up their spiritual vision so they could work in a whole new world of energies! A fact only given lip service by Steiner's followers, who never grasped the power of this new thinking.

There are several levels of the logik of the heart. The first level includes using the tableau for diagramming and comparing of elements of a whole. As said before, this is accomplished best by using large pieces of paper or whiteboards. Although using paper to outline ideas is nothing new, it is hardly ever taught as a way to enter into a higher experience of ideas.

The second level has to do with the discovery of living form in already existing structures. Whether we are looking at DNA strands or a diagram of the tongue, we see that there are organic patterns and levels in nearly everything. Covered later on is Steiner's famous control of thinking exercise in which a pencil is considered from seven archetypal perspectives. This exercise serves to help people to discover the living form and to think in levels of What? How? Why? Who?.

The third level has to do with applying the organic logic to writing, or to organizing our thoughts in order to give them an organic flow. This would include speaking organically, a fun and exciting challenge. The purpose of the Waldorf School was to model this thinking in lesson plan formats, curricula formats, and in the collaboration of the faculty's actions and thoughts. Additionally, between Bullinger's work and Rudolf Steiner's Philosophy of Freedom, a renewed Catholic or Protestant church could be founded which recognizes and practices this *biblical way* of thinking which Steiner further elaborated on. The third level also requires some study and re-creating of the thought-forms found in Steiner's Philosophy of Freedom or Theosophy. This study can be a purely intellectual activity without requiring any change of character, or *catharsis* which usually comes with intense heart-thinking reading.

The fourth level is the spiritual practice and eventual catharsis through the Philosophy of Freedom and other worthy books. Above and beyond the living form and its various applications comes the meditative practice. This practice can be done on several levels. The safer levels include personal or group study of the forms. *Systematic study and immersion initiate one into a healing state caused by the opening of the heart-chakra. Once the heart chakra is opened to a sufficient degree through the living-form meditation, the meditator begins to release all sorts of issues. These issues can manifest themselves in many ways and must be addressed and remedied.* Ideally, in conjunction with other activities, this organic-living heart-chakra meditation can be the method of creating a new "organic" thinker whose aura and presence supports others in the awakening of their heart-thinking. (O'Neil indicated that this thinking is also a systematic way to enter an inspired state of being. There are many ways of thinking about Steiner's work that I simply know nothing or hardly anything about. Thus the future is open to original researchers. Consider how original Rudolf Steiner was in everything he did. *There are levels of the heart-thinking and method of practice which must be revealed to people individually in quiet meditation, since they would cause great harm if certain meditative practices were carried out by those not given permission by higher worlds.*)

The Exoteric, Esoteric, and Renewed Human Being: The first four chapters have covered the exoteric or academic aspects of the heart thinking. I would like to give suggestions on how to practice and apply the external aspects of the four leveled method to two professions that may become the future vehicle for this organic "biblical thinking."

Spiritual institutions and schools could be the best organizations for the development of this thinking. The Orthodox, Catholic, Episcopal, and any church which follows a true Mass will have easier time understanding its role as a heart-thinking church. Rudolf Steiner co-created a renewed sacramental Christian church. His subtle choices in designing the church, liturgy (and its principal sections), organization, priest training, and Christology are the foundation of a heart-logik church. It would be quite an achievement if a mainline church would renew itself through heart-thinking. The renewal of clerical thinking would create priests and lay people who really understand the power of the heart-thinking.

The Waldorf Schools are another example of an institution that has never understood itself as a heart thinking institution. Although the Waldorf movement protects children from many harmful influences - the barrage of damaging tests, medications, meaningless pedagogical activities, ugliness of institutional education, educators without any imagination – Waldorf has yet to grasp its most esoteric role as a seed institution of the "Consciousness Soul" as Rudolf Steiner and Saul Bellow called it. The Consciousness Soul requires a different commitment than current civilization has in order to unfold. Waldorf education needs to renew its thinking if it is to realize its highest mission.

In his work Steiner pointed to numerous paths and exercises one can choose in order to develop oneself spiritually. Because we are in the New Age (the age of the Archangel Michael started in 1879) of Quantum physics, atonal music, abstract art, and so on, we should be inventing new institutions which have intellectually and spiritually dynamic roots. Steiner often lectured about how earlier authors and traditions encompassed many wonderful things. Today we are supposed to work hard to climb up to direct knowledge of the spiritual world, and the same requirement should exist in all subjects be they biology, physics, psychology, farming, and even physical exercises. In other words, the new thinking is preparation for understanding the old forms of our culture as well as the foundation for working on new forms and ways of being.

Let us in the next section considered how a liturgical church such as the Catholic or Christian Community, could be grasped anew within a heart-thinking framework.

I.   Renewing Sacramental Christianity

How can Christianity become alive again? Rudolf Steiner said that the liturgy and sacraments became necessary in the early church because the original Christian church gradually lost its sense of a direct connection to Christ. Thus he set out to renew and resuscitate the Catholic Mass, Christian Calendar, sermon and Sacraments.

There are other types of Christianity that seem to be related to Steiner's work. First is the work that the monks do in Mount Athos. Athos, according to Markides in his <u>Mountain of Silence</u>, has a living esoteric tradition alongside its formal Orthodox Christian worship which includes a daily four-hour mass, constant prayer and so on. The brothers and monks live in isolation and often have spiritual teachers who help them on their spiritual quest to "theosis" (complete immersion in God or in the eastern spiritual tradition called "enlightenment"). The monks have many interesting spiritual abilities which they keep for themselves, hardly a model for society. This lifestyle works for them, however, they don't really share their fruits of spiritual development with humanity.

In contradistinction to my use of the term organic, churches like the Organic Church have attempted to recapture this original experience by having Christ as their priest, and by allowing for a more inspired type of worship in which the congregants allow themselves to be lead to certain activities such as original songs, inspired prayers, healing and so on. This new movement resembles the original church lead not by a priest, but by the spirit itself. It is the original free style organicism of the foundling church.

Between old formal spiritual paths of orthodoxy and formless impsired church meetings, we have the possibility of re-enlivened church. For those who enjoy the structure of the liturgy, hierarchy, sacraments, transubstantiation, standard prayers, may want to understand their Christian life in terms of following Christ in a more form-filled fashion. In this sense, the tableau thinking may lend a hand.

The first question could be: what are the essential parts, functions, governance, life and social interactions of the church? This question is important to understanding how to think about church life organically. Because the church was already established it is essential to look for the organicism where it already exists as is the case with the format of the Mass, the Seven Sacraments, the Our Father Prayer, and possibly the five-fold sermon format which was derived originally from Aristotle!

The Christian Year: All religions follow a calendar. According to Steiner, each part of the year has a different energy and experience. Normally one gets caught up in the external drama of Easter or Christmas, but rarely does the Christian really take time to meditate on the spiritual climate of each part of the Christian year. Some people try to simply discount the spiritual uniqueness of Easter by saying it is simply an old pagan practice; or that Easter energy is Spring energy! Here is not the place to argue about our collective experience of the year. Let us consider the subdivisions of the Christian Year:

1. Christmas (Christ's Birth)
2. Epiphany (Christ's Baptism)
3. Easter
4. Ascension (40 days after Easter)
5. Whitsun (Pentecost) 50 days after Easter
6. St. John's Tide (June 24th) John was born six month before Jesus
7. Michaelmas (September 29th)

Do these seven Holy Days follow an organic heart-thinking format? Maybe, they do; maybe, they don't. The Ascension would be the highpoint or the Who?-level. Does any Christian group experience the course of the year in this way? The Catholic Calendar basically is without any significant happenings after Easter. In this sense Emil Bock and Steiner sought to rechristen the Christian Cycle of the Year.

The logik of the heart reveals a new seven-fold subdivision of the year. The first half of the year has to do with more Christ-centered activities while after Ascension we have descending festivals which are not readily recognized by Christendom. A holistic perspective would include St. John's Tide (a Summertime Christian Celebration) and Michaelmas (an Autumnal Christian Celebration). These Holidays are reflected in most churches by a change of colors on the altar and priest with the first half of the year having more dramatic color changes while the Whitsun, St. John's Tide, and Michaelmas displaying more subdued colors:

1. Advent (Four Sundays before Christmas) Blue with dark blue
2. Christmas (Christ's Birth Dec. 25 - Jan. 5) White with light lavender
3. Epiphany, (Christ's Baptism Jan. 6 plus 4 Sundays) Red-violet with dark red-violet
4. Passion Tide, (4 Sundays before Easter) Black with deep black
5. Easter Tide, Red with Green
6. Ascension (40 days after Easter) Red with gold
7. Whitsun (Pentecost 50 days after Easter, lasts three days in our observance) White with golden yellow
8. St. John's Tide (June 24th plus four Sundays) White with golden yellow
9. Michaelmas (September 29th plus four Sundays) Peach blossom (aka 'incarnat') with light green

Pericopes: Hans-Werner Schroeder wrote that Steiner's choice of bible readings (periscopes) require some thinking and explanation. Schroeder states that although the Christian Community's weekly pericopes are similar to the Anglican Book of Prayer, Steiner's new choices can be either clear, open to interpretation, or not given. Schroeder continues that the Gospels themselves have a very particular composition and follow a formative principle which gives "rise to an organic form – for example, the human body – or to an artistic design and compositions." (p. 8, The Gospel readings in the cycle of the year) Furthermore Schroeder states:

> There are sequences of readings in the gospels in which a particular motif undergoes an intensification: as can be seen in the sequence of parables, or in the healings. There are motifs which change and metamorphose, divide and reunite, thereby elucidating each other to allow a deeper understanding; for example, the love motif in the gospel of St. John in its stages as Eros, Philia and Agape, or sequence of settings such as sea, mountain, house, which in their succession indicate something beyond what words alone express.

Amazingly Schroeder claims the readings are based on the seven-fold human being with intensification and metamorphosis! Thus, one Sunday reading covers Eros, the next Philia, and the final one Agape. Schroeder's "formative principle" is nothing other than a What? How? Why? of Bible readings. He gives one fine example of the depth of the organicism of the gospels/pericope readings:

1. Peter's confession (Mark: 8: 27-38)
2. From the Sermon on the mount (Matt. 7:1-14
3. The lost sheep, the coin, the lost son (Luke 15:3-32)
4. The Twelve disciples are sent out (Luke 9:1-17)
5. The healing of the blind man (Luke 18: 35-43
6. The healing of the deaf mute (Mark 7:31-37)
7. The seventy disciples sent out (Luke 10:1-20)
8. Faith, gratitude, certainty (Luke 17:5-37)
9. From the Sermon on the Mount (Matt. 6:19-34)
10. The raising of the young man of Nain (Luke 7:11-17)

Schroeder notices the mirroring of line 2 and 9, 4 and 7, and even 1 and 10.

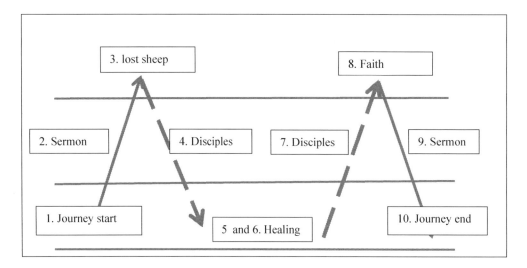

Schroeder goes on to show that: where gospel readings were carefully chosen (by Steiner), one finds organic form. Where there are no specific indications, the priest has the freedom to alter or complete their own organic form taking into account how the parts fit the whole! Schroeder points out that some years have fewer weeks and Sunday services so that this 10-form may be cut out of necessity to a nine form! Thus an opportunity arises for the priest to highlight an alternative structure. For example, the priest could make a nine-form, or a five-form plus a four-form. The mirroring and polarities would change, but the foundational logik of the heart remains consistent.

Anglican, Catholics, and free-thinking Christians could set the Gospel readings based on several organizing principles. So far we have: 1) content based decisions (readings correspond to the time of the year), 2) choices based on their spiritual significance, and 3) those based on their organic significance.

The Parts of the Mass: The next step would be to study the very structure of the Mass itself. The Christian Community Service has nearly the same four main parts of the Catholic Mass.

1. Gospel reading—hearing the good news from the realm of the angels;
2. Offertory—offering ourselves in response;
3. Transubstantiation—the transformation of what is offered;
4. Communion—receiving renewal in spiritual-physical form

Each of the four parts has subparts consisting various prayers and texts and actions (moving the text, bread and wine). The service has noticeable breaks as well as some subtle patterns. (Florin Lowndes has made some insightful discoveries about the Mass and the subtleties of organic form and movement hidden in it.) For example, a phrase is repeated seven times throughout the Steinerian Christian Community Mass: "Christ in you!" Upon careful examination, one could conclude that there is in addition to the four-fold structure, also a seven or eight-fold one too. Individual passages form the Christian Community Mass, although taken and rewritten from the Latin Mass of the Catholic Church by Steiner, have sentence for sentence, clause for clause beautiful and solid organic structures. The form of the entire Mass can be spoken according to different approaches: four fold approach; a seven fold approach, and a sentence for sentence approach.

Viewing the Catholic Mass from this perspective leads to some interesting questions about organic structure. There are several breakdowns of the Mass in addition to there being a Tridentine, post-tridentine, and pre-tridentine Mass. Catholics will have to make sense of this situation, and I imagine Anglicans will too. However, Steiner's recasting of the Tridentine Mass into a renewed fourfold form makes sense. It is somehow a confirmation that misunderstandings Catholics have with the actual parts of the Mass arise from the fact that today we have very little appreciation for form. (Some Catholics argue that post-tridentine Mass and its formal changes is the reason why church attendance declined!) From the point of view of this book's argument, these forms are part and parcel to all things Christian, and require some thought and artist apprehension.

Steiner, Schroeder, and even some Catholics believe that certain forms have a power and integrity that can't be explained by considering solely the contents of a prayer, Mass, or a bible passage. This organic-Christian way to order ideas was once the prized possession, as Steiner said, of highly developed spiritual adepts such as Jesus (who wrote the seven-fold our father) and others in the Church who were angelically guided, mostly likely unconsciously, to create the liturgical forms we have today.

When we look at a passage from the Mass Steiner rewrote of the Tridentine Mass, we see that every clause/sentence was constructed in organic form:

1. My heart be filled with Your pure life, Oh Christ.

2. *From my lips let flow the word purified by You.*

3. For if Your grace makes me worthy, my heart can be pure, and pure my word.

4. ***So live Your word worthily upon my lips, and borne by Your Spirit reach into those to whom it shall be proclaimed.***

5. ***Your blessing, Oh Christ, stream living through the word.***

6. May You be in my heart.

7. *May Your word flow from my lips.*

8. Then from a worthy source and in a right stream, Your gospel is proclaimed

The polarities become clear between the first (Christ) and the eighth (Christ's Gospel), the second (lips) and the seventh (lips), the third (heart) and the sixth (heart), and fourth (word) and fifth (word). The blatant repetitions give credence to the idea that in organic thinking that the form is more important than the contents. After all, don't the four gospels repeat nearly the same thing from four perspectives!? Again, one can underestimate the *form of such writings.*

Above we see how the sentence level contains clear forms. Since the entirety of the Mass is written in organic forms, then it should be spoken according to the levels, colors, polarity, and climbs. The question remains as to whether should each of the four main sections have a different tone and quality in the way it is spoken. The Catholic Mass is often delivered in rushed tempo and in a very matter of fact mode of speaking. With this new understanding, the priest could, for example, give a different quality when speaking the Creed compared to the way he would say the Penitential act, the Kyrie, and the Gloria.

How do we gauge this? First, speak the section according to its meaning and content. This seems obvious but often every part of the Mass is spoken in monotone. Some could object that the priest should keep his personality out of the service. The counter-argument could be made that the Mass may be a solemn affair, but it should also be a time of joy and good news. The priest should, therefore, bring love and joy to the fulfilling the duty of transubstantiation. Joy is a personal affair, and therefore, must come to fruition in individual modes of presentation. Rudolf Steiner once said that in our modern era it is actually the congregants in their connection to Christ that make the transubstantiation a reality. From this point of view, the priest can relax in his work by focusing on the glorious form of the Mass, and by highlighting the heart-thinking which has been essential to Christian practice.

There is flexibility in how the Mass can be spoken. The four parts could have four foundational tones: one for the reading, offertory, transubstantiation, and the communion. (The Catholic Rite has many *introductory* and *concluding* Rites, which they currently feel, create separate parts. These rites could be considered as parenthetic parts of a four-fold whole. Or the priest could give attention to the structure of each individual part: the various subsections within each of the four parts. Special attention could be given to each line of the creed and our Father prayer. The more priests and congregants know about the content and form of the Mass, the more this renewed sense of form can be experienced and experimented with.

(View the Catholic order of the Mass and see the level and parts, and if you can try to make sense of them. I certainly have trouble and I have studied this living thinking for decades. Is the Mass five-fold, four-fold, two-fold? In my opinion Steiner's fold-four schema is easier to manage mentally.)

Parts of the Catholic Mass
1. Introductory Rites
   Collect
2. Liturgy of the word
   Creed
3. Canon of the Mass
   Epiclesis
   Consecration
   Anamnesis
   Doxology
4. Communion Rite
   Rite of Peace
   Fraction
   Communion
5. Concluding Rite

When, in the future, the priest has analyzed every part and subpart of the Mass, new discoveries about the form will be made. Once this new Christian thinking has been grasped and internalized, each weekend the congregants could be surprised by the subtle changes of the spoken service that the priests make; those informed and immersed in the heart-thinking could have *an inner conversation with form of the Mass and the priest's manner of delivery*. A new, higher awareness and participation would become commonplace in the thinking of the church. Lovers of liturgical Christianity could find a home in this profound experience of the words, levels, and ultimately of transubstantiation itself.

The Sermon: The sermon traditionally comes from the Greek tradition and was continued by the Church Father, Chrysostom. He said that every priest should make the sermon a great oratory achievement. The sermon was an essential part of Catholicism coming not from the early Christian practice, but right out of the love of Greco-Roman oratory whose purpose was to entertain with eloquence and cleverness, with three or five well-argued points! Everyone knows that preaching is the life-blood of all protestant churches. Frank Viola points out that in his history book, <u>Pagan Christianity</u>, that the sermon itself is not biblical - since the Bible mentions that the people spoke freely, regularly interrupting each other, letting the spirit lead the meetings, there was not a lecturing, didactic pastor.

The Catholic Church seems to be confused about the role of the sermon, concluding recently that the sermon's task is to compete with popular media and to keep church goers interest and coming! Rome has asked that the sermon be kept as short as possible, under 8 minutes. In the Christian Community, although I have heard a wide range of sermon styles, the majority consist of comparing the Christian experience in the cycle of the year to various Goethean plant analogies e.g., one consistently hears phrases such as "slumbering forces" "imbuing". (This way of talking comes directly out of the Anthroposophical Society and can be considered dogmatic).

In the future heart-thinking church, the goal of the sermon would be to remind the congregation of existence of a spiritual way of thinking, and how to stay connected to Christ. Nevertheless, one could follow the Catholic and Protestant model with the addition of recasting the content of the sermon *in organic form*. In the future, sermon time becomes organic thinking time. Rudolf Steiner called this new type of thinking: Michaelic or Christ-imbued-thinking. The church could become the teacher of heart-thinking by making congregants aware of the new thinking.

Overview: What is left? The Bible has living form, the Mass has living form, the prayers have living form, sermons could have living form. The priest training would have to include, or reinvent itself to incorporate, the heart thinking. Finally, the church would have its own Christian organizing principle, one that understands life in all of its organic parts.

There are many aspects of the church where organic thinking and form are neither necessary nor applicable. In finance meetings, pastoral care, in day to day interaction one should not expect every pastor and parishioner to converse in the logik of the heart. The task for now is to highlight heart-thinking where it already exists. Also remember it is a teaching tool which is good to use in analyzing a topic and breaking it into its constituent parts: what? how? why? who? in the case of a church we have the:

1. What? The church building, various costs (salaries) and other foundational activities, upkeep and so on;
2. The How? The activities, service, meetings, choir, pastoral care;
3. The Why? The controlling body, pastor, board,
4. Who? Spiritual strivings, mission statement, ideals, future vision

One can see that these levels make sense and that the most difficult levels to maintain are the WHY? and possibly HOW? The why? level is steeped in human feelings, sympathies, and antipathies personal preferences. The tableau consciousness and artistic tools should be used to bring clarity to the controlling body, and the human, all-too-human opinions and "politicking" that one finds. When these levels have not been made clear to all, it is no wonder when all kinds of strife occurs. By reconnecting meditatively and by group discussion, the institution can concretely and effectively ask the WHO? or the spirit of the school for support: what is our ideal, mission, are we truly contemporary? Where do we need to make an inner change in the leadership first, in order to bring harmony to the outer organization?

In my opinion, church rarely serves new purposes of mankind. Just pick up any Church History text and check. Liturgical Christianity is supposed to strengthen our moral resolve by partaking in the body and blood of Christ and following the sacraments of the Church. Churches serve often the lowest common denominator, and, in the last century, have gone backwards theologically into a very un-Christian Christian fundamentalism. In the Ancient Church, beside the popular church where people gathered, there was also a gnostic and esoteric Christianity, which was parallel and available for the members with deeper spiritual longings for direct spiritual knowledge. Although these two Christianities had lived side by side in the early years, the early Roman Church declared certain gospels to be forbidden and certain practices heretical. Thus, spiritual Christianity was exterminated and forced underground where it still remains with a few individual masters remaining hidden.

Rudolf Steiner made a church where karma and spiritual development could be freely discussed, a church in which people could be free to pursue Christianity's highest gifts. The sacraments together with spiritual practices including meditation, working through and knowing one's karma, and teaching of a spiritual cosmology were given to be the foundation of a renewed church. Unfortunately, there are nearly no churches that openly practice the Western esoteric tradition in a way that casts this tradition in a modern form. The continued existence of the Christian Community is perhaps proof that the angels have not yet given up on the future possibility of this institution realizing its ultimate purpose: a church and its sacraments which understand how Christ stands within the practice of karma.

II.   Education and the Logik of the Heart

Rudolf Steiner's founded the Waldorf school in 1919, but wrote his first essay about Education as early as 1907. There was rarely anything Steiner did that on some level did not contain the logik of the heart. The 1907 essay called *"The Education of the Child: in light of spiritual science"* has a wonderful heart-thinking form. And, although there are many amazing pedagogical suggestions given by Steiner from 1919 to 1924, his unrecognized contribution is the very subtle utilization of the organic thinking in the curricula formats, lesson plan structures, and human developmental theory.

Rudolf Steiner's Waldorf educational ideas have created the single largest independent school movement in the world. Not surprisingly many of Steiner's educational ideas have been incorporated into main stream educational institutions in Europe, and so today it can be hard to appreciate the groundbreaking contribution he made. However, his logik of the heart as a method of thinking has never been officially recognized by the Waldorf schools. Waldorf reps do talk about heart-related qualities or hands-head-heart education. Much of Steiner's pedagogy helps to sustain an educational environment of warmth and gentleness - in short a "heartfelt education" as opposed to a merely intellectual/mechanical education. The thesis presented here is: not to change the "heartfeltness," but to add the logik of the heart and to go deeper.

I am not speaking as a detractor of the Waldorf movement. I love the Waldorf Educational Movement because it does fulfill the educational dream of having a school that educates through beauty, a pedagogy that understands child development, and has the methods to strengthen children on the path to adulthood. Even if half the Waldorf schools don't follow what Steiner said, or follow his suggestions in a very limiting, dogmatic fashion, the movement's existence is the last bastion of sanity in a world culture of Ritalin, medical fads (Vaccinations), Lunchables, and videogame babysitters. Every Waldorf conference I attended was full of the brightest and most caring teachers who put children's needs first, even against the bombardment of superficial and mindless trends of American culture. Often these teachers have worked in both the public/parochial and Waldorf systems, and heroically consecrate their lives to keeping the vision alive that children will someday be educated in a way that strengthens their innate gifts and powers.

The teachers' innate abilities must be developed first and foremost for Waldorf not to be a compromised project. Even though Waldorf teachers read about the *consciousness soul* in Rudolf Steiner's Theosophy, anthroposophical teachers as a rule have never considered or narrowed down in clear concepts what kind of thinking of qualitative thinking the *consciousness soul* moves in. Steiner thought that the Waldorf School's highest purpose was to be the inaugurator of the education for this *consciousness soul* faculty. This book is about the thinking aspect of the consciousness soul, and the other aspects need to be worked out. This will require training, a type of training that Rudolf Steiner was just beginning to put together with the resources and people available IN THOSE DAYS.

If Waldorf is simply going to continue following Rudolf Steiner's curriculum suggestions without reconsidering a more serious inner transformation of the teacher, the school will inch forward, *and backward*, never growing into its purpose. When I was in grad school, a fellow scholar said to me that Waldorf is blasé. I was shaken, and my dissertation accordingly was about a school that is already blasé like Summerhill, Ethical Culture, and Montessori! Waldorf people seem to be fond of arguing the expansion and contraction theory of institutional development. With Waldorf teacher training having been reduced from a full-fledged college of two years to weekend trainings for a few hours a week, one could guess the movement is again in a contraction phase, in spite of the new schools being founded. The bottom line is that Waldorf is expanding, however, not in a way in which people have grown to bring it to the level Steiner had wished. German Waldorf educators have documented this fact that the schools suffer from a lack of trained staff, and I guess the Germans 'in the know' watch in sadness and amazement how many Waldorf schools still *drone on* teaching the shell of the world's most radical pedagogy.

From this point of view, I think the movement needs to reconsider some points in addition to the heart-logik. Steiner's educational philosophy starts with a cosmological understanding of the human development. Some of his ideas which expand educational thinking far beyond his age and times (and beyond Waldorf practice as is seen in the gap in the literature of spiritual teacher development) include:

- Education especially in the early years must become a healing process. Unhealed teachers can't do this very well.

- Every generation has something new to bring to the earth in terms of ideas and impulses. Often the incarnated have not prepared the ideal circumstances for the coming generation to blossom.

- Each child has former incarnations and brings abilities whether God-given or earned in a prior lifetime.

- Each person carries karma both challenging and helpful to the present incarnation.

- Each person has a pre-life mission and/or soul group that they belong to.

- Each person is affected and supported by angels and other helpful beings.

- The teachers' task is to recognize/be open to their students possible past live genius and greatness as Plato, Caesar, Empress Theodora, Leonardo, and not to ever condescend them or treat the children as if they were little idiots. The teachers' task is to help the newly incarnated remember their higher abilities and virtues, not to tell them were Plato, Einstein and so on.

- Nutrient rich organic food is essential to the physical, mental, and spiritual growth of each child without which they may have trouble with their destiny.

- The health and appropriateness of our education during the first twenty-one years of life will be a decisive influence in our ability to grow into effective, mature, intuitive adults between the ages of 42 to 63.

- The developmental stages of children, young adults, adults, and the elderly must be heeded if human potential is to unfold to its fullest.

- Humans develop in seven year cycles which can be further broken down into 2 and 1/3rd year cycles. Teaching methods should change every 2 and 1/3rd years.

- The same main teacher instructs the same students from age 7 through 14. The definition of an elementary Waldorf teacher is more significant than in profane education. This relationship only works when it works for the teacher who then can guide them out of wisdom.

- The multiple intelligences must be educated in a developmentally appropriate manner with pedagogical methods that are also appropriate for that age group.

- Children should have a unified schooling experience which continues to age 21 if teachers can provide decent schooling that really serves their students.

- The teacher supports the child's development through meditation and prayer (love).

- The curricula and lesson plans choices and formats follow the logik of the heart.

- The Waldorf School's ultimate goal is to inaugurate a new type of thinking akin to Aristotle's mission of bringing the old logik.

Is society ready to fulfill these points of Waldorf education? Do Waldorf teachers really, truly believe that prior to their incarnation they were looking for new ways of being and thinking? Did they

100

find this new thinking in its totality? Are there institutions and trainings which practice this new thinking? Are we forcing children to give up their spiritual vision to fit our limited ways of knowing? In the following sections we have some reminders of where to find this heart thinking in old form Steiner gave nearly a century ago.

The Human life and the Nine-fold Human being: The first consideration is the nine fold human being. The first 63 years of our lives corresponds to the archetype of nine seven year cycles. Each seven year cycle is a period in which we develop one of our nine energy fields or bodies.

1. 0-7 are the physical body years
2. 7-14 are the ether body years
3. 14-21 are the astral body years
4. 21-28 are the sentient soul years
5. 28-35 are the intellectual soul years
6. 35-42 are the consciousness soul years
7. 42-49 are the spirit-self years
8. 49-56 are the life-spirit years
9. 56-63 are the spirit-man years

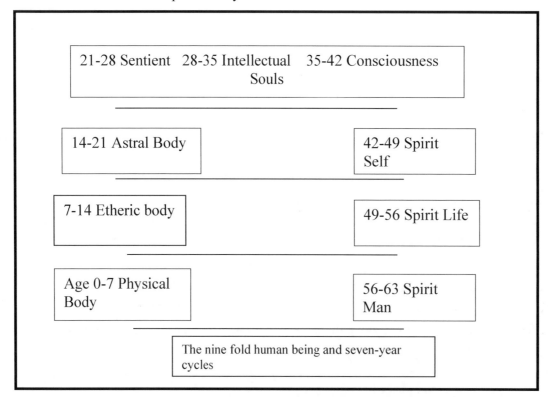

One can see that in organic form certain correspondences are evident. What the young children absorbed and what their early experiences provide them before the age of seven have an effect on what type of maturation process they will experience potentially in the Spirit Man years of 56 through 63. These early years of course have an effect on every seven-year cycle however there are certain key polarities between the etheric years and spirit-self years and so on.

The left side of the diagram shows the first three stages of life until age 21 or college age. In these first seven year cycles family, society, nation, and individuals give to us: we are receivers as we grow into independent beings. The middle years we seek and experience and gather. Hopefully by age 42 we begin to be of true service giving back to the society that nourished us. In this sense life is threefold.

As Americans, we may want to consider, as Steiner did, what amazing experiences could be provided for young people during the first 21 years of their lives. I can't imagine our pre-seven education of cramming knowledge is really what is best for the youngsters. Why is it that American education for pre-seven youngsters looks nearly identical to the education found in the elementary school? According to child developmental experts such as Pearce, Piaget, and so on this ignoring of developmental stages is unscientific and in fact damaging to brain development. This is a very serious Frankenstein streak in modern educators who do not want to allow for an experience which strengthens the child's sense of self. Every teacher of "gifted and talented" first graders I have met has admitted that the majority of children they crammed with knowledge eventually became mainstreamed ("ungifted" in a word) by high school! These cycles when understood fully will become the new basis of pedagogical science.

Seven-Year Cycles and Education: When diagrammed in the logik of the heart, the seven year cycles appear in a new light. If human development becomes the measure for educational action, then speculative nonsense of educators will come to an end. Educators want to ignore these natural biological and psychological stages by claiming that since children seem to enter for example formal operational thinking at different ages, one at age 6 and the other at age 8, that it is possible to lead children into formal operational thinking by way of "cognitive schemata." Ignoring these developmental markers - which are all easily established by a series of simple test questions - is the equivalent of sending a young colt prematurely into a horse race. Educators actually believe they are successful as they hammer away at the young children into they eventually draw upon parts of their brain that were only meant to be initiated well after age seven.

When the human being becomes the measure of all things, these seven-year cycles will become a kind of altar of worship. On the walls of schools children will see where they are in life on a big chart and follow their own development. Each year will become a special day in the life of children and they mark their development into a new stage. Maturation will be something to look forward to and we embrace each new soul capacity that comes with age. Human biography, our own biography, will be our true love, our theory of being human, our anthroposophy.

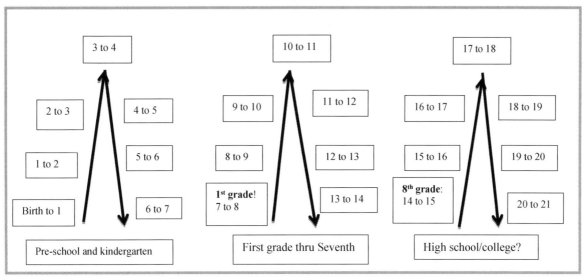

At age seven, the student is ready for first grade. At age fourteen for 8th grade. Today's society is terrified of waiting for children to reach age seven in order to start first grade. Evidently Sweden made it school law, but had to reverse the law because parents were so impatient having their children wait to learn. This addiction to state standards and state tests has done untold damage both developmentally and psychologically to children thus Sweden originally changed the age from 6 to 7 in order to lower the social service bill that comes from going to school too early!

If we waited a little for first grade and the children were truly ready, then the amount that could be memorized and covered in these seven grades would be phenomenal. American education waffles about endlessly, often exhausting its students by the time they finish college degree. Rudolf Steiner said for each new grade the main teacher should be experienced by the students as a completely new individual. The teacher develops and grows and changes with the children as he monitors their development through the seven-year cycle.

The seven year cycles are proximate. This is where the keen eye of educator or doctor come in handy in deciding when a child is ready for first grade. ***Most of the ADHD diagnoses start at age six and seven!*** We are still playing mad scientist by forcing them into first grade too early, and not following the natural development of children. Currently 2 million American minors take ADHD drugs, eight percent of the total population. *Pre-academic deficits in math and reading, as well as fine motor skills, are also more frequently observed in children with ADHD at the time of school entry* reports a website. Schools and parents should wait a year and see if ADHD magically disappears.

What could be achieved in a renewed high school would also be amazing. Without government regulations and the outdated requirement of having a college diploma, a seven-year cycle school for those between the age of 14 through 21. Steiner said that young adults could use this time not only to explore humanity's highest ideas, but also have experience in how the world really works. Imagine all the various ways people could learn to find independent livelihoods by experiencing how to grow their own food, research their own ideas and passions and enter in the adult world of work and creativity. Rudolf Steiner suggested that "high school" go until age 20 to 21, however things as we know it would have to change.

The logik of the heart requires us to look at the whole and see how the parts fit. Was Rudolf Steiner correct in asserting that children should be kept in a dreamy and less manipulative environment - an environment that currently regards 6 year olds as an educational problem that must be hurried through the system?

The 2 and 1/3rd year Cycles: In all my years of teaching, there has rarely been a book that presents the idea that lesson plan styles should change with the growing child. Rudolf Steiner is really the only exception to this trend. Even early educators like Pestalozzi, Froebel, and others didn't really have a sense for the true development of the child and this is reflected in their intellectualized pedagogies. For example, teachers are often given lesson plan directives which give a certain format for the subject matter taught. This format can be used for first graders or for 6th graders. Public and private schools see no difference between the two ages.

In Waldorf theory, one sees a radical difference between the lessons which are designed for 5 and 6 year olds, children ages 7 thru 9, and 10 thru 12, and so on. In fact, this sub-cycle, which is also noted by Montessori and Piaget, Steiner considered to be the best foundation. Most developmental researchers often recognize these subtle differences but have little pedagogical know-how to meet them. Because of the levelling nature of American society, I expect that these ages and stages will have to be made and considered anew especially in terms of first placing children in first grade at the appropriate age and keeping to the mode of thinking that is appropriate for that age. Waldorf has become watered down at best, and prep-schoolish at worst.

For Steiner and the logik of the heart, education should be foremost a curative process. Carefully following what the child demands from his education and not what ideology of the university or the demands of the economy will lead us to an actualization of the true seven-year cycle and what it truly requires. When we are able to follow solely what the child needs the school and the approach of the 2 and 1/3rd year cycle we will have a school of such force and children of such vigor only the best teachers of us will be able to lead them in honest fashion. The dismembering of children innate abilities through artificial diets, vaccinations, Television and videos, homework, Psychotropic medication, useless worksheets in school, and most of all educational method which prematurely engage abstract thinking, these dismembering elements keep children docile so that we never see a new generation, the very generation that through its insight and force of will ushers in a sensible and humane age.

College training in this logik should lead to an appreciation of the archetypal form of man. By allowing the children to be educated in a proper way from the very beginning we can look forward to the first generation of students who can monitor and trust in the archetype of the 63 year cycle. In the near future man will be the measure of all things.

Waldorf education barely carries this mission. Its curative work is kept to a minimum and the schools are famous especially around the sixth and seventh grade for being social failures. Review how Steiner built his curriculum from first grade to seventh grade. Observe how brilliant his choices are for each grade, how seventh grade require a reading of Schiller and Herder, how the curriculum storms ahead with real books which challenge even today's adults. Observe how much Waldorf has dumbed down its curriculum simply because it doesn't follow the 2 and 1/3rd cycle!

Curriculum in the Heart-Logik Format: Organizing curricula in the heart thinking format can be tricky. When it comes to education, some subjects usually precede others. For example, usually world history comes before European comes before American History. In Steiner's high school, modern Europe is first, second, ancient civilizations, third Medieval, fourth a synthesis of history. Does the subject matter fit the psychology of the age of the pupil? Is chronological order in fact not important in the teaching of history?

The literature/history curriculum of the Waldorf School shows some pretty interesting experiments in the logik of the heart. Required to make a curriculum first for an eight-grade sequence then for an addition high school sequence, Rudolf Steiner came up with an interesting format. In the diagram below we see the sleek polarities especially evident between grade 3, 6 and 11. Even where let's say the logik of the heart is not necessary or even expedient, Steiner ever so subtly sneaked it in. Every curriculum (math, foreign languages, and physics) of the school has its form. Had the eternally reverent Waldorf teachers working with Steiner asked him the simple question of why he made certain curricula decisions, this present book would not be necessary.

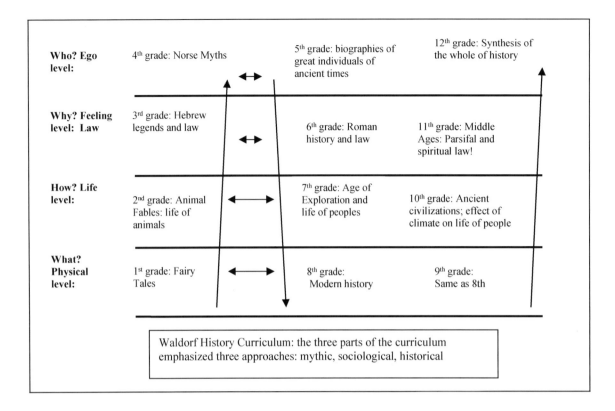

Of course in a true Waldorf school the school would be based on the seven-year cycle not on an eight-grade cycle. The polarities would have to be changed even if we kept the curricula identical.

Waldorf Lesson Plan: The Waldorf lesson plan is based on a three step process that covers two days. The first day teachers present the material and the students do an activity. The second day children recall what was done and draw conclusions about the process. Other popular Waldorf lesson plans require that in the third step the teacher posts the main ideas in picture form on the board. In physics class, the teacher presents an experiment, covers the details and the next the children find the lawful significance of the experiment. In any case Steiner gave these examples as ways to make a what? How? Why? lesson plan.

After mastering a three-fold lesson plan, Waldorf teachers could actually go on to make four-fold lesson plans or seven-fold lesson plan as subject matter and situation require! Below are the two examples Steiner gives on Logik of the heart lesson plan structures.

History Lesson Plan:
1) What? Give the facts in space and time
2) How? Add details and consider the first part of the lesson
3) Why? The next day, make judgments and reflect on the actions of the characters

Physics Lesson Plan:
1) What? Make an experiment
2) How? Repeat its stages
3) Why? The following day make hypotheses by reflecting on the phenomenon

Because of our expanded notion of heart-thinking, we could easily start to improvise by making the lesson plan into a 4-form, 5-form or 7-form. Waldorf representatives lecture dogmatically about the three-fold lesson plan without considering it origins. Even if you keep the three-fold structure you can still increase the number of sub-steps within each of the three main parts.

Reading and writing in the Logik of the Heart: The teaching strategies have been given in many instances by Rudolf Steiner especially for the elementary school years. However middle school and high school could be a place where this new thinking is met and taught consciously. Waldorf education still has the framework to do this because of the two-hour main lesson period and the fact that there are many great books required in the curriculum.

The organic thinking perspective will help scholars find the form of more and more books. Teachers will have in addition to the typical discussions of content, plot, genre, setting, and style the question of how the chapters of a book relate to one another in picture form. Charting the form of the book requires making synopses of each chapter and asking the question: how does chapter 1 relate to chapter 2? And chapter 2 to chapter 3? After reconstructing the elements of a story and sketching them out on the board, the class learns to think the totality of the book, how each chapter, section and part relates to the whole. By viewing The Republic or even The Great Gatsby, the author's vision of their book becomes a model of imitation or at least emulation. (It is amazing how form novels have. Whether Shelly or Dickens, each chapter is numbered and has a heading. Other great novels have parts, chapters, and chapter names such Dostoevsky's Crime and Punishment.)

This type of lesson would give depth to study. Working with novels or non-fiction in the organic way would provide the model and method of the author, the content and form become intelligible. Such a high level of understanding would also lead to higher quality of essays. When teachers begin to "see" the whole of a novel and not just its major points, then students and teachers will have a new capacity of thinking in totalities or wholes. Reading organically leads to writing organically and lecturing organically. More important, it leads to seeing complete pictures and overviews where hitherto fore unimagined inter-connections can be found.

The five-paragraph essay is a perfect tool. In the model used at the great hearts school system, students are required to find quotes from the consumables to put in the essays. The quotes write the essay and the student form their thesis by immersing themselves in various quotes. The result is by and large fantastic: students learn how to weave quotes into a very structured essay. In my experience, this rigid form allows the students to not only have a very concentrated theme in the essay, but also allows them to use many of the tools Steiner did: weaving quotes artistically into the essay, building paragraphs and sentences with great awareness for syntax, using grammar and punctuation creatively!

Young children and heart logik story telling: It is amazing how fairy tales already have such terrific forms. Each section of a fairy tale can be spoken in a different mood, tempo, and voice thereby highlighting polarity and other thought-laws. Here is the Seven Ravens, a seemingly beautiful and clear organic form and in diagram form:

1) What? Problem, brothers cursed at sister's birth: THERE was once a man who had seven sons, and still he had no daughter, however much he wished for one. At length his wife again gave him hope of a child, and when it came into the world it was a girl. The joy was great, but the child was sickly and small, and had to be privately baptized on account of its weakness. The father sent one of the boys in haste to the spring to fetch water for the baptism. The other six went with him, and as each of them wanted to be first to fill it, the jug fell into the well. There they stood and did not know what to do, and none of them dared to go home. As they still did not return, the father grew impatient, and said, "They have certainly forgotten it for some game, the wicked boys!" He became afraid that the girl would have to die without being baptized, and in his anger cried, "I wish the boys were all turned into ravens."

2) How? Brothers flew and sister grew: Hardly was the word spoken before he heard a whirring of wings over his head in the air, looked up and saw seven coal-black ravens flying away. The parents could not recall the curse, and however sad they were at the loss of their seven sons, they still to some extent comforted themselves with their dear little daughter, who soon grew strong and every day became more beautiful. For a long time she did not know that she had had brothers, for her parents were careful not to mention them before her, but one day she accidentally heard some people saying of herself, "that the girl was certainly beautiful, but that in reality she was to blame for the misfortune which had befallen her seven brothers."

3) Why? Sister restless and prepares for mission: Then she was much troubled, and went to her father and mother and asked if it was true that she had had brothers, and what had become of them? The parents now dared keep the secret no longer, but said that what had befallen her brothers was the will of Heaven, and that her birth had only been the innocent cause. But the maiden took it to heart daily, and thought she must deliver her brothers. She had no rest or peace until she set out secretly, and went forth into the wide world to trace out her brothers and set them free, let it cost what it might. She took nothing with her but a little ring belonging to her parents as a keepsake, a loaf of bread against hunger, a little pitcher of water against thirst, and a little chair as a provision against weariness.

4) Why? Sister came to the Sun, stars and drumstick: And now she went continually onwards, far, far to the very end of the world. Then she came to the sun, but it was too hot and terrible, and devoured little children. Hastily she ran away, and ran to the moon, but it was far too cold, and also awful and malicious, and when it saw the child, it said, "I smell, I smell the flesh of men." On this she ran swiftly away, and came to the stars, which were kind and good to her, and each of them sat on its own particular little chair. But the morning star arose, and gave her the drumstick of a chicken, and said, "If you thou hast not that drumstick thou canst not open the Glass mountain, and in the Glass mountain are thy brothers."

5) How? Glass mountain, dwarf, cut finger, and eating the brothers food: The maiden took the drumstick, wrapped it carefully in a cloth, and went onwards again until she came to the Glass mountain. The door was shut, and she thought she would take out the drumstick; but when she undid the cloth, it was empty, and she had lost the good star's present. What was she now to do? She wished to rescue her brothers, and had no key to the glass mountain. The good sister took a knife, cut off one of her little fingers, put it in the door, and succeeded in opening it. When she had gone inside, a little dwarf came to meet her, who said, "My child, what are you looking for?" "I am looking for my brothers, the seven ravens," she replied. The dwarf said, "The lord ravens are not at home, but if you will wait here until they come, step in." Thereupon the little dwarf carried the ravens' dinner in, on seven little plates, and in seven little glasses, and the little sister ate a morsel from each plate, and from each little glass she took a sip, but in the last little glass she dropped the ring which she had brought away with her.

6) What? Sister frees the brothers: Suddenly she heard a whirring of wings and a rushing through the air, and then the little dwarf said, "Now the lord ravens are flying home." Then they came, and wanted to eat and drink, and looked for their little plates and glasses. Then said one after the other, "Who has eaten something from my plate? Who has drunk out of my little glass? It was a human mouth." And when the seventh came to the bottom of the glass, the ring rolled against his mouth. Then he looked at it, and saw that it was a ring belonging to his father and mother, and said, "God grant that our sister may be here, and then we shall be free." When the maiden, who was standing behind the door watching, heard that wish, she came forth, and on this all the ravens were restored to their human form again. And they embraced and kissed each other, and went joyfully home.

3) Sister restless and prepares for mission	4) Sister came to the Sun, stars and drumstick
2) Brothers flew and sister grew	5) Glass mountain, dwarf, cut finger, and eating the brothers food
1) Problem, brothers cursed at sister's birth	6) Sister frees the brothers

The first half of the story (sections 1, 2, 3) is the preparation for the daughters journey. The second half is the journey itself. Sections 1 and 6 have the problem and solution, or the family together. Sections 2 and 5 are actions. Sections 3 and 5 present a higher experience: 3 is about her resolve and 4 a meeting with the higher powers. The teacher would tell the story with a feeling of form, and this feeling would transfer to the students who would imitate their teacher's thought process.

III.   Exercises for Incorporating the Logik of the Heart

Very simple exercises lead to great things. The great architectonic forms of the bible chapters or The Philosophy of Freehood may appear overwhelming to the beginner. But with time and practice you will develop your own feel for living form. Use the new thinking questions for all of the little tasks you must undertake.

Some Basic Daily Exercises
Short Notes to others: To put yourself in the mood for organic writing, I recommend that you first review the four levels in your mind: blue, green, red, and yellow. Then with the colors and their corresponding moods in mind start to writing down notes.

Writing three- or four-sentence notes is a good way to start off. Start with your conclusion and build up to it. For example if you have a three-sentence note (what? how? Why?) begin with your conclusion (Why?) such as "I will bring your book tomorrow." Then go back to the what? "You left your book at my house." Now go to the How?: "I know you need it back as soon as possible."

What? You left your book at my house.
How? I know you need it back as soon as possible.
Why? I will bring it to you tomorrow!

Note the use of the past present and future tense – one for each level. I used an active verb for the second and third sentences. By switching the sentences around you can hear which works best for the levels. I could easily switch sentences two and three depending on what you are emphasizing. The key is to be conscious and deliberate in ordering your sentences.

Organizing Meeting: Meetings are a good occasion to take advantage of living form. Often various people present, discuss, and make decisions in meetings. Living form should help the flow and the logic of what is to be covered.

Meetings are often a waste of time and energy, but sometimes necessary for the running of a business or institution. Basic questions should be addressed: Is the meeting necessary? Does everyone need to be invited? The next question is how to organize them so that participants leave with a clear picture of what the overall purpose is.

Once you have the purpose of your meeting, then see if the components are related to one other by type or by quality.

Ascertain the purpose of your meeting: brainstorming, passing on necessary information, a combination of necessary announcements and inter-personnel exchanges. I used to organize my school's meeting agenda according to the order of importance:

What? Essential announcements for the running of the school led by our principal;

How? Short announcements by faculty or reminders for teachers;

Why? Discussion of difficult students and other student-teacher issues.

Who? Ideals. Comments for improving the school or discussions of pedagogy.

Thus the meeting goes from the essential to more theoretical aspects of the school. This model allowed a very talkative faculty to become focused on the necessary first. Nothing could be introduced into the meeting that was not on the agenda and no one was allowed to interject or interrupt the other speakers. Before this format everyone simply spoke whenever they wanted, often going on long tangents.

A well-organized meeting with a clear purpose should unfold according to the levels: the What?-level always sets the tone and mood of the meeting and should bring focus, define the parameters, and ground the group. The how?-level might require people to participate or have an application of the ideas presented in the what?-level. If the meeting only has a what?-level and how?-level, then the why?-level could be a reiteration or confirmation of what was discussed. The Why?-level gives a good indication of how the meeting went: are the participants clear or confused or both. The why?-level always brings a red color to the souls of the participants. Beware of the color: are the participants filled with sympathy or antipathy?

The rule of thumb is to organize your meetings in order of importance. One could start with life necessities such as financial issues or whatever it takes to run an institution i.e., the bottom line. Then proceed to the dynamic aspects necessary for getting stuff into motion. Third comes the tricky aspects where personal aspects come in. If your thinking is clear and organic, others in the meeting will feel it.

As the meeting chair, let yourself be inspired by a living form. In other words, let new forms pop into your head as you keep an open heart! Meeting could start out with a six-form but because of time or because a unseen important development in the meeting, it goes in a organically new direction.

Daily Schedule: Does the day necessarily unfold according to organic patterns? In a certain sense they do, but in another sense they do not. Some spiritual teachers suggest that one should sense what kind of day your day will be; and then, to the extent possible, determine how you want to experience it. We have a certain creative flexibility with the way we experience life.

In this living form way of thinking, we start with the who?-level of the day. We determine what *overall experience* we want to have: a productive day, a relaxed day, and quiet day. Thus we compose ourselves first thing in the morning, and gather our focus by setting up a pattern for our day at work. Once the pattern or what?-level has been set, we can then move into action or the how?-level. The day unfolds and after a certain amount of time of being productive at work we enter the why?- level. The why?-level has a dual possibility of either sympathy or antipathy; that is, we become conscious of how well our day is going, and how much we enjoy work or how shitty our day is filled with strife and grief. The day can be punctuated by lunch breaks and varying meetings so there may be a shifting between the how?, why? and who?-levels of the day. The key is to see the order and flow, to be conscious of it as it is unfolding, and if possible to work within the framework in a living manner.

Make the what?-level really clear and grounded; make the process or how?-level really dynamic; be weary or joyful in the why?-level. Sometimes a day can be a real mess and just let it unfold and give yourself a self-conscious distance that such an experience is necessary and has nothing to do with you. However, let the levels speak for themselves and don't force a level. Learn to ride a level like a wave. If you are giving a presentation, and it is not flowing, maybe you need to re-establish the What?-level. A good teacher knows when the material isn't flowing with the students and sometime we need to start over. Some students require a very long What?-level while other are more than ready to jump into the process oriented How?-level.

I like to make the why?-level clear in meetings and in teaching. During the Why?-level and the Who?-level of class, I often challenge the students by publically checking their grasp of the material. The tension which builds because of the questions often ends in a nice resolution because their grasp is often quite good. In other words, as a teacher I try to both create as well as allow the levels unfold. Days - when this does not go well, - send me back to reconsidering my preparation.

How are your evenings spent? Do you prepare for the next day by resting or by medicating yourself? Sleep is holy, so it is necessary to have enough and get to sleep by 11:00 pm. In spiritual thinking, sleep is a time when we excarnate and spend time in a meeting with our higher self or Genius. Sleep is more than simply a physiological resting of body processes. Also sleep is the best way to answer important questions and learning new material, that is sleep over newly learned material and difficult decisions.

It is also not a bad idea to read a book written in organic thinking before you fall asleep.

Once-a-week Speech Exercise: Steiner recommended that you carefully choose your words each day. Make Monday your day of organic speech. Before you speak, bring *form* to your words. Start with your conclusion, and lead up to it. In order to do this you will have to slow down your speech.

First, have something to say. Second, count the number of sentences you will use. Third, organize the sentences so they make sense organically: what? how? why? who? Fourth speak your sentences, and while speaking feel the color of each sentence: blue, green, red, and yellow.

The challenge is to continue this the whole day through. In the beginning you will sound stilted in your own mind. Colleagues may see you speaking a little slow on your speech exercise day, but it is good to slow down your speech 7x's in order that your words really encompass a divine pattern. Our culture would much benefit from a new way of speaking in which thoughts were carefully developed and reflected this organic logic of the heart.

Some other tips may be to sketch out what you are going to say ahead of time. Knowing that you have certain meetings or tasks, try to give those tasks a form ahead of time. Important phone calls, notes to co-workers, ordering at a diner all lend themselves to living form opportunities. Spontaneity may be lost by over-planning, but that will come with time.

Watch the reaction of those around you when you speak organically.

Artistic Exercises:

Steiner recommended considering and meditating on a simple man-made object such as a pencil or a needle. Interestingly enough, he gave the organic sequence so that the thoughts would flow in a dynamic archetypal form. Florin Lowndes suggests that one make a little seven-paragraph essay about the object and then turn the essay into a meditation of the seven perspectives of a pencil.

Write a paragraph about each of the following:

1. What?: Write about the shapes and materials that are used in the a simple lead pencil.
2. How?: Presents the steps that went into the manufacture of a pencil from raw materials to the finished product.
3. Why?: Discuss the design and function of the popular lead pencil. Why does it have a certain length and width?
4. Who?: Make conscious in written form the inventor of the modern pencil and his idea.
5. Why?: The necessity of the pencil for humanity. Moral implications etc.
6. How?: Archetypal overview: write about the history of all writing objects from the stylus to the super-cool pencil now in use.
7. What?: The last paragraph should give an glimpse into the different forms of pencils i.e., different colors, round or four-sided and so on.

Such an essay steers our thoughts away from arbitrary constructions into a dynamic way of thinking. Consider how each paragraph sticks to the topic of the pencil while at the same time presenting a completely different perspective of the same. These patterns imprint themselves on our thinking process and our thinking starts to a have a jumping or leaping quality as one is able to move quickly to new perspectives without being confused.

After you research and write your little essay, you can then meditate the content. Repeat each perspective aloud: what? the form and materiality; how? Discuss the manufacturing process and so on. Repeat each paragraph and their sentences every morning for five minutes. You can even think them backwards starting with the seventh paragraph and end with the first!

This activity leads to a feeling for the levels and form. One begins to see and feel into these qualities. With time you can begin to change the archetypes by substituting your own categories for the What? How? Why? and Who? You begin to become creative with the forms and thus discover new archetypes as Steiner himself did in the <u>Philosophy of Freehood</u>. Eventually the archetypes become as manifold as life itself.

Prayers, Mantras, and Poems: The goals of a prayer, poem, or Mantra can be many. By giving attention to the form, a new formal energy can be won. Already mentioned is *The Our Father* Prayer whose lines can be spoken easy according to the quality of the levels:

Blue level: Slow voice
Green level: more animated
Red level: given to feeling
Yellow level: conscious awareness or emphatic

The Our Father could be spoken in seven, four, two, or one voice(s) depending on one's perspective. Seven voices emphasize each petition; four voices, the four levels; two voices, the two halves or inversion; one voice, the totality.

Speech is an art, and finding the right voice for a poem or prayer can be challenging. In the line with the philosophy of this book is our challenge of highlighting the living form within a certain thought-form. Thus there may be a difference in approach between performing poetry at a club and experiencing poetry for the purpose of living form. The purpose of this section is to give you an activity you can practice every day that brings you into harmony with the levels of the new thinking.

The role of poetry, scripture reading, and prayers is to open our hearts. When poetry and prayer no longer serve this purpose, than their purpose needs to be renewed. What if poetry recitation, prayer, and mantras could again serve the purpose of opening up the chakra of the heart and throat?

Biography Study: A very important exercise for the soul is studying the patterns of biography. George O'Neil left behind a very important book called the <u>Human Life</u>. Each chapter sketches a different perspective on the stages and tasks of life. Although there are typical patterns and developmental stages that everyone follows, we all have our own archetype.

In the same way the archetypal plant has polarities and enhancements so does the form and graph of the human life. The plant unfolds in seven stages while the human life unfolds in nine main stages! Every seven years new forces are available to the human being. By charting our life stages, we begin to see patterns and cycles, and even polarities in the happenings, people, thoughts and passions in our history. O'Neil's book is fascinating because it shows that the living structures are part and parcel of life itself. In other words, life is filled with polarities and inter-connections.

According to O'Neil, because our life unfolds in stages, we can expect each seven-year cycle to confront us with challenges. O'Neil addresses such questions as: what are some of the challenges that individuals face between the years of twenty-eight and thirty-five? How are the challenges different from those during the years fifty-six to sixty-three? Not only are certain challenges particular to certain seven-year cycles, but, moreover, we need to do our own work if we are to unleash the potential forces of maturity! In other words only by working on ourselves - starting in our early thirties - do we access the spiritual-creative power that the gods grant us in our sixties and seventies! With great sadness, one sees retired individuals sitting in retirement homes unable to give leadership and wisdom to the younger generation often because with age they regressed into childish state filling their day with work, golf, drinks, and other dissipative activities. Will inner work someday be required by corporations?!

Personal Hygiene Exercises

Rudolf Steiner gave many exercises in his knowledge of higher worlds. The gist of all of the spiritual exercises is to have higher frequencies influence "lower" energies. Heart-logically speaking, the etheric level can bring harmony to the physical level, the soul-body can bring order to the ether body, and the ego ennobles all three lower bodies.

Each of our four bodies presents educational and sustenance needs. With the physical body, a young child needs healthy food otherwise they learn to eat junk food. What our parents model at a young age, our palate follows. Thus we develop physical addictions to unhealthy things. Look at how few people change their diet to vegetables until they are too sick to continue. I have plenty of friends who grew up on healthy organic food and home cooked meals and as a result they suffer terribly when they eat at cheap restaurants or nibble on processed foods. The same goes for exercise. Many of my friends have never played competitive sports or trained their bodies. Therefore they have no clue about the salutary effects of intense exercise. People learn to live in body which is used to poor nutrition and docility. Raw foods and real exercise are becoming the solid foundation of a new health culture.

With the etheric body the talk is about rhythm and cycles and breathing. As children we form habits and habitual thoughts and reactions. We repeat these thoughts and they slowly distort our energy currents and eventually our physical being. The life of habits can go both ways: good habits and bad habits. Where healthy food and exercise were essential to the physical body, certain types of activities are important for the etheric body. One notices children often love regularity; and religion and ritual are both good for children. They love story-time before bed, love to eat at the same time every day, they love to say prayers, hear the same songs, hear rhythmical and rhyming songs. Often people whose lives are a mess often benefit from a very structured lifestyle. It is easy to go workout if you have developed a rhythm. Your ether body's love of rhythm can carry you. Habits eventually become second nature and part of our physical being.

The astral, or soul body, is your system of agreeing or disagreeing with what you experience. Aesthetics in terms of architecture, music, clothing, poetry, and religious feeling all shape our astral body. Nietzsche said musical inspiration must be different for each person since that which stimulates the astral to higher creativity must be unique to each person. The astral body is shaped both by new thoughts and old habits and sympathies. Learning to ennoble our impulses through education and sociality refine our astral presence. Virtues such as tact, patience, helpfulness are part of the learning process. Allowing ourselves astral refreshment in terms of concerts, visiting art galleries, books written in truth and out of high ideals are important activities in life.

The Ego or I is a complex body. The education of the ego is based on clear thinking as well as allowing higher energies to manifest. The world consists of thought and our mind is permeated with thinking. Our mind is therefore able to grasp the workings of the universe because it lives in thought which is the very substance of the universe itself. In school, our ego helps us to learn about the visible world of science and the invisible world of mathematics and history. Eventually our ego has its highest need in discovering who we are, in self-reflection. Persistence in the face of disappointment and hopelessness is a great quality of the ego. True education requires us to practice overcoming our laziness and move toward higher truths. Hardship can often help the ego develop the power to do amazing things.

Rudolf Steiner's 10 exercises for Self-improvement. Using the Power of the Ego over the vagueness and nerves. Three Sets of Exercises in Self-Control "To Connect the Ego with the Deed"
The Exercises come in sets. Lopsided virtue is a Cardinal Sin. A tune-up takes many adjustments. Practice them all.

First Set of Exercises For Physical Stability			*Who is Boss? Man or mouse?*
	FIRST. ABSENT-MINDED AND FORGETFULNESS	Example: Visualize where you put things. Put in another place every night!	Picture surroundings
Control of the LIFE body over the Physical	**SECOND.** FOR JERKS AND CRAMPS	Example: Observe formation of letters. Draw them for 15 min.	Automaton?
	THIRD RECOLLECT EVENTS	Example: Review in Reverse the course of events, a tune, a play, your, a day. Write your diary backwards!	Float not in Time!

Second Set of Exercises For Mental Health **Control of the Soul body over the Life Body and to Consolidate life-processes**	**FOURTH** ATTENTION MAN AT WORK	Example: Watch what you do carefully! Do it consciously, be deliberate!	Drift not in Space!
	FIFTH MANNERISMS NOTA BENE	Example: Gestures, expressions, posture, walk. Verbal habits. Tones of voice.	See the oddities as others see them!
	SIXTH BE FLEXIBLE	Change a habit, a new handwriting. Shift hands to brush teeth, wield fork.	Get out of the rut!

C. For Personal Vigor and Self Possession	**SEVENTH** SAY NO	Self-Restraint. Deny yourself. Hold back. Child will imitate papa or teacher if he sees you doing it!	Pull in the Reins. Whoa Horse!
Ego Control over the soul body	**EIGHTH** ANTICIPATE OBJECTIONS	See PROs and CONS. Everything has two sides. List the views opposite your own.	Be Fair. At Least try.
	NINTH SAY YES	You decide and carry thru! Gurus eschew. Loudmouths hypnotize. Leave your doctor be!	Don't run to Mama!
	TENTH AND OBJECTIVE BE	Omit the personal, the I-feel, I-mean. Separate criticism from your Experience. If you see 10 asses, mention only one. Correct pupils every 7th mistake.	Facts Speak loudly

In the case of O'Neil exercises, we find their order in to be in the heart-logik. The exercises are also a wonderful sketch of how each of the four bodies works on the other. Much more could be said on how to carry them out. I also imagine having done many of the exercises that others may not be sure about their efficacy. In my experience, the people I met who practiced such exercises practice them in secret thereby rarely getting feedback about what part of their character they should work on. In the

116

future, groups should work on them really checking in with others on what some need to work on and check each other's' progress.

The first set of exercises requires the etheric to master the physical. The first exercise requires you to see form in the physical surroundings which normally appear as chaotic. Observe form and order. The beautiful form of your letters and the ordering of events in your day. Expand your consciousness to include the whole and the parts.

The second set of exercises can be summed up as: Bring awareness and intensity and playfulness to everything you do. Of course there are cultures that securitize too much as is the case in Germany and Japan where there is one right way to do something: places in which the motto is "hard work is more important than living life." Look at yourself for the clown that you are: too serious, bad posture, interrupter and so on. Lastly do something usual in an unusual way, be flexible, be playful.

The final set of exercises can characterized as keep silent. Don't act out every impulse, don't criticize, and don't look for sympathy. The ego can give form to the astral body which has its pet preferences and opinions.

The Pranic Tube Meditation and the Thinking of the Heart: Another very grounding and hygienic exercise is the newly coined "pranic tube" meditation. The meditation is essential for those who want to safely go the path of heart-thinking. Intensive study of sacred texts and Rudolf Steiner's work can quickly open the heart-chakra. This can be unwise to do without certain precautions.

The Pranic tube meditation prepares the auric space so that an open heart chakra is not vulnerable to attack or damage. The majority of human beings live in a state of closed-down-ness in which they are living in fear of others, and, worst of all, feel very uncomfortable with the open heart of others. Just look at how people greet each other, the tightness of their bodies, their heart-attacks, sexual dysfunction, headaches, and depression. Our current "shut down" culture is educating every new generation in exactly these damaging behaviors.

In order to make a new culture of the heart, the expansive auric exercise is very helpful. By filling your aura and chakras with light, expanding your auric field, sealing it holes and tears, and grounding yourself to the earths energy and uplifting yourself to the central sun, you begin to prepare to live in a energetically expanded state where heart thinking in its meditative form can be practiced safely and intensely.

The steps of the meditation go as follows:

Paragraph 1.
We will begin by taking three very deep breaths.
So: the first breath in… hold… and release.
Second breath in … hold… and release.
And third breath in… hold… and release.

Paragraph 2.
Continue breathing in a slow and easy gentle rhythm.
Allow your breath to fill your entire physical being from your head down to your feet.

Paragraph 3.
And now: bringing your attention to your crown, allow yourself to feel, sense, see your crown opening up, and your pranic tube begin to rise through your crown upwards through the sky, continuing upwards to the sky until your pranic tube meets your highest light source, the sun.

Paragraph 4.
And now: allow yourself - with every breath - to feel, sense, see that vibrant creative sun-energy move through your pranic tube.
Feeling that sunlight moving with every breath down through the sky.
Allowing yourself to feel that sunlight energy as it moves through your pranic tube down to your crown. Moving down through your throat, chest, bringing more sunlight energy with every breath, feeling that light as your pranic tube, filled with light continues to move downward, through your abdomen. Feel your base completely opening your pranic tube filled with light, moving downward through the crust of the earth down through many, many layers of the earth until your pranic tube filled with sunlight meets the very center, core of the earth.
Every breath, continuing to bring more sunlight energy moving through you, through your pranic tube, down to the core of the earth.

Paragraph 5.
As now: bringing up that creative, grounded earth energy back up, with every breath, through your pranic tube feeling that earth energy moving back up to the very many layers of the earth.
Every breath continuing to bring to more sunlight, and every breath continuing to bring up more grounded earth energy. Feel that earth energy moving up through your pranic tube to the crust into your base, entering through the body, upwards through the abdomen, trunk, chest, throat, continuing upwards to the head and continuing up through the pranic tube upwards until that earth energy by your pranic tube and through your pranic tube meets our highest light source, the sun.

Paragraph 6.
And now: with every breath bringing up the grounded earth energy, and bringing **down**, sunlight energy. Allow yourself to feel completely enlightened by highest light source, completely grounded by earth source - Heaven bound and earth bound, by your breath and by these energies.

Paragraph 7.
And now: bringing your attention to the front of your pranic tube, allow yourself to very gently create an opening in the front of your pranic tube and allow those energies, earth and sun, to come pouring out of that tube into auric field.
Repairing any damage you created: from the largest of tears and holes down to the very smallest of rips.

Every breath, bringing more sun and earth energy, bringing your attention to the pranic tube in the back of your heart space, very gently.

Paragraph 8.
Create an opening in the back of the pranic tube and allow those two sources of energy, earth and sun, to come pouring out into your auric field again. Repairing any damage you created from the largest of holes and tears down to the smallest rips.
With every breath, continuing to bring more earth and sun through your pranic tube into your field. Allow yourself to feel completely energized from the inside out, and again from the outside back in.

Paragraph 9.
Now that your auric field is in complete repair, feel yourself as whole and unique, separate and completely connected.
Allow yourself to continue by your breath and with your breath to bring more earth and sun energy expanding your auric field until you feel completely safe, knowing that nothing may enter this field that you have not invited and allowed. And with the breath, move anything which is inside that does not feel safe or comfortable for you.

Paragraph 9.
And now: Bringing your attention to the heart space in the back of your auric field gently close the opening that you have created in your pranic tube.
Bringing your attention to the front of your heart space in the front of your pranic tube very gently close the opening that you have created in the front of your pranic tube.
Keeping your tube open to heaven and earth and sun, every breath bringing those two energies through you, keeping you always grounded by the center-core of the earth, always enlightened by the sunlight-source.

Paragraph 10.
Once again we are going to take a very deep breath and hold it. And when you are ready and only when you are ready, open your eyes come back to "right here" and "right now"
So, a deep breath in and hold. And release. Enjoy!

This meditation grounds, energizes, and protects the chakras. When practicing the logik of the heart, the heart-chakra opens quickly. It is essential to have a full and protected auric field. Some spiritual practitioners do not have an energized and protective aura. For example, when they practice meditation, have profound sexual experience, and/or consciously choose to open their chakras, often the case is that their auric field is in no condition to provide the chakras protection. This becomes a kind of devil's circle in which a person can make enormous spiritual progress, but be compromised without even knowing it. Not having a full and vibrant aura is something that has to be remedied. Record this meditation and play it once a day to keep you in a grounded and expanded light-filled state!

Appendix I

Spiritual science does not want to usurp the place of Christianity; on the contrary it would like to be instrumental in making Christianity understood. Thus it becomes clear to us through spiritual science that the being whom we call Christ is to be recognized as the center of life on earth, that the Christian religion is the ultimate religion for the earth's whole future. Spiritual science shows us particularly that the pre-Christian religions outgrow their one-sidedness and come together in the Christian faith. It is not the desire of spiritual science to set something else in the place of Christianity; rather it wants to contribute to a deeper, more heartfelt understanding of Christianity.

To gain a better understanding of the archetype of the human being it may be helpful to consider its source. Rudolf Steiner wrote that human beings has in fact three energy bodies, three souls, and three spirit-bodies in their energy field and aura which appear to the seer as different layers of the aura. Thus a spiritually or morally advanced person will have an energy body which is substantially more differentiated and larger than a person who is committed to their lower drives and ideas.

As the human being develops these energy fields, through becoming wiser and more loving, the energy fields take on new forms and capacities. The soul is mediator between the body and the spirit body. Thus all learning done in the physical and spiritual realms is acquired in the 3 souls which Steiner says is centered in our I. All experience in the physical world or spiritual/intellectual world becomes part of our eternal being. Over many incarnations our physical body changes little but our aura and spiritual bodies grow larger through the ennobling of our lower energy bodies.

The three bodies are called the *physical body*[14], *etheric body*[15], and *soul body*[16]. What we normally call the body is in fact three subtle interpenetrating fields. Steiner says that the etheric body gives our physical body its formation and which we inherit from our parents. The etheric energy is "lighter" than the energy of the mineral body and in turn the soul body being of a finer energy allows transmissions from the soul and spirit bodies to the etheric and physical. These bodies have manifold functions: the physical body we know; but the etheric body supports in all our process and rhythms, memories, habits; the soul body is the seat of our drives, instincts, and lower passions. Through education, customs, and higher moral and philosophical ideas our "I" transforms these bodies into higher energy fields of the soul and spirit! Therefore every time one develops one's *physical body* through training, alters one's *etheric body* by learning new skills or changing habits, ennobles one's *soul body* by practicing art or by suppressing socially unacceptable passions the higher bodies of the soul and spirit are nourished.

The three souls are called the sentient[17], rational-feeling or intellectual[18], and the consciousness soul[19]. The three souls grow in their ability and function by working on the three bodies. The more the

---

[14] Steiner said: "This mineral structure built up in accordance with its function will be called in the following pages the *physical body* of man."

[15] Steiner wrote: "Mineral forces express themselves in crystals, and the formative life-force expresses itself in the species or forms of plant and animal life. The *ether body* is an organism that preserves the physical body from dissolution every moment during life."

[16] In regards to the soul body Steiner said this: "The force through which its limits are set, however, proceeds from the physical body. Thus, between the physical body and the ether body on the one hand, and the sentient soul on the other, another distinct member of the human constitution inserts itself. This is the *soul body* or sentient body."

[17] Steiner said this: "The activity by which sensation becomes a fact differs essentially from the operations of the formative life-force. By that activity an inner experience is called forth from these operations. Without this activity there would be a mere life-process such as we observe in plants. Imagine a man receiving impressions from all sides. Think of him as the source of the activity mentioned above, flowing out in all directions from which he is receiving these impressions. In all directions sensations arise in response to the stimuli. This fountain of activity is to be called the *sentient soul*. It is thought-power that has built ships, railways, telegraphs and telephones, and by far the greatest proportion of these conveniences

120

lower bodies are educated and worked on, the more the three souls can increase their activity. The three souls are the seat of our I which relates to the physical world and spiritual world through these three souls. The sentient soul thinks ways to make life convenient and comfortable since it is based in feeling. The intellectual soul carries the logical mind and its concern with external truth. Where Ancient Egypt and Renaissance Italy show the power of a culture grounded in the sentient soul by their harmonious artistic, political, and religious creations, Greece and France, on the other hand with their intellectualism and argumentative spirit, present examples of cultures dominated by intellectual soul activity. The part of our soul which leads us beyond our own pet preferences and theories to truth, is called the consciousness soul. The three bodies relate to the three souls in the following way:

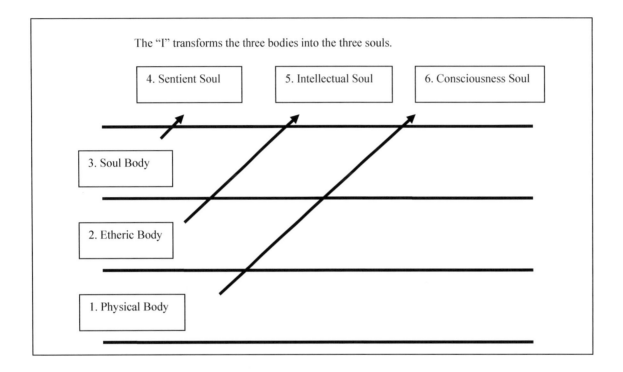

Out of the three bodies is created the three souls and the three spirit bodies. Steiner's model includes therefore body, soul, and spirit, however each having three aspects. The spirit aspects are formed by the activity of the "I" and become permanent features of the individual. Steiner writes:

In the "I" the spirit is alive. The spirit sends its rays into the "I" and lives in it as in a sheath or veil, just as the "I" lives in its sheaths, the body and soul. The spirit develops the "I" from within,

serves only to satisfy the needs of sentient souls. Through the sentient soul man is related to the animals. In animals also we observe the presence of sensations, impulses, instincts and passions. The animal, however, obeys these immediately and they do not become interwoven with independent thoughts thereby transcending the immediate experiences."

[18] Steiner reported: "The mere sentient soul, therefore, differs from the evolved higher member of the soul that brings thinking into its service. This soul that is served by thought will be termed the intellectual soul. It could also be called the *rational-feeling soul*."

[19] According to Steiner: "The consciousness soul is thus distinguished as a member of the soul distinct from the intellectual soul, which is still entangled in the sensations, impulses and passions. Everyone knows how a man at first counts as true what he prefers in his feelings and desires. Only that truth is permanent, however, that has freed itself from all flavor of such sympathy and antipathy of feeling. The truth is true even if all personal feelings revolt against it. That part of the soul in which this truth lives will be called *consciousness soul*."

outwards; the mineral world develops it from without, inwards. The spirit forming and living as "I" will be called *spirit self* because it manifests as the "I," or ego, or self of man. There could be no color sensations without physical eyes, and there could be no intuitions without the higher thinking of the *spirit self*.

The work on the astral body or soul body prepares the *spirit self* [20] for its task of intuition. The transformed etheric body forms the *life spirit* [21] which comes about by changing habits and deeply rooted character traits. The final member of the human being is the *spirit man* which is formed by working on the physical body.

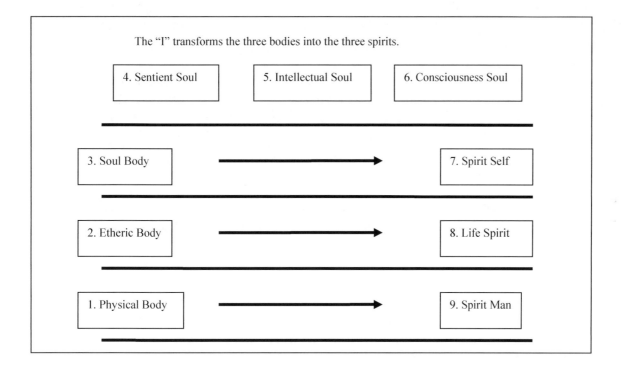

The nine-fold human being is the archetypal picture of the human being. The seven-fold, three-fold, and eight-fold are all variations or contractions of this model. The basic breakdown consists in the first five

---

[20] Through this work, however, higher stages of the being of man are reached. Through it, man develops new members of his being. These lie as the concealed behind what is manifest to him. Not only can he become master of the soul by working on the latter through the power of the ego so that the soul drives the concealed into manifestation, but he can also extend this work. He can extend it to the astral body. The I thus takes possession of this astral body by uniting itself with the latter's hidden nature. This astral body, overcome and transformed by the ego, may be called the *spirit self*. (This is what, in connection with oriental wisdom, is called "manas.") In the spirit self we have a higher member of man's being, one which, so to speak, exists within it as a germ and which emerges more and more as it actively works upon itself.

[21] The work upon the ether body is, however, more intensive than the work upon the astral body, for what is concealed in the former is enveloped by two veils, while the concealed in the astral body is veiled by only one. It is possible to form a concept of the difference in the work on these two bodies by pointing to certain changes that can take place in man in the course of his development. Let us call to mind how certain human soul qualities develop when the ego is working upon the soul; how passion and desire, joy and sorrow may change. It is only necessary to think back to the time of childhood. At that time, what was man's source of pleasure? What caused him pain? What has he learned in addition to what he was able to do in childhood? All this is only an expression of the way the ego has gained mastery over the astral body. For this body is the bearer of pleasure and pain, of joy and sorrow. Compare this with how little certain other qualities of man change in the course of time, for example, his temperament, the deeper peculiarities of his character, and so forth. A person, hot-tempered as a child, will often retain certain aspects of this violent temper in *later life*.

members (physical body through the intellectual soul) which are on the more sensual side of the human experience, while the consciousness soul and the other members draw from the spiritual side.

The details of the nine-fold human being help shed light on how a nine-form is written. The first famous nine-form is the nine (!) beatitudes in the New Testament. Those who are offended by new age or radically interpretative translation may not want to see eye to eye on this theme. For those who are tired of the simplistic interpretation of ancient scripture, may be pleased with Steiner's living-form.

Quotations from Steiner's lecture on the Beatitudes: Steiner gave the following in a lecture on the Beatitudes. One should keep in mind that Steiner believed that Christ's coming was a central event in the spiritual evolution of humanity. This event has consequences for everyone not simply believers. In other words the true understanding of Christ and Jesus leads us to an event of cosmic significance which transcends religions and sectarian preferences.

"Christ Jesus Himself expressed, in the most penetrating thoughts, the fulfillment of the times in the Sermon on the Mount, as it is called. This was by no means a sermon for the masses. The Gospels read, "When Christ saw the multitudes of people, He withdrew from them and revealed Himself to His disciples." To them He disclosed that man, in ancient times, could become God-imbued during states of ecstasy. While outside his ego, he was blissful and had direct experience with the spiritual world from which he could draw spiritual and health-giving forces.

"But now - so said Christ Jesus to His disciples - a man can become God-imbued who becomes permeated within himself with the God and Christ impulse, and can unite himself as an ego with this impulse. In the past, he alone could ascend to spiritual spheres who was filled with divine streamings from them. Only he, as possessor of the spirit, could be called blessed. Such a man was a seer in the old sense and he was a rare personality. The majority of the people had become beggars in the spirit. *Now, however, those who sought the Kingdom of Heaven could find it through their own egos.*

What occurs in such an important epoch in world evolution always affects the whole of humanity. If only a single member of a man's being is affected, the others all respond. *All the members of his being — the physical and etheric bodies, the sentient, rational and consciousness souls, the ego, and even the higher soul members — receive new life through the nearness of the Kingdom of Heaven.* These teachings are in complete accord with the teachings of primeval wisdom:

1. In order for an individual to enter the spiritual world in earlier times, the etheric body had to be slightly separated from the physical body, which was thus formed in a special way. Christ Jesus therefore said in regard to the **physical body**, "Blessed are the beggars, the poor in spirit, for if they develop their ego-ruled bodies in the right way, they will find the Kingdom of Heaven."
2. Of the **etheric body** He said, "Formerly, men could be healed of illnesses of the body and soul by ascending into the spiritual world in a state of ecstasy. Now those who suffer and are filled with the spirit of God can be healed and comforted by finding the source, the comfort, within themselves."
3. Of the **astral body** He said, "In former times those whose astral bodies were beset by wild and tempestuous passions could only be subdued when equanimity, peace and purification streamed to them from divine spiritual beings." Now men should find the strength within their own egos, through the indwelling Christ, to purify the astral body on earth. Thus, the new influence in the astral body had to be presented by saying, "Blessed and God-imbued in their astral bodies are those who foster calmness and equanimity within themselves; all comfort and well-being on earth shall be their reward."
4. The fourth beatitude refers to the **sentient soul**. The ego of him who purifies himself in his sentient soul and seeks a higher development, will become permeated with the Christ. In his heart he will thirst for righteousness; he will become pervaded with godliness and his ego will become sufficient unto itself.

5. The next member is the **rational soul**. In the sentient soul the ego is in dull slumber; it only awakens in the rational soul. Because the ego sleeps in the sentient soul, we cannot find in another man the ego that truly makes him a human being. Before an individual has developed the ego within himself, he must allow his sentient soul to grow into higher worlds to be able to perceive something there. But when he has developed himself in his rational soul, he can perceive the person next to him. Where all those members previously referred to are concerned, we must bear in mind what was given them in earlier realms. It is only the rational soul that can fill itself with what flows from man to man. In the fifth beatitude the sentence structure will have to take on a special form. The subject and the predicate must be alike, since it concerns what the ego develops within itself. The fifth beatitude says, "He who develops compassion and mercy shall find compassion in others."

6. The next sentence of the Beatitudes refers to the **consciousness soul**. Through it the ego comes into being as pure ego and becomes capable of receiving God into itself. If man can elevate himself to such a degree, he can perceive within himself that drop of the divine, his ego; through his purified consciousness soul he can see God. The sixth sentence of the Beatitudes must, therefore, refer to God. The external physical expression for the ego and the consciousness soul is the blood, and where it brings itself most clearly to expression is in the heart, as expression of the purified ego. Christ said, therefore, "Blessed are the pure in heart, for they shall see God." Thus, we are shown how in the most intimate sense the heart is the expression of the ego, the divine in man.

7. Now let us advance to what is higher than the consciousness soul, to manas, buddhi and atman, or spirit self, life spirit and spirit man. Contemporary man may well develop the three members of the soul but not until the distant future will he be able to develop the higher members, spirit self, life spirit and spirit man. These cannot as yet live in themselves in man; for this to occur he must look up to higher beings. His spirit self is not yet in him; only in the future will it suffuse him. Man is not yet sufficiently evolved to take the spirit self completely into himself. In this respect he is still at the beginning of his development and is like a vessel that is gradually receiving it. This is indicated in the seventh sentence of the Beatitudes. At first, the **spirit self** can only weave into man and fill him with its warmth. Only through the deed of Christ is it brought down to earth as the power of love and harmony. Therefore, Christ says, "Blessed are those who draw the spirit-self down into themselves, for they shall become the children of God." This points man upward to higher worlds.

8. Further on, mention is made of what will be brought about in the future, but it will encounter in ever-increasing measure the opposition of the present time and be fiercely rejected. It is said in the eighth sentence of the Beatitudes, "God-imbued or blessed are they who are persecuted for righteousness sake, For they will be fulfilled in themselves with the Kingdom of Heaven, with **life spirit** or Buddhi."

9. Connected with this we find references also to the special mission of Christ Himself, in the sentence that reads, "Christ's intimate disciples may consider themselves blessed if they have to suffer persecution for His sake." This is a faint allusion to **spirit man** or atman, which will be imparted to us in the distant future.

"Thus, in the Sermon on the Mount the great message that the Kingdom of Heaven is at hand is proclaimed. In the course of these events the mystery of human evolution was fulfilled in Palestine. Man had reached a degree of maturity in all the members of his being so that he was able with his purified physical forces to receive the Christ impulse directly into himself. So it came to pass that the God-man Christ merged with the human being Jesus of Nazareth and these united forces permeated the earth for three years with their powers. This had to happen so that man would not lose completely his connection with the spiritual world during Kali Yuga."

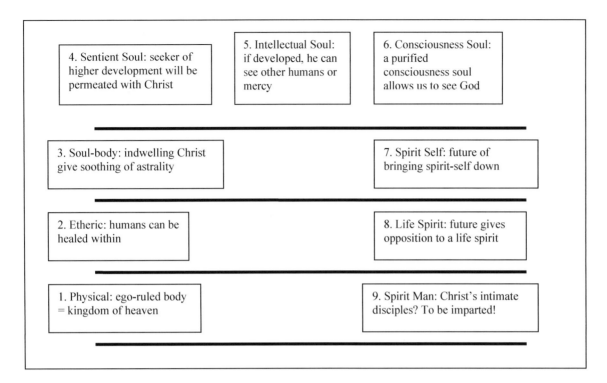

Each of the three sections presents a different aspect of our human archetype. The first three give the fundamentals: Christ's presence in our ego. The second three, sentences four through six, advocate a necessary training via a higher development and purification. The final three discuss the future of bringing down spiritual bodies as true disciples of the Christ. Thus we have in the beginning of Christian teaching, although in hidden form according to Steiner, the archetype of the human being.

There are some wonderful parallels in philosophical form to the beatitudes in Steiner *Preface* to the <u>Philosophy of Freehood</u>. This *Preface* talks about the living form in a fairly direct manner. Steiner says that there are two questions. The first question has to do with a new way of viewing or thinking that supports all knowledge and experience. Steiner never names this thinking "living form" but it clear from his work this is what is intended. The second question has to do with freehood: that is, the ability to leave our conditioned self behind and receive intuitions for new/free (unconditioned) ideas for action. Freehood does not come without exertion, practice, and self-education.

In the same fashion as the beatitudes, the last four members of the thought-form carry the future of humankind. In sentences 6 through 9 Steiner writes how in a certain soul-state we confront our freehood possibility. Notice how in these sentences there is always an "if": soul state in six; if it did not confront in seven; depends on the point of view in eight; if the soul region is found in nine.

If we relate the beatitudes to these nine sentences we see the similarity of the future in sentences seven through nine. The reader literally must be ready to engage a new type of thinking, to confront the possibility of freehood. The idea of freehood is inextricably connected with the realization of becoming Christ-like in the spiritual sense of the word. For Steiner says we know Christ in Freehood as our helping guide. There is no other way.

1. There are two root-questions of the human soul-life toward which everything is directed that will be discussed in this book.
2. The first question is whether there is a possibility to view the human being in such a way that this view proves itself to be the support for everything else which comes to meet the human being through experience or science and which gives him the feeling that it could not support itself.
3. Thereby one could easily be driven by doubt and critical judgment into the realm of uncertainty.

4. The other question is this: can the human being, as a creature of will, claim free will for himself, or is such freehood a mere illusion, which arises in him because he is not aware of the workings of necessity on which, as any other natural event, his will depends?

5. No artificial spinning of thoughts calls this question forth.

6. It comes to the soul quite naturally in a particular state of the soul.

7. And one can feel that something in the soul would decline, from what it should be, if it did not for once confront with the mightiest possible earnest questioning the two possibilities: freehood or necessity of will.

8. In this book it will be shown that the soul-experiences, which the human being must discover through the second question, depend upon which point of view he is able to take toward the first.

9. The attempt is made to prove that there is a certain view of the human being which can support his other knowledge; and furthermore, to point out that with this view a justification is won for the idea of freehood of will, if only that soul-region is first found in which free will can unfold itself.

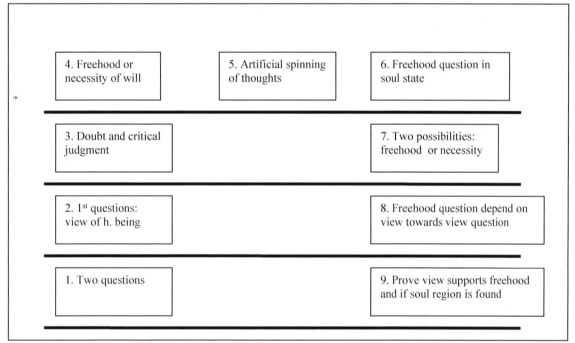

The archetype of the nine-form has three parts. It has as well future aspects starting in the sixth member of the form. The sixth member, the consciousness soul member is a strictly spirit member unlike the intellectual or sentient soul. In the beatitudes this is captured by the transition in five (seeing man) to seeing God in six. Here in the *Preface* freehood only appears to the mature individual who is ready to live in a higher awareness.

One could say that Steiner reworked past spiritual texts in order to fit his nine-fold system. But with so many examples of prayers, the mass, credo, it is hard for me to imagine that this thinking, although not unique to Christianity, doesn't have an intimate connection to the heart of Christ and the redemption of thinking.

***

For those ready to go deeper, the second section presents one way of tackling the inner aspect of the heart-thinking.

Study Guide
to the
Philosophy of Freehood

Once asked, for which of his books he would be remembered as writer, Rudolf Steiner answered: for my Philosophy of Freehood.

It was with this book that he laid the foundations for his later works, and it was to this book he again and again referred, up to the very last in his <u>Autobiography</u> and the <u>Letters to Members</u>, as the one bearing the essence of the task to which he had devoted his life.

And this task, by and large as we see it now, was the formulation in terms appropriate for the consciousness of man today and for times to come, of the means by which men can once more place themselves in waking relationship to the creative world of spirit. The world in which all things have their origin, from which human beings come and to which they return.

The foundations for such a path of knowledge had to be laid in the sphere of cognition. In the sphere where old forces of instinctive thinking were dying out, involving themselves in contradiction and despair, and in which new forces of life, new powers of living cognition had to be engendered for the future development of mankind. The language of this sphere is philosophy.

But let it not be thought that this book was to be a new philosophy. The age of intellectual world conceptions was over. Hegel had come and gone. The mystics of idea-perception belonged to history and their greatness is not to be undervalued. But their appropriateness is no longer of these times. What this <u>Philosophy of Freehood</u> purported to be was the expression of the struggle of the individual modern soul in conquest of spiritual reality and the discovery of the reality of his own being.

Rudolf Steiner, while writing it, was not concerned with philosophy as such, nor with teaching in philosophic terms, but with working out for himself the means of expression which, in its very thought-formation could bring about the transformation of those forces which had been brought to the highest possible peak in pure scientific thinking and now could become the spring board for the final leap into new realms. The pure thinking of science (rightly understood) is the sole avenue leading to the spirituality of the future.

George O'Neil, 1961

Introduction

While studying in Germany in 1992, I took part in a seminar that introduced me to The Philosophy of Freehood. The very first chapter, with its contention of whether we can truly be conscious of the reasons why we choose an action, captivated me. I was so excited by the book that I made synopses of the first seven chapters and sent them to my father. My instructor, Frank Teichmann, was a superb teacher who was able to apply Steiner's insights to the most challenging situations in scientific research and moral conduct.

Midway through Teichmann's seminar, I met another Steinerian scholar, Florin Lowndes. He intimated that there was a special method of thinking hidden within the paragraphs of The Philosophy of Freehood. Lowndes made use of color diagrams to highlight the compositional character of Steiner's "idea-art" as it weaves through the paragraph-structures of his book. Already pleased with the content, I was overjoyed that I had come upon this new method of thinking, which seemed to fill a deep longing or sense that something had been missing from my life.

I was not alone in my enthusiasm for this new thinking. Lowndes' seminars had touched a chord in the souls of the German Anthroposophists. In order to broaden my own knowledge of this new thinking in The Philosophy of Freehood, I organized a study group with my classmates in our dormitory at the University of Tuebingen. Interest in Steiner's new thinking had grown so quickly in a mere two-year period that the members of the various study groups from Germany, France and the United States came together for a retreat at Oberlin House in France to discuss the founding of a new-thinking center based on the study of The Philosophy of Freehood. About 40 individuals - including anthroposophically oriented university students, Waldorf teachers, branch members, Christian Community priests, and Anthroposophical doctors - shared their hopes that the new thinking would become a popular renewal movement within Anthroposophy.

When I returned to the United States in 1995, I started a Philosophy of Freehood study group in New York City. I had to provide my own translations of the book since the existing ones (Wilson and Stebbing) had substantially altered the structure of the paragraphs and sentences from the original German text. In the new thinking approach to Steiner's work, each paragraph and sentence is carefully composed to create dynamic wave-forms. If too much liberty is taken in the translation, these wave-forms are distorted or lost. While writing my doctoral dissertation on Steiner's use of the new thinking in the conception of his Waldorf educational philosophy, I led new thinking study groups at the NYC Branch, Sunbridge College, and even my apartment. The work was rewarding and the participants were engaged, and although I was unsure of what to do next, I knew more needed to be published about this new method of study.

One could ask the question why an awareness of this new thinking is not already more widespread. George O'Neil, an American anthroposophist who dedicated his life to researching and practicing Steiner's new thinking, had already illustrated the form and method hidden within the pages and paragraphs of The Philosophy of Freehood in his 1961 workbook (mimeograph copies).[22] He was not an obscure figure in Anthroposophy as he led the New York Branch with Henry Barnes for decades. In spite of the fact that he made his research results public through various classes and seminars, O'Neil's students never seemed to grasp the inner aspects of this new thinking. This is particularly evident in the lack of publications about Steiner's method of writing.

The study guide is a collection of ideas and experiences which I gleaned from conversations and workshops with Florin Lowndes, his book Das Erwecken des Herz-denkens (Freies Geistesleben), from George O'Neil's precious manuscript, A Work-book to the Philosophy of Spiritual Activity, and from

---

[22] George O'Neil, "A Work-book to the Philosophy of Spiritual Activity" available at the Steiner Library or at www.organicthinking.org.

years of study and meditation with <u>The Philosophy of Freehood</u>. I wanted to give enough material to allow the reader to work through the book, however without giving away all the details of the forms.

The choice to replace "freedom" with "freehood" in the title better reflects Rudolf Steiner's original intention. The German word "Freiheit" translates literally into free-hood which like knighthood, brotherhood, motherhood, implies a way of being or an activity of the mind and heart. "Free-dom," like kingdom, points to a plot of land where one can do as one pleases. It would be nice to have a new word in English such as "freehood" which captures the spirit of striving for and keeping our minds in this active state. The new title, <u>The Philosophy of Freehood</u>, indicates the beginning of a new understanding of the purpose of the book: a dynamic artistic consciousness.

This book is an instrument, written in such a way that the reader who devotes himself to it with the necessary intensity can, by means of the manner in which the thoughts have been composed, awaken in himself the capacity for intuition.

Knowledge is acquired when thoughts are introduced once into the soul with sufficient force and conviction. When these thoughts were repeatedly brought into consciousness in an organic way, so that one grows out of the other, building up in the process a totality, then forces of the soul-life which otherwise are scattered in daily life, are concentrated, united and focused. What had been an aptitude for unfolding thoughts in a coherent way, now gradually becomes a power of inner perceiving, an inner vision for broad trains of thought. There is born the intuitive power of grasping at one glance what logically can be worked out in time but with painstaking effort and continually fraught with the possibility of error. Thinking becomes a seeing, a seeing that at the same time is thinking.

George O'Neil, 1961

Chapter One, The Content

The Content and Argument of the Philosophy of Freehood: I have never met anyone who did not enjoy their study of <u>The Philosophy of Freehood</u>. The argument of the book prances along defeating opponents and quoting advocates of freehood. It is refreshing when the big names of philosophy are exposed for their theoretical follies. Steiner's book announces the end of complicated philosophy and offers a universal philosophy which embraces life and empowers the reader.

The first half of the book states that: our thinking is not a process of spinning thoughts in our heads, but rather that our thinking gives us a true knowledge of the very substance (information) of the world. It is a fascinating study in what actual thinking is, and how we use it to have direct knowledge of ourselves and the world. Steiner's work is valuable to everyone because he defines in every day terms concepts such as: monism and dualism, thinking, subjective and objective, objects of knowledge, ideas, feelings, various philosophic schools of thought, and the knowing process.

The second half of the book answers the question of whether we can act freely based on the argument set forth in the first half of the book - that human beings have no limits to knowledge. A free action means that *we* are the originator of a new idea (new knowledge) which then becomes a motive for an action, that is then translated into a concrete action. In this light, all laws and moral ideas were once created by human beings. Historically speaking, "free-thinkers" are the ones who have intuited new moral ideas which then entered into society and became part of traditional morality and law. We, as individuals, may not necessarily make fabulous contributions to the legal system or moral codes in this life time, but we do have the possibility of transcending conventional moral ideas through our own *free* inspirations.

Human beings develop into their freehood over time. Nature gives us our existence; society, its laws and customs; and the free spirit shapes his own moral and practical life anew, striving to transcend aspects of inherited habits of one's gender, race, religion, and nation. Steiner states that freehood is inherent in human beings, and an important part of freehood is the motivation to improve the welfare and freehood of others. Evolution in the Steinerian sense is nothing short of the moral and social progress of everyone on earth toward their own individual values and freehood. In a world where everyone can pursue their own ethical goals without hurting others, our own inner moral voice of freehood will guide us, as individuals, to satisfy our own unique needs. Participating in our freehood, our highest moral calling, is, according to Steiner, living in God.

After reading such a conclusion it is difficult to suppress the desire to work on one's path to freehood and service to humanity. If everyone in college were taught that the goal of life was to live in service to humanity by working on intuitive capacities, and to develop your own personal ethical code by listening to your own inner voice, then our graduates may not despair as they enter into the "real world." It is never too late to work on freehood. May the next several chapters inspire you to continue on this path to your own inner voice.

Steiner's method of writing supports Freehood: <u>The Philosophy of Freehood</u> not only conveys information about knowledge and freehood, but also embodies a new method of thinking. In order for our thinking to be free it needs to flow in dynamic-living archetypal patterns. Rudolf Steiner used an organic type of logic in which the thought-process climbs and descends through a series of flowing perspectives. For this reason, Steiner's philosophy and writing style could be termed organic "point-of-viewism."

When reading <u>The Philosophy of Freehood</u> we have, on the one hand, the content that entertains and empowers the reader to seek out the source of their own free will. On the other hand, we have chapters, paragraphs and sentences which are structured in wave-like patterns with an inner mirroring of themes and subject matter. What is the purpose of this organic structure? Steiner wanted the content of the book to be seen in picture form so that the readers become accustomed to viewing ideas as harmonious arrangements or "compositions." By meditating on these structures one develops the ability to see from the whole-to-the-parts, and the parts-to-the-whole. Ideally, organic structures can be integrated into one's own writings, imbuing them with archetypal forms that every reader can intuit while reading.

<u>*The Philosophy of Freehood*</u> *and group work*: Steiner expected that people would study this text in a group setting. When individuals gather in regular meetings, the group creates a certain energetic dynamic. However, it is often difficult to find even two people who can successfully work together without conflict. Our age requires a text and a type of group study in which social skills and freehood are practiced. There is a promise from Rupert Sheldrake which claims that when a significant number of individuals practice a new behavior, an energetic field of influence permeates the universal consciousness. When a "hundred monkeys" practice freehood, then there is a powerful opportunity for the world to open itself naturally to a new freehood impulse.

How does a new thinking group read and study? Customarily, each person produces synopses of a chapter and its paragraphs and presents them to the group in their own words. This wrestling with the text in a group setting allows the individual to draw from the energy of the group in the development of their intuitive faculties. Each person's synopses should simplify the text so that the other members of the group can hear original interpretations of the content clearly.

This simple method of recreating the content in its organic structure has a bonding effect on the group. By learning to listen to others and staying true to the text in the presentation, individuals release their intellectualized and competitive attitudes and accept different styles of communicating. We learn to listen to the other individuals, really listen, by moving beyond our own expectations of what should be said and find *that* inner quiet where the other's real voice can be heard. This is the beginnings of a new social life.

Some Aspects of Freehood: Freehood is a medium for expressing our unique passions, feelings, desires, and ideas. We want to articulate the creative impulses within us. Each of us has passion to varying degrees and freehood is the constructive means for living out our passions. The study of <u>The Philosophy of Freehood</u> addresses this issue by opening up our rigid thinking to new ideas and capacities. In the study of flexible dynamic thinking, we learn to uplift our passions into the ideal world where they can bear fruit.

There are many aspects to this philosophy. We have the content of <u>The Philosophy of Freehood</u> which is a series of logical points made about how we can experience our freehood. Steiner calls this the **Science of Freehood**. Then comes the organic-dynamic movement and pictures of the text, which flow through the four levels and colors, as described in the coming chapters. This we call the **Art of Freehood**, which includes the art of being social in freehood. And finally, by participating in a thinking "ritual" of each chapter, we practice the **Religion of Freehood**.

Compared with the current abstract thinking, the new thinking is one that takes on the quality of picturing, where thoughts stand side by side rather than follow each other in logical sequence. Anschauendes Denken it is called, and this 'seeing power' once it reaches maturity, is experienced as the living within the stream of flowing thought-life itself. It has freed itself from the mirroring physiological basis of the brain and has taken on life. The new thinking is living thinking.

George O'Neil, 1961

Chapter 2, Principles of Organic Logic

The Archetypal Plant: What is an organic form? Johann Wolfgang Von Goethe wrote about four perspectives from which we can observe the living process of a plant. These perspectives are rhythm (expansion and contraction), enhancement (climb and swoop), polarity, and inversion.

All living things breathe and have an internal rhythmical quality. In Goethe's archetypal plant, the form of the plant breathes as each stage contracts and expands, as in the contracting seed and expanding leaf, the contracting bud and expanding flower and so on. We find rhythm in all living thought-forms and life processes.

If these movements are then taken together as they progress through the living process of the plant, we can visualize Goethe's second perspective, called enhancement (also called climb and swoop, or intensification). With the passage of time, a plant becomes ever more complex and intricate in its structure (in the case of humans, we *can* become ever more complex and wise with age). The plant "enhances" as it climbs upward to the sun, becoming ever more complex in form. It then transforms into a flower, and then swoops or descends downward to the earth returning to the seed stage once more.

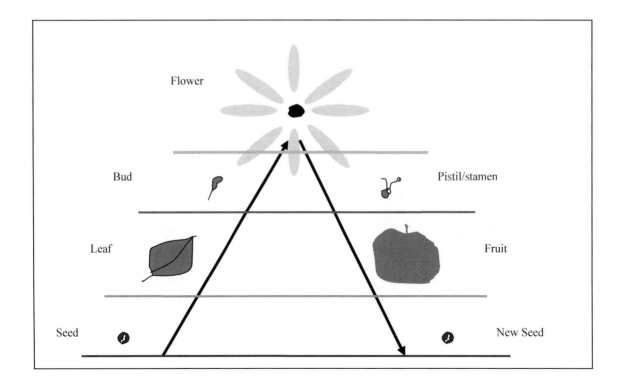

Polarity is the perspective of subtle contrast. Each of the four levels of the plant contains a polarity: the old seed is polar to the new seed; the leaf (responsible for feeding the plant) is polar to the fruit (responsible for providing nutrition for the seed); the bud is polar to the pistil/stamen in that the bud receives its growth impetus from within but the pistil/stamen from without (pollination). Thus there are three polarities inherent in the form of the plant with the flower containing a pseudo-polarity, or contrast, of the petals and the flower center.

The fourth perspective is called inversion, or turning inside-out. One can actually see the first three stages of the plant and its growth as they palpable to the eye. At the flower stage an inversion takes place and the last four stages have hidden and internalized processes. Generally speaking, the first three stages and their processes are two-dimensional, while the last four stages are three-dimensional.

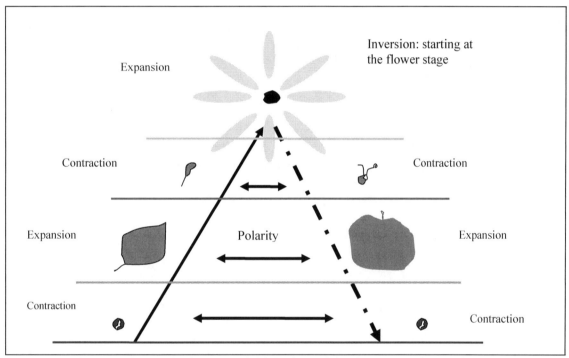

In Goethe's archetypal plant, Rudolf Steiner found an organic model which could justify and support his organic logic. Steiner called the four perspectives "metamorphosis of the plant." We add to the laws of normal logical thinking (syllogism), four new perspectives each one building on the other.♥

Organic thinking is the logic of life: Before we get into the chapters of The Philosophy of Freehood, it is necessary to further clarify the qualities of the four levels so we can understand this new living logic. Steiner revisited the ancient notion that there are four kingdoms of nature: mineral, plant, animal, and human. Each kingdom has its own unique traits or qualities: the mineral has form; the plant, form and life; the animal, form, life and feeling; and the human being form, life, feeling and self-reflection. In spiritual literature, these traits are similarly reflected within the four main energy fields: the physical body, the life or etheric body, the feeling or astral body, and the ego or I-body. Rudolf Steiner wrote about and mentioned these four bodies or energy fields in many of his books and lectures, thereby reminding the reader of their importance to his work.

♥ Lowndes assigned each stage of the plant's process to a certain level of development that embodied specific qualities: the blue level (seed) has a static quality; the green level (leaf and fruit) a dynamic quality; the red level (bud and pistil/stamen) an inner quality; and the yellow level (the flower) an individual quality.

136

Steiner on one occasion called this four-level approach, the "human being systematic."
The four fold human being, and its various manifestations, became for him the archetypal pattern for "stringing" together thoughts, ideas, chapters, and paragraphs. He captured the traits of this archetypal pattern with the four questions: what? how? why? and who?. These questions serve as scaffolding around which we can organize our ideas. They represent universal organic patterns which speak to an unconscious need for our thoughts to flow in a 'natural' way. The four levels always move from the concrete to the abstract, or from the what? to the who?

As with the archetypal plant, the physical level has the characteristic of being static or of consisting of form and material. The life level represents the dynamic, growth, method, time, creation and so on. The feeling, or astral level, contains the instinctual, aesthetic, goal-oriented, sympathy/antipathy, and comparisons. The ego level represents the most abstract of the levels: essence, thinking, definitions, new ideas, inner person, principles, and self-reflection.

Ego Level:	The Who? Idea, self-reflection, statement, essence, invention, thinking, personality
Astral Level:	The Why? consciousness, design, purpose, goal, feeling, contrast
Life Level:	The How? method, life, dynamic, movement, time, process
Physical Level:	The What? material, form, static, dead, facts,

All undertakings - any decisions we set into action – can be considered in light of the stages and questions of the organic logic. When traveling, we begin with our destination (the who? or idea level) but proceed from the physical level. Do we take a car, bus, sneakers, airplane? With this question we address the what?-level or the physical aspect of our travel. Then, based on our destination, we find a route and decide on a time of travel (the how level?). While on our way to our destination, we take into consideration the tempo, rest stops, or modify our trip for a more scenic route, or even rush quickly to our destination (the why? or feeling level). We arrive at the destination and fulfill the who? level, in other words we realize our original wish to reach our destination.

    Now let's consider the following activities of house building and pizza making in their organic order. We see how every plan requires a series of steps through the four levels. We always start with our idea and then proceed through the steps or levels of the organic logic to eventually realize our goal.

	House Building	Pizza Making
Who?	4. Architect's plan/ finished house	4. Idea of pizza/ finished pizza
Why?	3. Modifications	3. Checking for desired crispiness
How?	2. Construction	2. Cooking
What?	1. Materials	1. Ingredients

    The what?, how?, why?, and who? levels serve as guides for the interval quality of this new form of thinking and therefore are not to be answered literally.

The Basic Forms: Rudolf Steiner's entire Philosophy of Freehood ascends and descends utilizing the questions what? how? why? and who? as a scaffold. While this may at first appear to be a rigid schema, in Steiner's hands it becomes a diverse musical score of philosophical ideas, a jazz score. Even though the writing moves through these questions, it is never repetitive and each chapter challenges the preceding one, thus giving the reader new and varying perspectives on this organic logic.

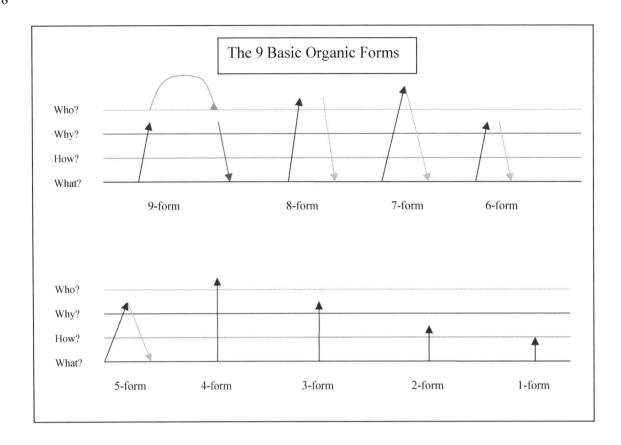

As shown in the diagram above, Steiner primarily used nine basic organic forms in composing his thought forms in <u>The Philosophy of Freehood</u>. These nine can be divided into two main types of organic forms: linear and polar. A linear form, one that moves through 1-, 2-, 3-, or 4- questions (ascending only) has neither mirroring nor polarity. However, 5-, 6-, 7-, 8-, and 9-forms all have polarity, thus answering the questions on the ascent and descent. The chapters, paragraphs and sentences are structured according to various combinations of these forms. All forms however, proceed from the what? to the how? and so on consistently in that progression and never proceed arbitrarily, i.e., from the how? to the why? to the what? level. George O'Neil and Florin Lowndes established a canon of forms observed in Steiner's work, a list of which appears in the quick reference section in the Appendix.

A Glimpse at the Forms of the <u>Philosophy of Freehood</u>: The challenge comes now in studying the book for its forms as well as its content. Each chapter presents a different organic pattern. The goal is to practice each chapter and to learn its form to the extent that you grasp the thought-pattern and can apply it to your own work.

All of the organic patterns in the chapters have symmetrical forms. Often a chapter has several forms 'going on' at once, which will be explained later on. These forms will appear as abstractions at first, but once you start making your own synopses you will see the patterns fairly quickly. Some of them are very challenging though. It is not uncommon to wrestle with a chapter until there is an "a-ha" moment and the parts start to fall together into a coherent whole.

Below we have a diagram of the first seven chapters and their organic forms. The details are not given, but one can see the general movement of climb and swoop through the four levels. Many of the forms have a similar pattern, but on closer inspection the emphasis is slightly different (compare chapters 3 and 4). *I would like to give the reader a chance to first attempt to find some of the forms on their own*; so don't cheat by memorizing these forms first before you begin your study.

The first thing one notices is that the colors and parts of the curves often mirror each other. There are varying forms and tempos to the chapters. When you start on your journey through <u>The Philosophy of Freehood</u>, you can draw your own conclusions and have your own experiences with the form and the content.   It is important to note here that these forms are not written in stone, and that new interpretations and configurations might be possible. This new thinking is still in its infancy and future enthusiasts may find other modes of characterizing these thought forms.

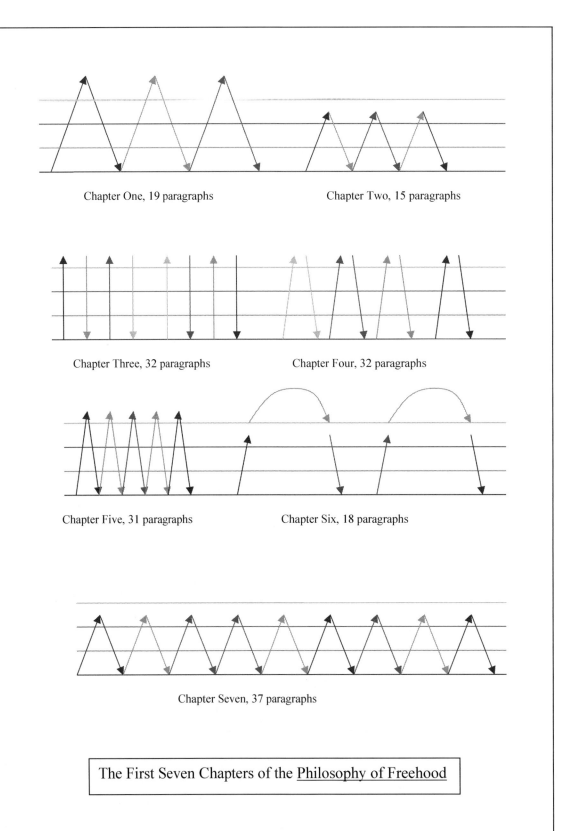

Chapter One, 19 paragraphs

Chapter Two, 15 paragraphs

Chapter Three, 32 paragraphs

Chapter Four, 32 paragraphs

Chapter Five, 31 paragraphs

Chapter Six, 18 paragraphs

Chapter Seven, 37 paragraphs

The First Seven Chapters of the <u>Philosophy of Freehood</u>

Of recent time, thought has been given to the source of great creative impulses, to the appearance of decisive trends in history. Where do Ideas come from? What of the creative process whereby new insights are born? Intuition, Inspiration are acknowledged facts. Scientific Imagination is highly rewarded. But the burning question is never answered: how can it be taught? How can it be brought into the service of man? What in essence is this purely human way of thinking?

To the answer of these questions this book was dedicated, and as the only answer to them, has still, 70 years later, yet to find recognition.

George O'Neil, 1961

The goal of our study of this book is acquisition of a thinking to which no man today is born, and no schooling so far prepares him. It is new to the degree that it is as yet unrecognized not alone outside, but also often within the very circles established for the cultivation of Anthroposophy. This cannot be stressed sufficiently.

George O'Neil, 1961

Chapter Three, Practice

The Big Picture: The Philosophy of Freehood contains fourteen main chapters, a "fifteenth chapter," a preface, two appendices, and eleven addenda. When you begin your study, it is quite fun to sketch the whole book ever so lightly, to get a feel for its proportions, just as an artist makes broad stokes before filling in the details. The goal is to see the book as a living organism.

The paragraphs and sentences of the text are numbered. Before each paragraph, you will always see two numbers, such as "1/14," which tells you that paragraph one has fourteen sentences. This is necessary in order to keep track of the correct paragraph-count which is not always easy to establish because of unorthodox uses of punctuation. Steiner used dashes, quotes, and so on sometimes in conventional, and other times in very unconventional ways. For example, there are a few places where a dash appears in the middle of a paragraph. These dashes signify parenthetical remarks that neither add to the thought form of the chapter nor constitute new paragraphs. Therefore, the numerical headings at the start of these remarks include a letter, i.e. 12a/10. The dashes in the *Preface to the new 1918 revised edition* and the addenda, in contrast, *are considered new paragraphs* as Steiner subsequently changed his mind about the function of the dash later in his career!

Because he was never confronted about his particular style of writing while alive, no one knows with 100% certainty if our manner of numbering his text is absolutely correct in all cases. What we do know is that the fourteen chapters of the book are written in organic form. We have already mentioned that the paragraphs create an organic form, and in fact the sentences within the paragraphs do as well. To do justice to all these levels of organic form, this translation attempts to capture the sentence and clause structure of the original German text. I based my translation on Michael Wilson's and William Lindeman's excellent work and tried, to the best of my ability, to use more contemporary language without sacrificing Steiner's organic syntactical structure.

How to study The Philosophy of Freehood: Reading the book can be rewarding, in itself. However, a truly energizing experience comes from reading, working out synopses of the content and sketching out the diagrams. The reason for this is that studying the thoughts in their wave-form engages and intensifies our chakric activity. For now, let us focus on how we begin to develop our wave-form diagrams.

The first step is to summarize each paragraph as you are reading through the text, capturing the main ideas without including too many details. These summaries or condensements should be no longer than a sentence or two (if the paragraph is very long), and each condensement-sentence should be further condensed into catchwords!

Condensing is a great skill to learn. The art of condensing and coming up with catchwords can lead to profound insights into what *any* author is doing. The important thing is to practice mastering Steiner's ideas and finding their organic forms.

There are aspects of Steiner's writing where questions may arise during the condensement process. Steiner used quotations and other forms of punctuation in new and "artistic" ways. For example, in chapter one, *Conscious Human Action*, he quotes Spinoza at length beginning in the middle of paragraph two. The quote continues for two more paragraphs which should each be condensed into sentences and catchwords. It is of interest to follow how Steiner wove Spinoza's quote into his own organic forms. Yes, Spinoza's quote was in part in organic form – at least at the sentence level. In practice, such quotations usually follow colons and, for our purposes of having an accurate sentence-count, new sentences come after periods not after colons.

Continue making synopses (condensements) for each paragraph and each chapter in the book. Chapter one has nineteen paragraphs and once you have completed your study of it, you should have nineteen synopses and the accompanying catchwords or catch-phrases. If, in the beginning, you decide to borrow condensements from me or George, you still have the sentence level to grapple with and, if you wish, Steiner has 20 other "virgin" books you can work with.

After reading and condensing the entire book, you should have condensements for:

- the two starter texts, the *Preface to the new 1918 revised edition* and the *Second Appendix*;

- the fourteen primary chapters of the book;

- chapter "15" *The Consequences of Monism*;

- and the dangling texts of the eleven addenda;

- and the *First Appendix*.

There is enough material in the fourteen chapters to work with for several years. (I myself spent years just on the *Preface 1918* and *Second Appendix*.) Once you have your synopses in front of you and you begin to sketch out the forms, it is then possible to experience how the parts live in the whole and scan their every contour. There is a special energy in this activity.

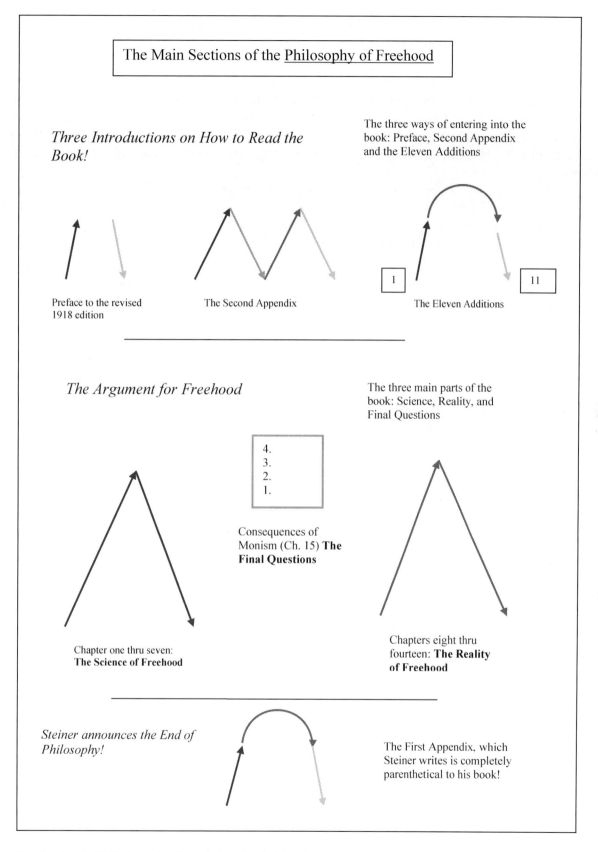

The Main Sections of the Philosophy of Freehood

Three Introductions on How to Read the Book!

The three ways of entering into the book: Preface, Second Appendix and the Eleven Additions

Preface to the revised 1918 edition

The Second Appendix

1   The Eleven Additions   11

The Argument for Freehood

The three main parts of the book: Science, Reality, and Final Questions

4.
3.
2.
1.

Consequences of Monism (Ch. 15) **The Final Questions**

Chapter one thru seven: **The Science of Freehood**

Chapters eight thru fourteen: **The Reality of Freehood**

Steiner announces the End of Philosophy!

The First Appendix, which Steiner writes is completely parenthetical to his book!

Group Study: Rudolf Steiner believed that individuals should come together to study philosophical and spiritual texts. He wrote his books utilizing this organic method because he thought that by reading them in this form, it would harmonize the energetic bodies of the participants. The group process consists of a rhythmical breathing pattern of presenting and listening. One person presents a series of paragraphs while the others listen and offer corrections or compliments. All the members go through this process.

There are two main ways to approach group study of Steiner's text. The most basic level of group work, *requiring no outside preparation*, involves reading the text aloud and making synopses together. Sometimes this can be tricky, since it can be challenging for the participants to agree on one essential idea (condensement) from each paragraph. Once a chapter is finished then the group can jointly determine its organic form and discuss the inter-connections, such as enhancements and polarities, of the paragraphs.

A more committed group will have its participants prepare synopses and a diagram of a chapter, including the enhancement, polarity and inversion of each wave-form, *before* their meetings. Each member of the group will then, in turn, present the whole chapter from their notes. If there are six group members, we should hear six relatively different synopses of the chapter. In my experience, there is no better way to *own* the text then to work at this higher level of commitment. It allows for a more rapid mastery of the content, which assists in a deeper understanding of the polarities and structure and a better visualization of the flow of the form. When finishing a chapter, the last meeting all participants present the whole chapter without any notes!

The goal of group work is to have a moving experience while studying The Philosophy of Freehood. By working with others, one is able to enjoy their own insights and those of the other members of the group more immediately. Total immersion in the text, its waves and colors, and organic relationships begins to work on the heart and mind of the group. Participants may see that as they continue to work together, those less intellectual may show some new genius, the bellicose more gentleness, and the distracted more focus.

Meditation on the Organic-Forms: When we meditate, we bring our awareness to a single object. The chapters of The Philosophy of Freehood become objects of meditation in which the mind moves through the steps/levels of the organic thought-structures. We begin to associate our synopses and one-word condensements with the colors and qualities of the four levels as we meditate on each individual aspect of a chapter.

The meditation differs from the group work in that now we re-create the chapters out of our tableau consciousness in silence. We scan each curve, up and down, forwards and backwards, until we have mastered the thought-sequence and color-quality of each level. We begin to *feel* the nuance of each paragraph as we slowly transcend the content (catchwords and synopses); and with every breath we enter into a new paragraph. *Chapter one* has nineteen paragraphs, so we have nineteen slow breaths as we move through the levels and waves of the chapter.

Steiner recommended we review a chapter fifty times, in the same way a musician practices his scales. Imagine each paragraph, sentence and condensement to be akin to a note on these scales, and through repetition, we familiarize ourselves with their qualities until we can view them from a myriad of different aspects – backwards, forwards and inwards. This new form of meditation is actually quite simple. One must only trust that these thought-forms lead to a new and exciting experience.

To achieve this living in thought as distinct from building in logical thought units, and letting the personal feeling determine the pattern of words, we first must become master in highest degree of content, utterly eliminating the arbitrariness of personal preference and emphasis. Says Goethe: to have the whole thing in your heart, you must have conned its every part. To which Rudolf Steiner has added: first read for substance, then read again for form.

In contemplating the totality of a living thought-organism, correspondences and symmetries, previously unseen, begin to emerge, each illuminating the other. Meanings come forth, never before expected, revealing interdependence and mutual support. The whole is experienced as a web of interrelationships. An Idea is experienced as a weaving interplay of single thoughts, each reflecting the whole as experienceable from its single aspect.

George O'Neil, 1961

Chapter 4, The Keys to the Book

There are certain concepts which are necessary prerequisites to understanding living thinking as it appears in written texts. These concepts are in George's quote above:

1. The parts only have meaning in their context. To know the form of a chapter means to first know it in its entirety i.e., all of the paragraphs and their content.

2. Chapters, paragraphs, and sentences are not inherently "physical," "etheric," or "astral." One may *not* read a random sentence from Steiner's book aloud and ask: "which level is this sentence on?" Dynamic sounding sentences may be etheric in one paragraph but physical in another.

3. Steiner's thought-forms consist of slight repetitions of the same idea. If there are six paragraphs in a chapter, then one should experience the same idea recast six times from six different points of view. In contemplating a six-paragraph chapter, one can best penetrate its meaning by considering it from the perspectives of enhancement and polarity.

George O'Neil's work was misunderstood by his contemporaries because they did not understand these Goethean and Steinerian concepts. Keep in mind when looking for the levels that everything is contextual.

Patience is necessary when reading the text. Steiner wrote the text in a particular style that prevents it from being easily recalled. While working on the texts, note taking is very important because one can see the development more clearly.

"Preface to the new revised 1918 edition" and "The Second Appendix": The *Preface …1918* and the *Second Appendix* contain the keys to the book. Both texts provide hints about how to grasp the organic thinking and the content of <u>The Philosophy of Freehood</u>. The *Second Appendix* explains that philosophy can become an "organic-living science," which, like art, also has a compositional element. When concepts take on an artistic existence as they do in <u>The Philosophy of Freehood</u>, says Steiner, a new active consciousness is possible. This new consciousness is able to "survey" concepts and bring them

into a living order that "benefits" us on all levels. The *Preface ... 1918* emphasizes that the book can be life-changing if it is read in a "living" way by entering into the particular method in which it is written.

Another intriguing fact about these two starter texts is that they include all nine basic forms used throughout the rest of the book. Thus, an examination of the *Preface ...1918* and the *Second Appendix* can offer us an opportunity to quickly and concisely familiarize ourselves with these basic thought-forms in preparation for our study of the other sections.

Below, I have provided the text of the *Preface...1918* and the *Second Appendix* in order to not only exemplify these nine basic thought forms, but also to illustrate how to begin to create condensements and catchwords. While reading the text, look for the key concepts in each paragraph without interpreting too much. I have included my own synopses and catchwords, which are by no means perfect but meant only as examples for creating your own. You will notice subtle repetitions of the main concepts of these texts in each paragraph. At the end of each text are the schema and diagrams to help you view the entire thought-forms.

*

PREFACE TO THE NEW REVISED 1918 EDITION of the <u>Philosophy of Freehood</u>

1/9
1. There are two root-questions of the human soul-life toward which everything is directed that will be discussed in this book.
2. The first question is whether there is a possibility to view the human being in such a way that this view proves itself to be the support for everything else which comes to meet the human being through experience or science and which gives him the feeling that it could not support itself.
3. Thereby one could easily be driven by doubt and critical judgment into the realm of uncertainty.
4. The other question is this: can the human being, as a creature of will, claim free will for himself, or is such freehood a mere illusion, which arises in him because he is not aware of the workings of necessity on which, as any other natural event, his will depends?
5. No artificial spinning of thoughts calls this question forth.
6. It comes to the soul quite naturally in a particular state of the soul.
7. And one can feel that something in the soul would decline, from what it should be, if it did not for once confront with the mightiest possible earnest questioning the two possibilities: freehood or necessity of will.
8. In this book it will be shown that the soul-experiences, which the human being must discover through the second question, depend upon which point of view he is able to take toward the first.
9. The attempt is made to prove that there is a certain view of the human being which can support his other knowledge; and furthermore, to point out that with this view a justification is won for the idea of freehood of will, if only that soul-region is first found in which free will can unfold itself.

Catchwords and Synopsis of paragraph 1/9:
two questions – *two main questions in the book: view of human being and freehood: the second question is dependent on first question and requires a special soul region*

2/5
1. The view, which is under discussion here in reference to these two questions, presents itself as one that, once attained, can be integrated as a member of the truly living soul life.
2. There is no theoretical answer given that, once acquired, can be carried about as a conviction merely preserved in the memory.
3. This kind of answer would be only an illusory one for the type of thinking which is the foundation of this book.
4. Not such a finished, fixed answer is given, rather a definite region of soul-experience is referred to, in which one may, through the inner activity of the soul itself, answer the question livingly anew at any moment he requires.
5. The true view of this region will give the one who eventually finds the soul-sphere where these questions unfold that which he needs for these two riddles of life, so that he may, so empowered, enter further into the widths and depths of this enigmatic human life, into which need and destiny impel him to wander.

Catchword and Synopsis of paragraph 2/5:
A living answer – *view can become part of the soul and answer the question livingly*!

3/1
6. A kind of knowledge seems thereby to be pointed to which, through its own inner life and by the connectedness of this inner life to the whole life of the human soul, proves its correctness and usefulness.

Catchword and Synopsis of paragraph 3/1:
Unique Knowledge – *knowledge because of its importance to the soul it is correct and useful.*

4/10
1. This is what I thought about the content of the book when I wrote it down twenty-five years ago.
2. Today, too, I have to write down such sentences if I want to characterize the purpose of the thoughts of this book.
3. At the original writing I limited myself to say no *more* than that, which in the *utmost closest sense* is connected with the two basic questions, referred to here.
4. If someone should be amazed that he finds in the book no reference to that region of the world of spiritual experience which came to expression in my later writings, he should bear in mind that in those days I did not however want to give a description of results of spiritual research but I wanted to build first the foundation on which such results could rest.
5. This <u>Philosophy of Freehood</u> does not contain any such specific spiritual results any more than it contains specific results of other fields of knowledge; but he who strives to attain certainty for such cognition cannot, in my view, ignore that which it does indeed contain.
6. What is said in the book can be acceptable to anyone who, for whatever reasons of his own, does not want anything to do with the results of my spiritual scientific research.
7. To the one, however, who can regard these spiritual scientific results, as something toward which he is attracted, what has been attempted here will also be important.
8. It is this: to prove how an open-minded consideration of these two questions which are fundamental for *all* knowing, leads to the view that the human being *lives* in a true *spiritual world*.
9. In this book the attempt is made to justify cognition of the spiritual world *before* entering into actual spiritual experience.
10. And this justification is so undertaken that in these chapters one need not look at my later valid experiences in order to find acceptable what is said here, if one is able or wants to enter into the particular style of the writing itself.

Catchword and Synopsis of 4/10:
Value of Knowledge – The book gives the foundation of spiritual work and a foundation for science if one can enter into the writing style itself.

5/5
1. Thus it seems to me that this book on the one hand assumes a position completely independent of my actual spiritual scientific writings; yet on the other hand it also stands in the closest possible connection to them.
2. These considerations brought me now, after twenty-five years, to republish the content of the text almost completely unchanged in all essentials.
3. I have only made somewhat longer additions to a number of sections.
4. The experiences I made with the incorrect interpretations of what I said caused me to publish comprehensive commentaries.
5. I changed only those places where what I said a quarter of a century ago seemed to me inappropriately formulated for the present time.
(Only a person wanting to discredit me could find occasion on the basis of the changes made *in this way*, to say that I have changed my fundamental conviction.)

Catchword and Synopsis of Paragraph 5/5:
How the book changed – the book has almost no changes except addendum and some modern formulations

6/6
1. The book has been sold out for many years.
2. I nevertheless hesitated for a long time with the completion of this new edition and it seems to me, in following the line of thought in the previous section, that today the same should be expressed which I asserted twenty-five years ago in reference to these questions.

3. I have asked myself again and again whether I might not discuss several topics of the numerous contemporary philosophical views put forward since the publication of the first edition.

4. To do this in a way acceptable to me was impossible in recent times because of the demands of my pure spiritual scientific research.

5. Yet I have convinced myself now after a most intense review of present day philosophical work, that as tempting as such a discussion in itself would be, it is for what should be said through my book, not to be included in the same.

6. What seemed to me necessary to say, from the point of view of the <u>Philosophy of Freehood</u> about the most recent philosophical directions can be found in the second volume of my <u>Riddles of Philosophy</u>.

Catchword and Synopsis of Paragraph 6/6:

2ⁿᵈ book – Steiner questions whether to add to his book, but instead refers to another book, <u>Riddles of Philosophy</u>.

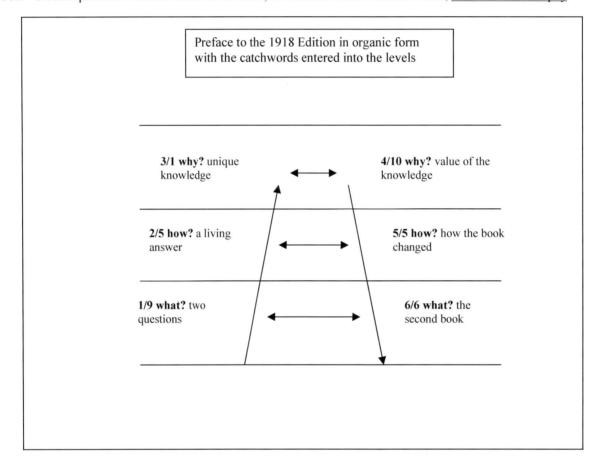

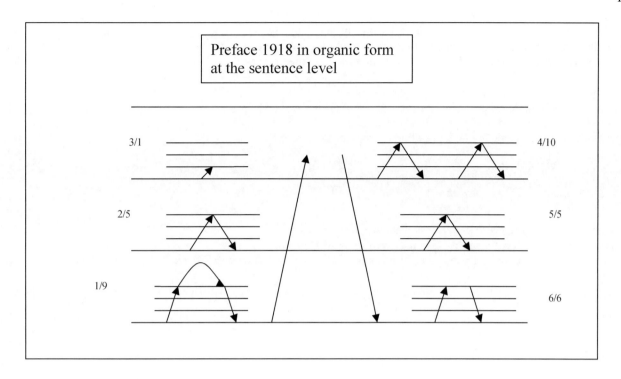

*

THE SECOND APPENDIX

1/3
1. In what follows will be reproduced in all its essentials that which stood as a kind of "preface" in the first edition of this book.
2. I placed it here as an "appendix," since it reflects the type of thinking in which I wrote it twenty-five years ago, and not because it adds to the content of the book.
3. I did not want to leave it out completely for the simple reason, that time and again the opinion surfaces that I have something to suppress of my earlier writings because of my later spiritual writings.

Catchword and synopsis of 1/3:
Text reprinted – Former preface is reprinted as appendix because of the type of thinking and because of accusations of suppression.

2/4
1. Our age can only want to draw *truth* out of the depths of man's being. *
2. Of Schiller's well-known two paths:

      "Truth seek we both, you in outer life,
        I within the heart, and each will find it for sure.
        Is the eye healthy so it meets the Creator outside;
        Is the heart healthy then it reflects inwardly the World"
the present age will benefit more from the second.
3. A truth that comes to us from the outside always carries the stamp of uncertainty.
4. Only what appears as truth to each and every one of us in his own inner being is what we want to believe.

Catchword and Synopsis of 2/4:
Two Paths – Our age benefits from Schiller's heart-path to truth, not head path

* Footnote: Only the first introductory paragraphs have been completely omitted from this work, which today appear to me totally unessential. What is said in the remaining paragraphs however, seems to me necessary to say in the present because of and in spite of the natural scientific manner of thinking of our contemporaries.

3/3

1. Only truth can bring us certainty in the development of our individual powers.
2. Whoever is tormented by doubt his powers are lamed.
3. In a world that is puzzling to him he can find no goal for his creativity.

Catchword and Synopsis of 3/3
Value of Truth – Truth gives certainty, power, a goal and creativity

4/4

1. We no longer want merely to *believe*; we want to *know*.
2. Belief requires the accepting of truths, which we cannot fully grasp.
3. However, what we do not fully grasp undermines our individuality, which wants to experience everything with its deepest inner being.
4. Only that *knowing* satisfies us that subjects itself to no external norms, but springs instead out of the inner life of the personality.

Catchword and Synopsis of 4/4:
Our knowledge – We want knowledge that springs from out inner life.

5/3

1. We also do not want a form of knowing, which is fixed for all eternity in rigid academic rules and is kept in compendia valid for all time.
2. We hold that each of us is justified in starting from firsthand experiences, from immediate life conditions, and from there climbing to a knowledge of the whole universe.
3. We strive for certainty in knowing, but each in his own unique way.

Catchword and Synopsis of 5/3:
Compendia vs. individual knowledge – We don't want rules but first hand experience and individual knowing

6/6

1. Our scientific theories should also no longer take the position that our acceptance of them was a matter of absolute coercion.
2. None of us would give a title to an academic work such as *Fichte* once did: "A Crystal Clear Report to the Public at Large on the Actual Nature of Modern Philosophy.
3. *An Attempt to Compel Readers to Understand*."
4. Today nobody should be compelled to understand.
5. We are not asking for acceptance or agreement from anyone who is not driven by a specific need to form his own personal worldview.
6. Nowadays we also do not want to cram knowledge into the unripe human being, the child, instead we try to develop his faculties so that he will not have to be *compelled* to understand, but *will* want to understand.

Catchword and Synopsis of 6/6:
2 types of education – Fichte coercion method and develop faculties look for individual needs

7/5

1. I am under no illusion in regard to this characteristic of my time.
2. I know that generic mass-ified culture [individualitaetloses Schablonentum] lives and spreads itself throughout society.
3. But I know just as well that many of my contemporaries seek to set up their lives according to the direction indicated here.
4. To them I want to dedicate this work.
5. It should not lead down "the only possible" path to truth, but it should *tell* about the path one has taken, for whom truth is what it is all about.

Catchword and Synopsis of 7/5:

Book dedicated – our age has a generic culture; Steiner dedicates his book to people who have individual needs

8/6
1. The book leads at first into more abstract spheres where thought must take on sharp contours in order to come to certain points.
2. However, the reader will be led out of these dry concepts and into concrete life.
3. I am certainly of the opinion that one must lift oneself into the ether world of concepts, if one wants to penetrate existence in all directions.
4. He who only knows how to have pleasure through his senses, doesn't know life's finest pleasures.
5. The eastern masters have their disciples spend years in a life of renunciation and asceticism before they disclose to them what they themselves know.
6. The West no longer requires pious practices and ascetic exercises for scientific knowledge, but what is needed instead is the good will that leads to withdrawing oneself for short periods of time from the firsthand impressions of life and entering into the spheres of the pure thought world.

Catchword and Synopsis of 8/6:
Book's Western path of concepts – the eastern path of renunciation vs. the western path short periods of study

9/16
1. There are many realms of life.
2. Every single one has developed a particular science for itself.
3. Life itself, however, is a unity and the more the sciences* are striving to research in their own specialized areas the more they distance themselves from the view of the living unity of the world.
4. There must be a type of knowing that seeks in the specialized 'sciences' that which is necessary to lead us back once more to the wholeness of life.
5. The specialized researcher wants through his own knowledge to gain an understanding of the world and its workings; in this book the goal is a philosophical one: science shall itself become organic-living.
6. The specialized sciences are preliminary stages of the science striven for here.
7. A similar relationship predominates in the arts.
8. The composer works on the basis of the theory of composition.
9. The latter is the sum of knowledge whose possession is a necessary precondition of composing.
10. In composing, the laws of the theory of composition serve life itself, serve actual reality.
11. In exactly the same sense, philosophy is a creative *art*.
12. All genuine philosophers are *concept-artists*.
13. Through them, human ideas became artistic materials and the scientific method became artistic technique.
14. Thereby, abstract thinking gains concrete, individual life.
15. Ideas become life-powers.
16. We have then not just a knowing about things but we have made Knowing instead into an actual, self-governing organism; our authentic, active consciousness has placed itself above a mere passive receiving of truths.

Catchword and Synopsis of 9/16:
Self-governing consciousness – The new organic-living science has a compositional character in which ideas become life-powers and knowledge relates truths into a self governing organism!

10/3
1. How philosophy as art relates to the *freehood* of the human being, what freehood is, and whether we are active in our freehood or able to become active: this is the main question of my book.
2. All other scientific explanations are included here only because they provide an explanation, in my opinion, about those things that are of importance to human beings.
3. A "*Philosophy of Freehood*" shall be given in these pages.

Catchword and Synopsis of 10/3:
Freehood question – How philosophy as an art relates to freehood

_____

11/4
1. All scientific endeavors would be only a satisfying of idle curiosity, if they did not strive toward uplifting the *existential worth of the human personality.*
2. The sciences attain their true value only by demonstrating the human significance of their results.
3. Not the refinement of any single capacity of soul can be the final goal of individuality, but rather the development of all the faculties slumbering within us.
4. Knowledge only has value when it contributes to the *all-sided* unfolding of the *whole* human nature.

Catchword and Synopsis of 11/4:
True value of science – science must uplift human beings and unfold their latent capacities

12/1
1. This book, therefore, conceives the relationship between scientific knowledge and life not in such a way that man has to bow down before the idea and consecrate his forces to its service, but rather in the sense that the human being masters the world of ideas in order to make use of it for his *human* goals, which transcend the mere scientific.

Catchword and Synopsis of 12/1:
Empower world of ideas – book conceives relationship between life and science to empower us for human goals not mere scientific ones

13/1
1. One must experience and place oneself consciously above the Idea; *otherwise* one falls into its servitude.

Catchword and Synopsis of 13/1:
Mastering or serving the Idea –

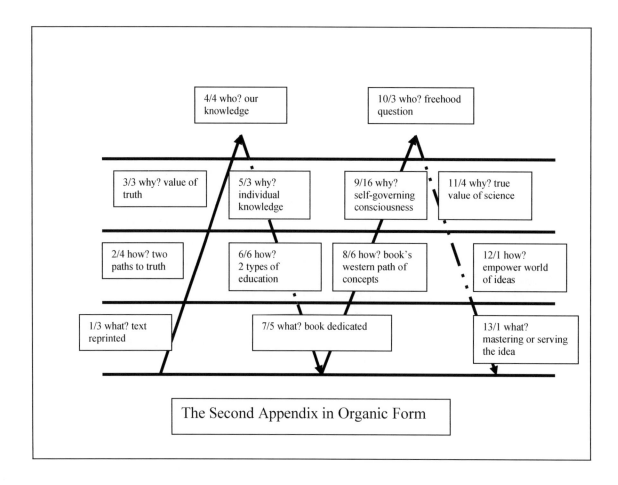

*

A closer look at the nine basic forms: In the next section, we repeat the same exercise as above, but now at the sentence level. As mentioned earlier, Steiner placed the nine basic forms into the *Preface... 1918* and *Second Appendix* so that students could have a foundation from which to work before they mastered the whole book. By examining these texts at the sentence level, we can better visualize these thought-forms and become better acquainted with each one's specific quality. Here are the diagrams of the nine basic forms once again.

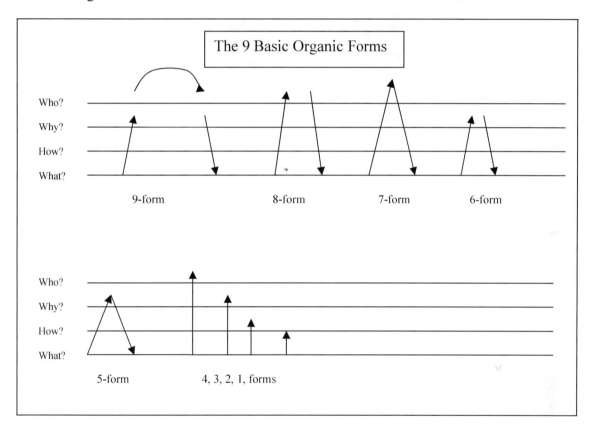

The 9-fold organic form: Paragraph 1/9 of the *Preface to the revised 1918 Edition* is an example of a very special form in Steiner's work. Structurally speaking, the nine-fold organic forms are composed of three groups of three sentences with the topic shifting in each group. Sentences four through six, all on the ego level, share the same topic (in paragraph 1/9 - the freehood question). But here it is worth noting that sentence four answers the question why?, sentence five how?, and sentence six what? while at the same time collectively answering the question who?

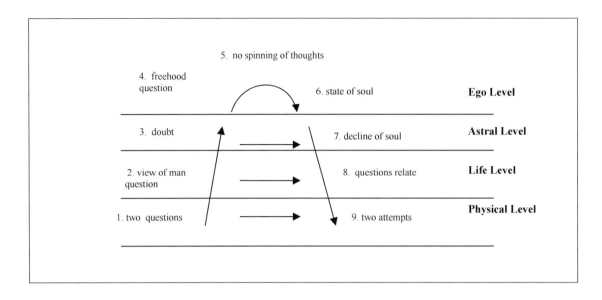

Paragraph 1/9 from the *Preface 1918*

1. There are two root-questions of the human soul-life toward which everything is directed that will be discussed in this book.

2. The first question is whether there is a possibility to view the human being in such a way that this view proves itself to be the support for everything else which comes to meet the human being through experience or science and which gives him the feeling that it could not support itself.

3. Thereby one could easily be driven by doubt and critical judgment into the realm of uncertainty.

4. The other question is this: can the human being, as a creature of will, claim free will for himself, or is such freehood a mere illusion, which arises in him because he is not aware of the workings of necessity on which, as any other natural event, his will depends?

5. No artificial spinning of thoughts calls this question forth.

6. It comes to the soul quite naturally in a particular state of the soul.

7. And one can feel that something in the soul would decline, from what it should be, if it did not for once confront with the mightiest possible earnest questioning the two possibilities: freehood or necessity of will.

8. In this book it will be shown that the soul-experiences, which the human being must discover through the second question, depend upon which point of view he is able to take toward the first.

9. The attempt is made to prove that there is a certain view of the human being which can support his other knowledge; and furthermore, to point out that with this view a justification is won for the idea of freehood of will, if only that soul-region is first found in which free will can unfold itself.

In addition to the three-foldness of the structure there is the polar nature of the nine-form. The first four sentences in paragraph 1/9 present "two questions," sentence five inverts the form by judging the preceding four sentences, and sentences six through nine discuss the conditions under which the questions can be addressed. Namely, only those readers who can fulfill these requirements can enter into the promise of the book:

       *If they reach a particular soul state
       *If they confront their own Freehood
       *If they are capable of the right point of view of the human being
       *If they find the soul region for unfolding free will

Steiner sets up fairly strong polarities between the sentences of this paragraph:

1 and 9 (2 questions and 2 attempts),

2 and 8 (1ˢᵗ question),
3 and 7 (doubt and feeling the soul decline),
4 and 6 (freehood question and individuals who regard it).
Nine-fold forms have a very subtle gestalt that requires much study.

The 8-fold organic form: Next to paragraph 1/9 *Preface*, paragraph 9/16 of the *Second Appendix* contains some of the most essential information about the nature of the heart-thinking. Steiner argues that the way to wholeness is to take the elements of science and relate them in an artistic-musical-compositional manner; and thereby, to develop a new idea consciousness, a compositional-consciousness! The goal of the book is to make consciousness itself organic-living.

Paragraph 9/16 from the Second Appendix:
1. There are many realms of life.
2. Every single one has developed a particular science for itself.
3. Life itself, however, is a unity and the more the sciences are striving to research in their own specialized areas the more they distance themselves from the view of the living unity of the world.
4. There must be a type of knowing that seeks in the specialized 'sciences' that which is necessary to lead us back once more to the wholeness of life.
5. The specialized researcher wants through his own knowledge to gain an understanding of the world and its workings; in this book the goal is a philosophical one: science shall itself become organic-living.
6. The specialized sciences are preliminary stages of the science striven for here.
7. A similar relationship predominates in the arts.
8. The composer works on the basis of the theory of composition.
9. The latter is the sum of knowledge whose possession is a necessary precondition of composing.
10. In composing, the laws of the theory of composition serve life itself, serve actual reality.
11. In exactly the same sense, philosophy is a creative *art*.
12. All genuine philosophers are *concept-artists*.
13. Through them, human ideas became artistic materials and the scientific method became artistic technique.
14. Thereby, abstract thinking gains concrete, individual life.
15. Ideas become life-powers.
16. We have then not just a knowing about things but we have made knowing instead into an actual, self-governing organism; our authentic, active consciousness has placed itself above a mere passive receiving of truths.

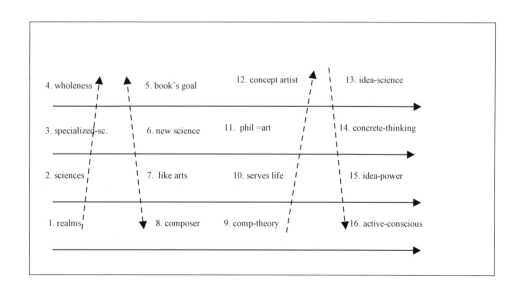

The polarities in 9/16 are based on a 'problem and solution' model. For example, in sentence 1 the 'problem' is the "many realms of life," in sentence 8 the solution is the composer (he who brings the elements into a whole). Between sentence 2 and 7, the polarity is: the "sciences" find their complement in the arts; between sentences 3 and 6, the old specialized sciences find their fulfillment in a "new science" arising out of their results. The problem of wholeness in knowing in sentence 4 finds its solution in the organic science of sentence 5.

These polarities are subtle and they can be continued even to include the second half of 9/16.

The 7-fold and 6-fold Organic Forms: There is no example of the seven-fold form at the sentence level in the two texts, but we do see it at the paragraph-level in the *Second Appendix* (see the diagram above). The seven and six-forms generally have the same archetypal structure, except that the seven-form has its own ego-level paragraph, unlike the six-form.

In paragraph 6/6 of the Second Appendix there is solid six-form. The first three sentence cover coercive theories and Fichte's book while the second three sentences cover today's need for individual learning. Important to note here is how in sentence two Steiner quotes the title and makes two sentences by placing it after a colon.

6/6
1. Our scientific theories should also no longer take the position that our acceptance of them was a matter of absolute coercion.
2. None of us would give a title to an academic work such as *Fichte* once did: "A Crystal Clear Report to the Public at Large on the Actual Nature of Modern Philosophy.
3. *An Attempt to Compel Readers to Understand.*"
4. Today nobody should be compelled to understand.
5. We are not asking for acceptance or agreement from anyone who is not driven by a specific need to form his own personal worldview.
6. Nowadays we also do not want to cram knowledge into the unripe human being, the child, instead we try to develop his faculties so that he will not have to be *compelled* to understand, but *will* want to understand.

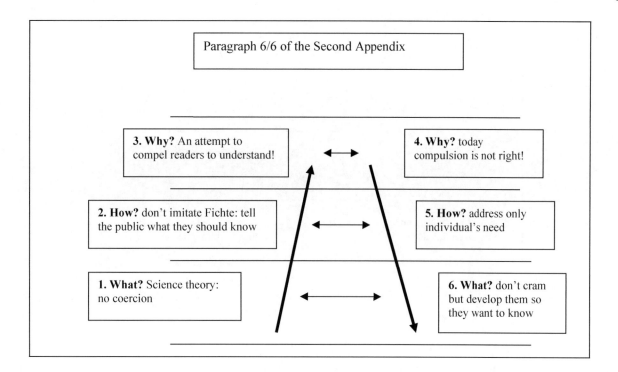

There are nice polarities between the first and second halves. The problem of coercion is answered by what the individual needs of today require in order to learn. The basic questions of what? how? and why? are answered pretty straightforwardly.

Example of the 5-fold Organic Form: Paragraph 2/5 of the *Preface to the revised 1918 Edition* clarifies how the question concerning the view of the human being can be answered by its integration, not memorization. The first two sentences present the "view" in its un-integrated form. In contrast, the last two sentences present the "view" in its living, integrated form. Sentence 3 declares that the type of thinking, organic-living, is the foundation of the book.

Sentence 1 and 5 create a solid polarity: the not-yet-integrated view of sentence 1 is integrated into the soul in sentence 5. The theoretical memorized answer of sentence 2 becomes a living soul activity in sentence 4. This paragraph is an excellent model for writing exercises because of the clarity of the polarities.

2/5
1. The view, which is under discussion here in reference to these two questions, presents itself as one that, once attained, can be integrated as a member of the truly living soul life.
2. There is no theoretical answer given that, once acquired, can be carried about as a conviction merely preserved in the memory.
3. This kind of answer would be only an illusory one for the type of thinking which is the foundation of this book.
4. Not such a finished, fixed answer is given, rather a definite region of soul-experience is referred to, in which one may, through the inner activity of the soul itself, answer the question livingly anew at any moment he requires.
5. The true view of this region will give the one who eventually finds the soul-sphere where these questions unfold that which he needs for these two riddles of life, so that he may, so empowered, enter further into the widths and depths of this enigmatic human life, into which need and destiny impel him to wander.

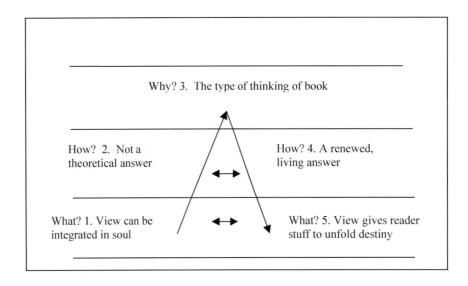

The 4-fold Organic Form: This 4-form is from paragraph 11/4 of the *Second Appendix*. The main topic in each of these sentences revolves around the value of knowledge/science. Each sentence answers the questions of the levels quite clearly.

11/4
1. All scientific endeavors would be only a satisfying of idle curiosity, if they did not strive toward uplifting the *existential worth of the human personality*.
2. The sciences attain their true value only by demonstrating the human significance of their results.
3. Not the refinement of any single capacity of soul can be the final goal of individuality, but rather the development of all the faculties slumbering within us.
4. Knowledge only has value when it contributes to the all sided unfolding of the *whole* human nature.

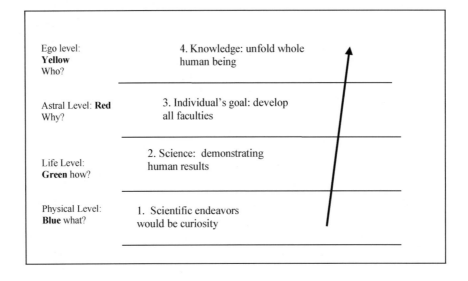

The 3-fold Organic Form: This paragraph is 1/3 of the *Second Appendix*. (The fourth, or ego level, is not represented directly by a sentence.) Each sentence clearly embodies the levels, particularly the astral or 3rd sentence, filled with feeling and conflict.

Grammatically, this paragraph has a classical organic pattern of passive verb (will be reproduced), active verb (placed), and model auxiliary (want). In this way Steiner expressed the static (what?), active (how?), and feeling (why?) levels through verb forms.

1/3

1. In what follows will be reproduced in all its essentials that which stood as a kind of "preface" in the first edition of this book.

2. I placed it here as an "appendix," since it reflects the type of thinking in which I wrote it twenty-five years ago, and not because it adds to the content of the book.

3. I did not want to leave it out completely for the simple reason, that time and again the opinion surfaces that I have something to suppress of my earlier writings because of my later spiritual writings.

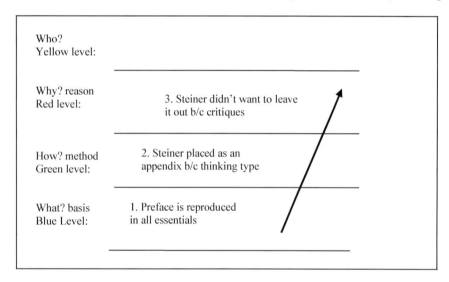

The 2- and 1-fold Organic Forms: There are only three examples of two- and one-fold paragraphs in the *Preface 1918* and the *Second Appendix*. From a certain point of view there is simply not much to consider. However, we can always consider what role such a short paragraph plays in an essay.

Usually a two-sentence paragraph has a movement from concrete to abstract, or some other duality – as opposed to building blocks which is the case with the 3- and 4-sentence paragraphs. In the next example we see the first sentence talks about the introductory paragraphs (unessential) in sentence one vs. the "remaining" paragraphs (essential) of sentence two!

From the footnote to the paragraph 2/4 of the *Second Appendix*:

1. Only the first introductory paragraphs have been completely omitted from this work, which today appear to me totally unessential.

2. What is said in the remaining paragraphs, however, seems to me necessary to say in the present because of and in spite of the natural scientific manner of thinking of our contemporaries.

A one-sentence paragraph, at least as Steiner uses them, seems to emphasize some important point. (Although the exact same thing can be said about a 30-sentence paragraph.) A one-sentence paragraph can be a very long thought with many clauses requiring deep contemplation, or a very profound kind of show-stopper utterance. In the *Preface 1918* and the *Second Appendix* there are two examples.

In paragraph 3/1 of the *Preface 1918*, we see a long sentence consisting of at least three clauses. Steiner was discussing how the questions, when answered in a living way, can become a type of knowledge with an inner life which provides the soul with a new grasp on truth. Its content is esoteric to say the least. One is forced to stop at this paragraph and considered carefully what is said.

1. – A kind of knowledge seems thereby to be pointed to which, through its own inner life and by the connectedness of this inner life to the whole life of the human soul, proves its correctness and usefulness.

The final sentence of the *Second Appendix,* paragraph 1/13 also has a kind of show-stopper quality. Steiner concludes this chapter by saying you can either be a master or slave to the idea. He doesn't leave room for interpretation.

13/1

1. One must experience and place oneself consciously above the Idea; *otherwise* one falls into its servitude.

*

A closer look at Steiner's structures: The new thinking has to do with qualitative differences. In order to bring about the inter-relationships and interval quality of enhancement and polarity. When Steiner created an enhancement in chapter titles, paragraphs, sentences, and even in clauses, he employed many stylistic devices.

We already mentioned some standard patterns for creating an enhancement on the sentence level by using a specific verb forms: passive (physical level), active (etheric), conditional (astral). Other methods for creating enhancement on the sentence level are: creating varying sentence rhythms; using unusual or strong words in each sentence; and observing the context i.e., what precedes and follows a given sentence.

The translator's dilemma consists in keeping the syntax close to Steiner's original structure without sacrificing readability in English. Let us look at a copy of the German original *Preface to the revised 1918 edition* of the <u>Philosophy of Freehood</u>. With this highlighted copy and translation with indented clauses, we can see how much attention Steiner gave to formation of the sentences and clauses. Opponents of George's organic-form research have kept their eyes closed to some of the most amazing achievements of Steiner's career. Below we have an analysis of the first paragraph of the *Preface 1918*.

Grammatical Structures in the Preface 1918 according to clauses: A note on my abbreviations. MC = Main Clause, DC = Dependent Clauses. MD1, MD2 and so on signify the depth of the dependency.

Why study Steiner's clauses? In sentence four we see three main clauses in the sentence about "freehood" but only one main clause in sentence two for the "view" question. Steiner used grammar to emphasize certain points.

In sentence nine we find the same emphasis when Steiner uses three DC's for the freehood question, but only two DC's for the view question!

Another nice example is sentence two. Each clause follows the organic form of the what? how? why? who? why? how? what? These organic-living structures are completely ignored, of course, in other translations. Maybe in the future we will have a text which purposively, and possibly in an awkward English, reproduces or transliterates these structures. Future researchers will could work out a complete study of Steiner's syntax.

First Sentence:
1. **MC**   **Zwei Wurzelfragen des menschlichen Seelenlebens sind es,**
2. DC1   nach denen hingeordnet ist alles,
3. DC2   was durch dieses Buch besprochen werden soll.

English translation: **There are two root-questions of the human soul-life**
                    toward which everything is directed
                    that will be discussed in this book.

Second Sentence:
1. **MC** **Die eine ist,**
2. DC1   ob es eine Möglichkeit gibt,
3. DC2   die menschliche Wesenheit so anzuschauen,
4. DC3   daß diese Anschauung sich als Stütze erweist für alles andere,
5. DC4   was durch Erleben oder Wissenschaft an den Menschen herankommt,
6. DC5   wovon er aber die Empfindung hat,
7. DC6   es könne sich nicht selber stützen.

          The first question is
           whether there is a possibility
             to view the human being in such a way
               that this view proves itself to be the support for everything else
                 which comes to meet the human being through experience or science and
                 which gives him the feeling
                   that it could not support itself.

Third Sentence:
1. **MC** **Es könne von Zweifel und kritischem Urteil in den Bereich des Ungewissen getrieben werden.**

Thereby one could easily be driven by doubt and critical judgment into the realm of uncertainty.

Fourth Sentence:
1. **MC** **Die andere Frage ist die:**
2. **MC** **Darf sich der Mensch als wollendes Wesen die Freiheit zuschreiben,**
3. **MC** **oder ist diese Freiheit eine bloße Illusion,**
4. DC1   die in ihm entsteht,
5. DC2   weil er die Fäden der Notwendigkeit nicht durchschaut,
6. DC3   an denen sein Wollen ebenso hängt wie ein Naturgeschehen?

      The other question is this:
      can the human being, as a creature of will, claim free will for himself,
      or is such freehood a mere illusion,
        which arises in him

because he is not aware of the workings of necessity
on which, as any other natural event, his will depends?

Fifth Sentence:
1. **MC   Nicht ein künstliches Gedankengespinst ruft diese Frage hervor.**

No artificial spinning of thoughts calls this question forth.

Sixth Sentence:
1. **MC   Sie tritt ganz naturgemäß in einer bestimmten Verfassung der Seele vor diese hin.**
It comes to the soul quite naturally in a particular state of the soul.

Seventh Sentence:
1. **MC   Und man kann fühlen,**
2. DC1   es ginge der Seele etwas ab von dem, ,
3. DC2   was sie sein soll
4. DC2   wenn sie nicht vor die zwei Möglichkeiten: Freiheit oder Notwendigkeit
des Wollens, einmal mit einem möglichst großen Frageernst sich gestellt sähe.

And one can feel
that something in the soul would decline,
from what it should be,
if it did not for once confront with the mightiest possible earnest questioning the two   possibilities: freehood or necessity of will.

Eighth Sentence:
1. **MC   In dieser Schrift soll gezeigt werden,**
2. DC1   daß die Seelenerlebnisse,
3. DC2   welche der Mensch durch die zweite Frage erfahren muß,
(DC1)   davon abhängen,
4. DC2   welchen Gesichtspunkt er gegenüber der ersten einzunehmen vermag.

In this book it will be shown
that the soul-experiences,
which the human being must discover through the second question,
depend upon
which point of view he is able to take toward the first.

Ninth Sentence:
1. **MC   Der Versuch wird gemacht, nachzuweisen,**
2. DC1   daß es eine Anschauung über die menschliche Wesenheit gibt,
3. DC2   welche die übrige Erkenntnis stützen kann;
4. **MC   und der weitere, darauf hinzudeuten,**
5. MC1   daß mit dieser Anschauung für die Idee der Freiheit des Willens eine volle
Berechtigung gewonnen wird,
6. MC 2   wenn nur erst das Seelengebiet gefunden ist,
7. MC3   auf dem das freie Wollen sich entfalten kann.

The attempt is made to prove
that there is a certain view of the human being
which can support his other knowledge;

and furthermore, to point out
> that with this view a justification is won for the idea of freehood of will,
>> if only that soul-region is first found
>>> in which free will can unfold itself.

*

A-Whole-to-the-Parts Approach to the Chapters: What is an effective way to approach the chapters when studying their form? From the whole to the parts. In a true organic structure, chapters and paragraphs will only make sense by comparing one to the other. The thought-movement, scanning the text back and forth and across, brings our thinking into a completely new comparative holistic consciousness.

Our first step is to make synopses of all the paragraphs in a chapter. Some paragraphs are larger than others and may require several sentences for a synopsis. However, the catchwords should stay short and concise, capturing the essence, not a recapitulation. From the catchwords and synopses, O'Neil saw that certain patterns would occur in clusters of paragraphs. These patterns are sometimes so obvious that one is astounded that it took so long for Steinerians to locate them; while others are so subtle that one almost has to have a personal epiphany into the possibility of such a pattern. Chapter One, *Conscious Human Action* is an example of a cut and dry form which follows the what? how? why? who? without stretching the imagination. Chapter Five is pretty challenging to the point where one wonders if there is such a thing as organic thinking at all – or maybe it is a skill best left for geniuses such as O'Neil and Steiner. The liberating aspect about true organic thinking and writing is: it is not supposed to bowl you over with an exaggerated aesthetic or formality of the levels.

Let us view chapter one from our organic perspectives. Below are my synopses of chapter one. (There is a numbered copy of Chapter I at the end of the book.) The catchwords are bold type and in the next section entered onto the diagram of the forms.

Chapter I, Conscious Human Action

1/14 What? **Freehood question?** Freedom question is posed and its supporters and detractors argue; modern day thinking (Strauss) rejects freedom as indifferent choice, however, Steiner makes clear there is a reason for choosing.

2/10 How? **Freedom-Opponents answer** Present day opponents (Herbert Spencer) attack freedom of choice, liberty to desire or not the origin of which is found in Spinoza's idea of a free necessity of nature (God) not free decision.

3/5 Why? **Spinoza's stone analogy** Spinoza writes all created things are like a rolling stone are determined to exist and act in a fixed manner by an external cause and non inner necessity.

4/6 Who? **Spinoza's freedom** Spinoza continues that the stone, like man, believes it is free because it is conscious of its striving and desire, but does not know the causes just as the child freely desires milk, the angry boy, the coward, and the drunk.

5/16 Inner Why? **Spinoza's error** It is easy to detect Spinoza's error (man overlooks that a cause drives him) because we can be conscious of the causes, are all human actions of the same kind (drunk v. statesman) this has caused endless confusion because the point is to whether a known motive has the same compulsion as an organic process.

6/6 Inner How? **Hartmann's unfree motives** Eduard Von Hartmann says human willing is determined from circumstances without and from within i.e. character determines a mental picture determines motive – Steiner says there is no differentiation between conscious and unconscious motive.

7/3 What? **Connecting Freehood question ?** We are at a standpoint and consider whether the question should be posed in a one sided way or should it be connected?

8/3 How? **Conscious motives then freehood?** The question of judging a conscious and unconscious motive of action will determine our position to the question of inner freedom.

9/3 Why? **Knowledge of reasons** The question of having knowledge of the reasons for action has been neglected because the knower and doer have not been synthesized i.e. the one who acts out of knowledge.

10/2 Who? **Freehood defined by Kant** Someone defined freedom as the control of reason, purpose, and deliberate decision- not animal passions.

11/3 Inner Why? **Compulsion of reason** The definition above does not differentiate between the compulsion of reason and the compulsion of passion for a rational decision has the same necessity as hunger and thereby my freedom is an illusion.

12/2 Inner How? **Motives determine will** Another expression runs to be free means to be able to do as you want not want as you want because Hamerling says your will is determined by motives.

13/6 What? **No freehood with such motives** Again (Hamerling) there is no difference between conscious and unconscious motives and freedom has no meaning if I must want something and the main question is whether a motive is forced on me with necessity (against my thinking reason).

14/1 How? **How of the decision** The question is how the decision comes about within me, not its execution.

15/13 Why? **Rational thinking, not analogies** The human beings rational thinking distinguishes him from other beings over against modern science which groups together the movement of a stone and the volition of a donkey and the human being (modern science, Paul Ree) who doesn't see the possibility of a conscious motive.

16/1 Who? **Steiner says stop** Enough examples of freedom opponents who don't know what freedom is.

17/6 Inner Why? **Knowing the reasons** Knowing a reason for an action poses question of the significance of thinking as Hegel says thinking gives human action its characteristic stamp.

18/20 Inner How? **Gemuet, thought, motives, love** highest human actions are always permeated by thought however love pity and patriotism are not from the cold intellect. The Gemuet does not create the motives but presupposes them. Love when it is beyond sexual instinct depends on mental pictures since thought is father of the feeling. Love blinds to failings, open the eyes to good qualities and mental pictures of good qualities allows love to awaken in the soul.

19/2 What? **Question of thinking** No matter the standpoint, the question of human action presupposes thinking origin, and to the next question.

When we put the catchwords into diagram form we get the following.

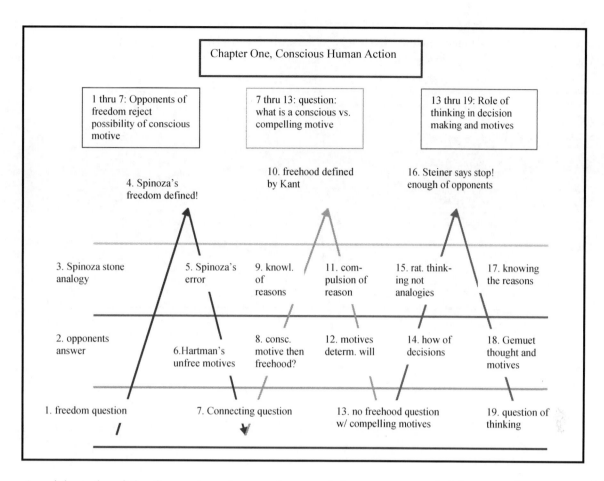

A quick study of the forms show how each curve (of seven paragraphs) has an enhancement of blue, green, and red highlighting the movement from concrete (blue curve) to dynamic (green curve) to abstract (red). When imitating such a form in your own writing you can borrow this straightforward climb. Notice how every seventh paragraph the topic "question" is addressed. Of course not all chapters lend themselves to such quick and easy analysis.

My synopses are slightly biased in favor of highlighting the four levels and their questions. O'Neil was expert at finding new appellations for the levels and I have experimented much with the names of the levels. I thought that questions (what?), motives (how?), analogy/knowledge (why?), and definitions (who?) work well. Therefore each paragraph could read something like this: what we do, how we do it, why we do it, what is the main idea.

In the next diagram is an example of how the forms would appear in the first curve (paragraphs 1-7) of the chapter one. We see the levels within the levels. It is difficult to fit in catchwords into every single sentence-form. The reader will have to get a large piece of paper and do this for himself. It is a wonderful experience to have mastered a chapter on this detailed level.

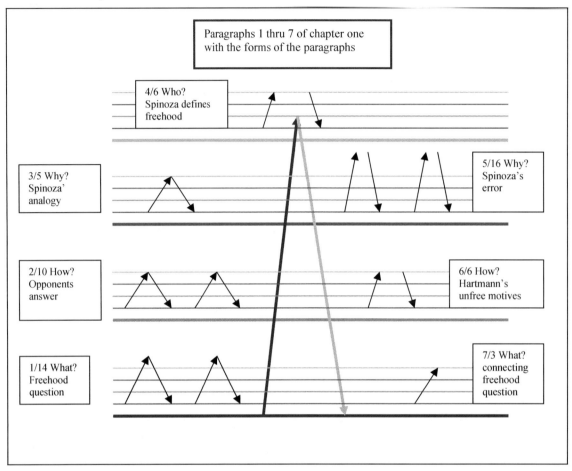

APPENDIX A
The Forms of the Philosophy of Freehood

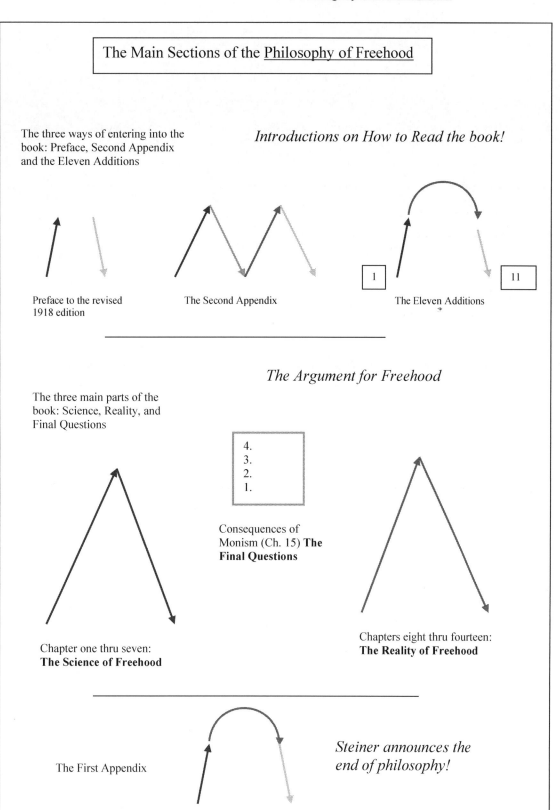

The Main Sections of the Philosophy of Freehood

The three ways of entering into the book: Preface, Second Appendix and the Eleven Additions

Introductions on How to Read the book!

Preface to the revised 1918 edition

The Second Appendix

1   11

The Eleven Additions

The Argument for Freehood

The three main parts of the book: Science, Reality, and Final Questions

4.
3.
2.
1.

Consequences of Monism (Ch. 15) **The Final Questions**

Chapter one thru seven: **The Science of Freehood**

Chapters eight thru fourteen: **The Reality of Freehood**

The First Appendix

Steiner announces the end of philosophy!

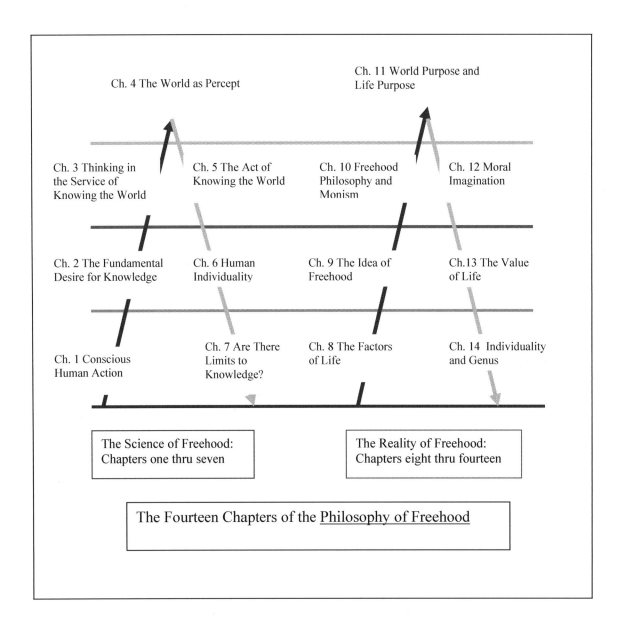

Ch. 4 The World as Percept

Ch. 11 World Purpose and
Life Purpose

Ch. 3 Thinking in
the Service of
Knowing the World

Ch. 5 The Act of
Knowing the World

Ch. 10 Freehood
Philosophy and
Monism

Ch. 12 Moral
Imagination

Ch. 2 The Fundamental
Desire for Knowledge

Ch. 6 Human
Individuality

Ch. 9 The Idea of
Freehood

Ch.13 The Value
of Life

Ch. 1 Conscious
Human Action

Ch. 7 Are There
Limits to
Knowledge?

Ch. 8 The Factors
of Life

Ch. 14 Individuality
and Genus

The Science of Freehood:
Chapters one thru seven

The Reality of Freehood:
Chapters eight thru fourteen

The Fourteen Chapters of the Philosophy of Freehood

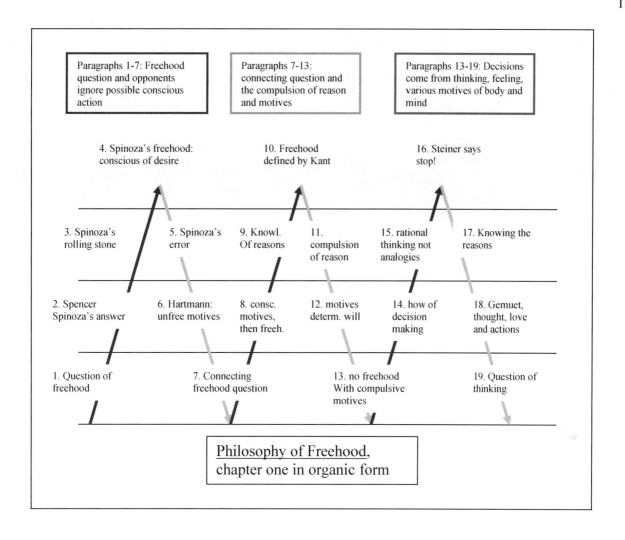

Philosophy of Freehood,
chapter one in organic form

170

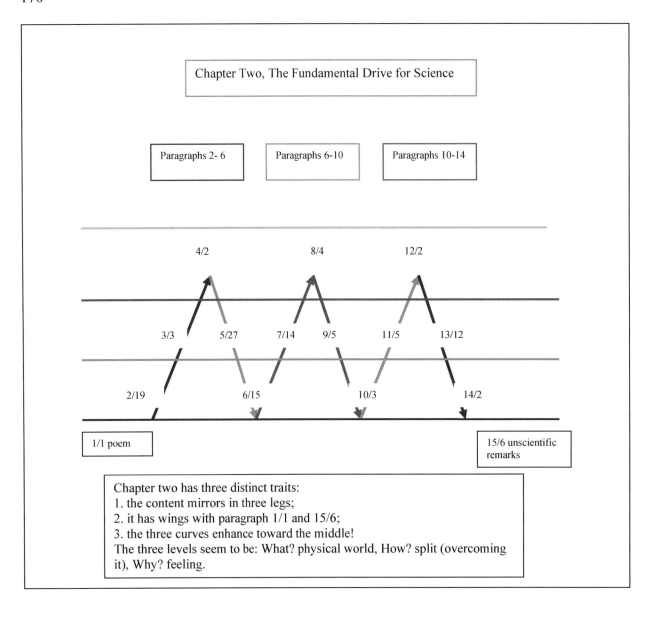

Chapter Two, The Fundamental Drive for Science

Paragraphs 2- 6   Paragraphs 6-10   Paragraphs 10-14

4/2   8/4   12/2

3/3   5/27   7/14   9/5   11/5   13/12

2/19   6/15   10/3   14/2

1/1 poem

15/6 unscientific remarks

Chapter two has three distinct traits:
1. the content mirrors in three legs;
2. it has wings with paragraph 1/1 and 15/6;
3. the three curves enhance toward the middle!
The three levels seem to be: What? physical world, How? split (overcoming it), Why? feeling.

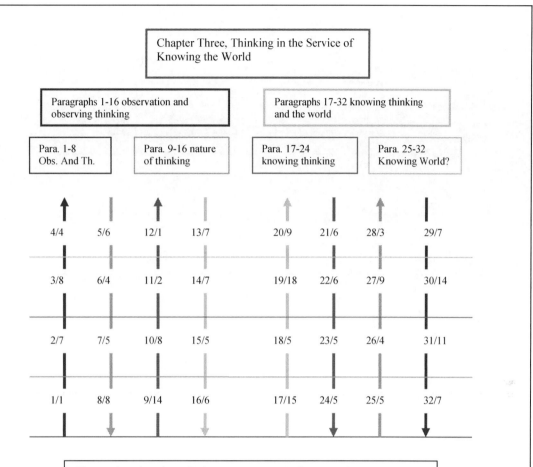

Chapter Three, Thinking in the Service of Knowing the World

Paragraphs 1-16 observation and observing thinking

Paragraphs 17-32 knowing thinking and the world

Para. 1-8 Obs. And Th.

Para. 9-16 nature of thinking

Para. 17-24 knowing thinking

Para. 25-32 Knowing World?

4/4	5/6	12/1	13/7	20/9	21/6	28/3	29/7
3/8	6/4	11/2	14/7	19/18	22/6	27/9	30/14
2/7	7/5	10/8	15/5	18/5	23/5	26/4	31/11
1/1	8/8	9/14	16/6	17/15	24/5	25/5	32/7

Chapter three has three distinct movements: 1) the two main parts observing thinking (1-16) vs. knowing thinking (17-32); 2) the general enhancement consisting the four groups of eight; 3) the eight parts which mirror each other qualitatively. The four levels can be loosely termed: what? objects (of study); how? activity; why? consciousness; who? new ideas.

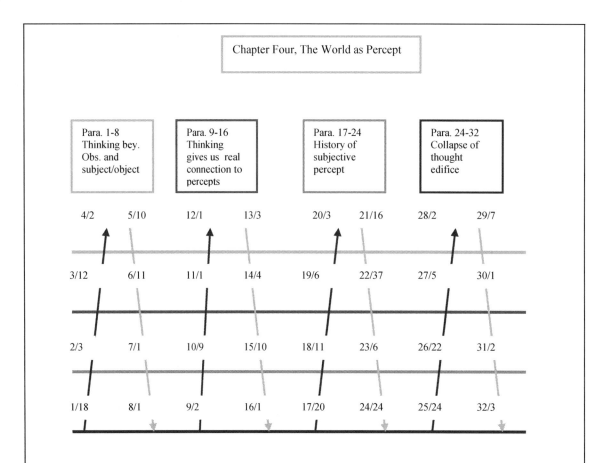

Chapter Four, The World as Percept

Para. 1-8
Thinking bey.
Obs. and
subject/object

Para. 9-16
Thinking
gives us real
connection to
percepts

Para. 17-24
History of
subjective
percept

Para. 24-32
Collapse of
thought
edifice

4/2	5/10	12/1	13/3	20/3	21/16	28/2	29/7
3/12	6/11	11/1	14/4	19/6	22/37	27/5	30/1
2/3	7/1	10/9	15/10	18/11	23/6	26/22	31/2
1/18	8/1	9/2	16/1	17/20	24/24	25/24	32/3

Chapter four has similar form to chapter three but with a different emphasis. Chapter four has a reverse form in that the general movement moves from the yellow (paragraphs 1-8) down to the blue (paragraphs 24-32). And unlike chapter three, chapter four has no mirroring. The four levels can be seen as: what? Consciousness, how? thinking, why? corrections, and who? essentials.

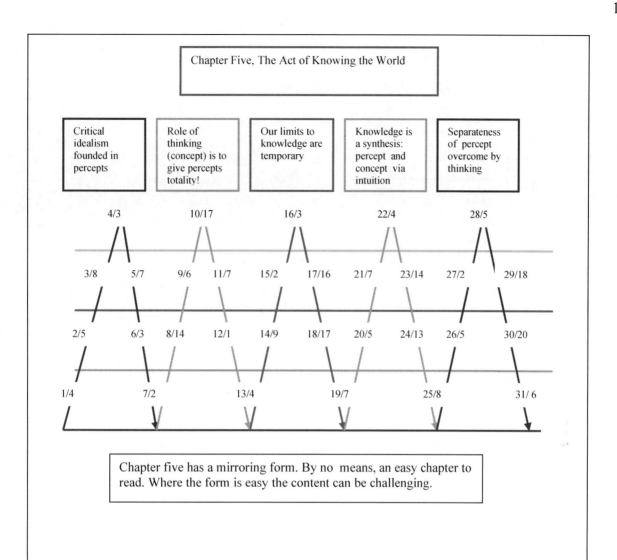

Chapter Five, The Act of Knowing the World

Critical idealism founded in percepts

Role of thinking (concept) is to give percepts totality!

Our limits to knowledge are temporary

Knowledge is a synthesis: percept and concept via intuition

Separateness of percept overcome by thinking

4/3   10/17   16/3   22/4   28/5

3/8   5/7   9/6   11/7   15/2   17/16   21/7   23/14   27/2   29/18

2/5   6/3   8/14   12/1   14/9   18/17   20/5   24/13   26/5   30/20

1/4   7/2   13/4   19/7   25/8   31/6

Chapter five has a mirroring form. By no means, an easy chapter to read. Where the form is easy the content can be challenging.

174

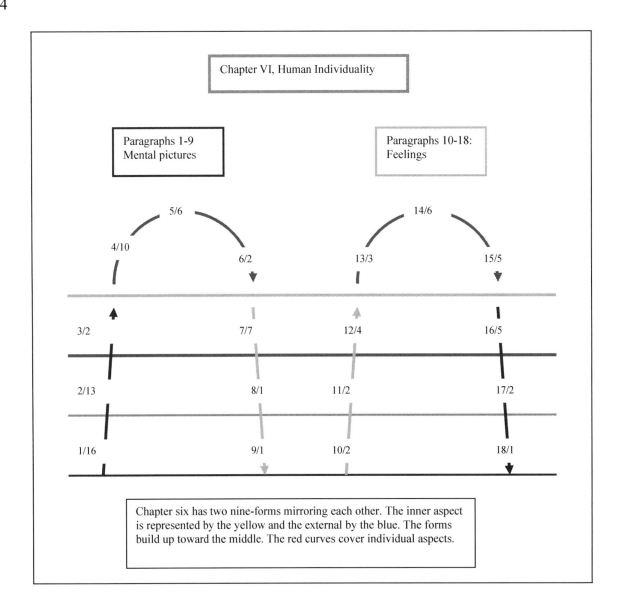

Chapter VI, Human Individuality

Paragraphs 1-9
Mental pictures

Paragraphs 10-18:
Feelings

5/6

14/6

4/10

6/2

13/3

15/5

3/2

7/7

12/4

16/5

2/13

8/1

11/2

17/2

1/16

9/1

10/2

18/1

Chapter six has two nine-forms mirroring each other. The inner aspect
is represented by the yellow and the external by the blue. The forms
build up toward the middle. The red curves cover individual aspects.

Chapter VII, Are There Limits To Knowledge?

Monism/ dualism and their main ideas

From NR to MR: world view described

From MR to Monism:

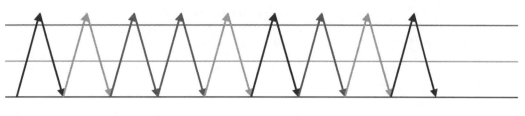

1   13   25   37

Chapter six and seven have variations on nine forms. Chapter seven has a very detailed nine-form in which each aspects has a distinct color. The center piece goes red, green, blue losing thereby its symmetry but illustrating the three aspects of sentient, intellectual, and consciousness soul.

176

Chapters Eight through Fourteen in the
Philosophy of Freehood in Organic form

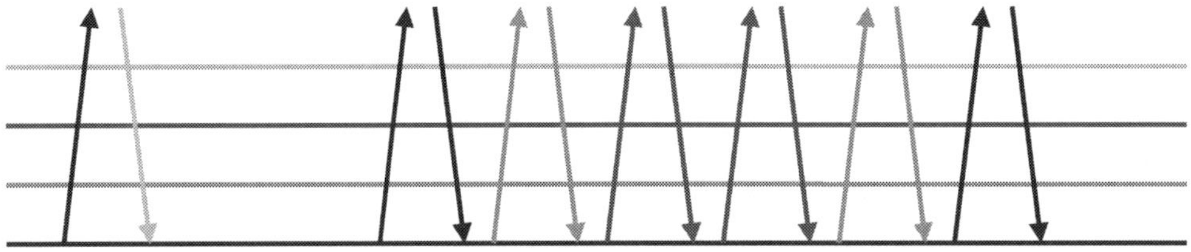

**Chapter VIII, The
Factors of Life**
consisting of an 8-form

Chapter IX, The Idea of Freehood
consisting of 6 x 8-forms mirroring

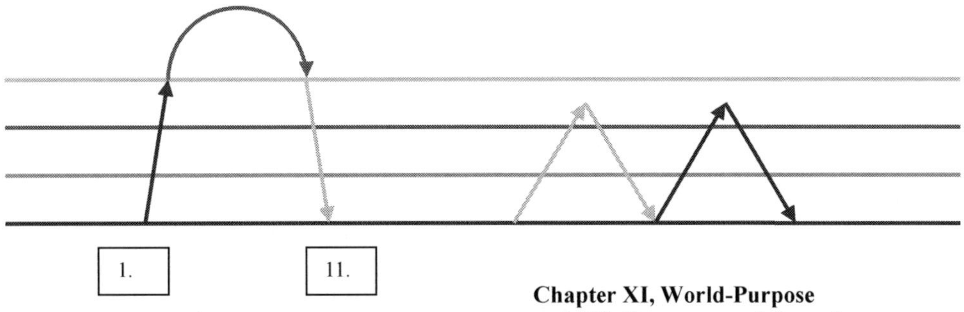

1.   11.

**Chapter X, Freehood Philosophy
and Monism** consisting of a 9-form
with two wings making an 11-form

**Chapter XI, World-Purpose
and Life-Purpose** consisting of
two connecting 5-forms, a very
unusual 9-form!

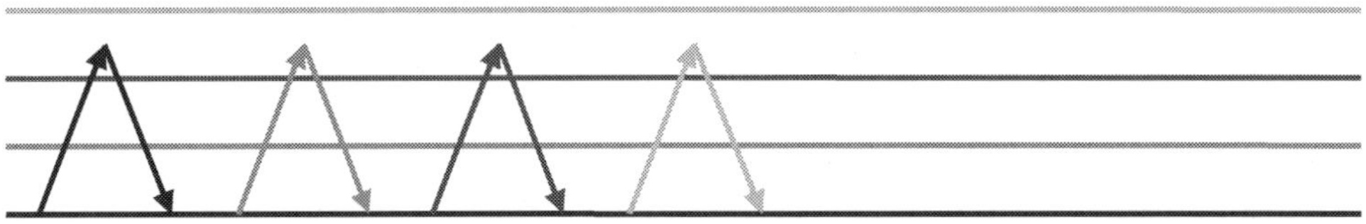

Chapter XII Moral Imagination consisting
of twenty paragraphs of four 5-forms.

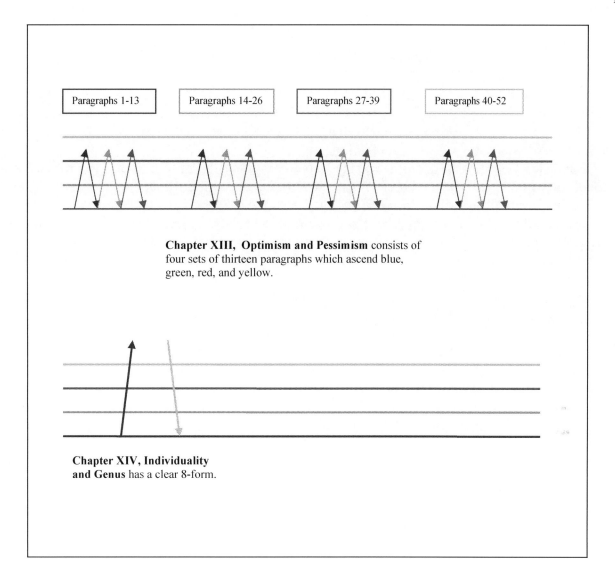

Paragraphs 1-13   Paragraphs 14-26   Paragraphs 27-39   Paragraphs 40-52

Chapter XIII, Optimism and Pessimism consists of
four sets of thirteen paragraphs which ascend blue,
green, red, and yellow.

**Chapter XIV, Individuality
and Genus** has a clear 8-form.

Appendix B
Out of the Work of George O'Neil

This Appendix B gives samples of George's work out of his original manuscript. This is not his only manuscript as he worked out the form and content of many of Steiner's books and lectures. He was famous for lecturing on the form of the Gettysburg Address. Our website has several of his old handouts which he gave his students (www.organicthinking.org).

I included George's work (some scanned, some rewritten) because he has given us such a nice precedent for working with Steiner's new logic. He conceptualized the whole book as a seed, listed the fourteen chapters and their themes in form, and presented the *Preface 1918* and the 11 *Addenda* as key texts. Compared to other interpreters of Steiner's work, George's style has a free and masterful quality, his writing is entertaining without losing its seriousness. I recommend reviewing George's work after you have done some on your own first. The genius of his condensements can be underappreciated if you have not, at least, made your own first.

George and Gisela O'Neil died in 1988 leaving their work in Florin Lowndes' hands. Florin diligently published George's The Human Life in English and German and in 1990's published The Enlivening of the Chakra of the Heart and Das Erwecken des Herzdenkens. Florin has quite a few of O'Neil's gems such as his journals, details about how to meditate in the new thinking way, and countless other documents still unavailable to the public. Although organized Anthroposophy is sure to decline within the next decade, I believe George's work will live on in spite of the obstacles (obstacles such as a general disinterest in the new thinking by Steiner's followers, and the hoarding of his research findings by George's former students). Even if the 'esoteric' O'Neil is not public, at least the exoteric Steiner will soon be.

I know there will be readers who will want to research more of Steiner's work especially his other books. Thus it is essential to review all of O'Neil's research in order to work out an effective approach for this universal method of thinking. In this way, George's name will be given the honor and due diligence it deserves.

From George O'Neil's Notes on The Philosophy of Freehood:

"Once asked, for which of his books he would be remembered as writer, Rudolf Steiner answered: for my Philosophy of Freehood.

It was with this book that he laid the foundations for his later works, and it was to this book he again and again referred, up to the very last in his Autobiography and the Letters to Members, as the one bearing the essence of the task to which he had devoted his life.

And this task, by and large as we it now, was the formulation in terms appropriate for the consciousness of man today and for times to come, of the means by which men can once more place themselves in waking relationship to the creative world of the spirit. The world in which all things have their origin, from which human beings come and to which they return.

The foundations for such a path of knowledge had to be laid in the sphere of cognition. In the sphere where old forces of instinctive thinking were dying out, involving themselves in contradiction and despair, and in which new forces of life, new powers of living cognition had to be engendered for the future development of mankind. The language of this sphere is philosophy.

But let it not be thought that this book was to be a new philosophy. The age of intellectual world conceptions was over. Hegel had come and gone. The mystics of idea-perception belonged to history and their greatness is not to be undervalued. But their appropriateness is no longer of these times. What this <u>Philosophy of Freehood</u> purported to be was the expression of the struggle of the individual modern soul in conquest of spiritual reality and the discovery of the reality of his own being.

Rudolf Steiner, while writing it, was not concerned with philosophy as such, nor with teaching in philosophic terms, but with working out for himself the means of expression which, in its very thought-formation could bring about the transformation of those forces which had been brought to the highest possible peak in pure scientific thinking and now could become the spring board for a final leap into new realms. The pure thinking of science (rightly understood) is the sole avenue leading to the spirituality of the future.

*

Of recent time, thought has been given to the source of great creative impulses, to the appearance of decisive trends in history. Where do Ideas come from? What of the creative process whereby new insights are born? Intuition, Inspiration are acknowledged facts. Scientific Imagination is highly rewarded. But the burning question is never answered: how can it be taught? How can it be brought into the service of man? What in essence is this purely human way of thinking?

To the answer of these questions this book was dedicated, and as the only answer to them, has still, 70 years later, yet to find recognition.

*

This book is an instrument, written in such a way that the reader who devotes himself to it with the necessary intensity can, by means of the manner in which the thoughts have been composed, awaken in himself the capacity for intuition.

Knowledge is acquired when thoughts are introduced once into the soul with sufficient force and conviction. When these thoughts were repeatedly brought into consciousness into an organic way, so that one grows out of the other, building up in the process a totality, then forces of the soul-life which otherwise are scattered in daily life, are concentrated, united and focused. What had been an aptitude for unfolding thoughts in a coherent way, now gradually becomes a power of inner perceiving, an inner vision for broad trains of thought. There is born the intuitive power of grasping at one glance what logically can be worked out in time but with painstaking effort and continually fraught with possibility of error. Thinking becomes a seeing, a seeing that at the same time is thinking.

*

The goal of our study of this book is acquisition of a thinking to which no man today is born, and no schooling so far prepares him. It is new to the degree that it is as yet unrecognized not alone outside, but also often within the very circles established for the cultivation of Anthroposophy. This cannot be stressed sufficiently.

Compared with the current abstract thinking, the new thinking is one that takes on the quality of picturing, where thoughts stand side by side rather than follow each other in logical sequence. Anschauendes Denken it is called, and this 'seeing power' once it reaches maturity, is experienced as the living within the stream of flowing thought-life. It has freed itself from the mirroring physiological basis of the brain and has taken on life. The new thinking is living thinking.

To achieve this living in thought as distinct form building in logical thought units, and letting the personal feeling determine the pattern of words, we first must become master in highest degree of content, utterly eliminating the arbitrariness of personal preference and emphasis. Says Goethe: to have the whole thing in your heart, you must have conned its every part. To which Rudolf Steiner has added: first read for substance, then read again for form.

In contemplating the totality of a living thought-organism, correspondences and symmetries. Previously unseen, begin to emerge, each illuminating the other. Meanings come forth, never before expected, revealing interdependence and mutual support. The whole is experienced as a web of interrelationships. An Idea is experienced as a weaving interplay of single thoughts, each reflecting the whole as experienceable from its single aspect."

I. CONSCIOUS HUMAN ACTION (DAS BEWUSSTE MENSCHLICHE HANDELN)

A. No Freedom - Unconscious Motivation
B. Freedom through Reason - Do Motives Compell?
C. Freedom Not Understood - The Leading Role of Thinking.

GESTALT: 19 P. - 3 linked 7's - Rising Intensity.
QUALITY: A struggle with the hidden, or occult, by the unssing.

If one has kept up with recent literature, one knows how diversely
the Freedom-Idea is interpreted today. Attention should be given to
the chapter's threefold title itself, in order to limit the scope.
Which aspects are stressed, which excluded?

As he proceeds, the reader will encounter famous names. These also
represent viewpoints extant today. They should be listed and their
viewpoints compared with one another. There is significance in the
order in which they appear. Note that Hegel stands outside the
other seven.

Pictorially expressed, this is the tale of the seven blind men who
came to see the elephant. The elephant is no easy beast to interpret
if you can't see. Neither is man's relation to his spirit being.

If the world's notable philosophic figures have misconstrued the
inner creative process by which man can consciously give themselves
their motives, - if something which seems obvious must suffer
distortion for intellectual reasons, can we not expect that we too,
as individuals, have hazy notions of this thing called FREEDOM?

The English language is in this case no help: liberty, independence,
free-choice, free-speech, free-thought, and freedom of this or that;
the word Free-dom itself, Free-domain, is an old landholders' term,
and like all the above, a purely political notion, expressing
human rights bestowed by law.

"FREIHEIT", (literally Free-hood) implies a state or spiritual
condition of the individual. Its non-existence in English was the
reason why Rudolf Steiner adviced the translators that his book
in English be entitled: THE PHILOSOPHY OF SPIRITUAL ACTIVITY.
Someday, we may have the courage to coin the word 'Free-hood'.
Until then, whenever we read or hear the word 'Freedom' in connection with this text, the echo from within must be SPIRITUAL
ACTIVITY.

After the reader has carefully analysed these seven typical views
of 'what freedom is not', and has fully grasped the irrelevance
of any connection between 'freedom' and the unconscious or animal
nature of man, and has seen that 'free-choice' is a verbal shell,
he is faced with finding the real meaning of 'consciousness'. It
may be of help here, to remind ourselves of its derivation:
con-scious = with-science, or knowing activity. We may imagine
we know what it means to be conscious, but when pinned down, can
I be humanly conscious without thinking ? Aware, certainly, in
an animal way, but not humanly conscious, until I think about
what I perceive.

To round out a good discussion of the chapter, a students' group
should go to town on P 18. Is love possible without thinking? -
That should end the meeting on a warm note.

Chapter I - 19ᵃ - Conscious Human Action □

{A} No Freedom - {B} Freedom through Reason - {C} Freedom Not Understood -
Unconscious Motivation — Do Motives Compel? — The Leading Role of Thinking

The question: is man free? polar views

{1} Strauss: an illusion

main attacks:
freedom of choice
{2} Spencer: free desire
{3} Spinoza: free necessity

1

2

3 — Spinoza: Stone analogy. Outer cause

4 — Spinoza: child, angry boy, coward, drunk. (consc. of desires, ignorant of cause)

5 — error: man can be conscious of causes. lack of distinction

6 — {4} Hartmann: outer & inner causes: motive & character. No distinction consc./unconsc.

7 — question onesided? Other question?

8 — difference conscious motive - unconsc. urge

9 — knowledge of reasons? Separation of acting & knowing man

10 — {5} sayings (Kant?) man free, if ruled by reasons, purposes & decisions

11 — do reasons, purposes & decisions compel?

12 — 'To do what we will': {6} Hammering: the strongest motive wins

13 — no distinction consc./unconsc. — Are there only compelling motives?

14 — {7} Thee - ass invisible causes — importance: how decision rises in man

15 — man/animal difference through thinking

16 — Many fight against freedom - don't know what it is

17 — consc. action: origin & meaning of thinking. {8} Hegel: thinking turns (soul) to spirit

18 — motives are permeated by thought. From head to heart (love)

19 — question is presupposed: origin of thinking

183

The "Philosophy of Spiritual Activity"
    an Organic Structure

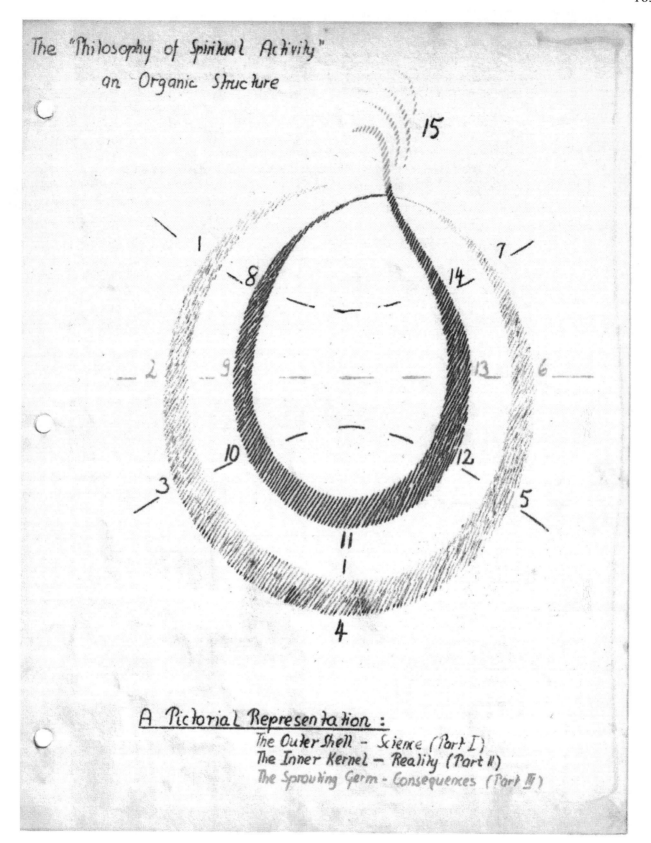

A Pictorial Representation :
        The Outer Shell – Science (Part I)
        The Inner Kernel – Reality (Part II)
        The Sprouting Germ – Consequences (Part III)

184

Part I: The Science of Spiritual Activity (Freedom)

IV The World as Percept
A Thinking transcends object & subject
B Relation of percept to conscious subject
C Derived viewpoints – resulting from correction – the "thought-edifice"
D Collapse of modern thought-edifice

III Thinking in Service of World Comprehension △
A Nature of observed TH:
  a Points of departure (TH & Obs)
  b Obs. of TH – the exceptional st.
  c Reasons why TH is not obs.
B Value of observed TH:
  c¹ Firm point – importance of obs. TH
  b¹ Creating the obj. of obs.
  a² TH = the 'fulcrum' for grasp of world

II The Basic Striving for Knowledge ~
A The Split
B Unsuccessful Efforts
C The Way out

I Conscious Human Action ▭
A No freedom – unconscious motivation
B Freedom through reason – do motives compel?
C Freedom not understood – the leading role of thinking

V The Act of Knowing the World △
A Representation World of Crit./Idealist
B Neglect of thinking – no totality
C Cognition & human organization
B¹ Percept + Concept a totality through TH
A¹ Percept as separation, TH = the link

VI The Human Individuality ro

I Representation
A External views P&R
B Concept of R
C Significance of R. experience & reality (Life as universal being

II Feeling
A¹ Role of feeling for practical life
B¹ Concept of indiv. life
C¹ Signif. of feeling Life as indiv. being

VII Are There limits to Knowledge? ▭
A Our dualistic inheritance: limits of knowledge & metaphysics
  1 The 'concept' game.
  2 Barriers overcome (M: no fixed limits)
  3 D accounted for: a 'meta-real' assumed
B Realism in three steps: Naive/NR/MR
  4 Naive man's view
  5 Assumption of naive realism
  6 From NR to MR
C Steiner's Monism & Hartman's Inductive Inference
  7 Why MR can merge into Monism
  8 Monism: a human way of cognition
  9 Hartman's 'percept game': ind./inference

Part II: The Reality of Spiritual Activity (Freedom)

XI World-Purpose and Life-Purpose (Destination of Man) ⊙
A Monism: Purpose only in human action. Not in: Nature, man's destiny, history, world-order.
B Dualism: Laws of nature are purpose of God. Hammerling: Instincts, form of organism, wonders of creation.

X Freedom-Philosophy and Monism △
A Moral Norms of HR - The Unfree
B The unfree & the free- determined by P or Int./I
C Philosophy of freedom. The free spirit.

IX The Idea of Freedom ~
I How will arises in man (science of freedom)
A Thinking & Human Organization
Experienced Thinking - Ego & Will
B The Springs of action (character)
(Individual Life)
Conditionings - Thinking Aptitude
C The Motives (Thoughts)
The Ladder - The Highest Levels
II Conditions for free moral action
(reality of freedom)
C True Individualism (prerequisites)
Capacity for Intuition - Love of the deed.
B Free Action (Presuppositions)
Realizing the freedom Idea - finding one's own concept
A The free spirit & society
From man to free spirit - work ahead!

VIII The Factors of Life □
Thinking, Feeling, Will - How they are related to man and world.
The two aberrations:
A Mysticism B Voluntarism

XII The Moral Imagination △
(Darwinism & Morality)
A Elements of free action.
B Results of free action become objects of Knowledge. Evolution in Nat. & Ethics
C Ethical Individualism as spiritualized evolution
D Freedom as perfect form of human action.

XIII The Value of Life (Optimism & Pess.) ~
A The Elements:
a Two views: Optimism
b Pessimism
c Experience: Pleasure/Pain
B Striking the Balance:
a Hartman's balance through reason
b Life's balance: quantity counts
c Experience: facts must be checked.
C Evaluation: a Pessimism as source of selfless conduct - not selfless
b Values measured
c Desire (not Pain) as measure of joy
D Mature Human Striving:
a Balance-No influence on human will.
b Spiritual desires & high ideals
c The mature man - his own master. Freedom.

XIV Individuality and Genus □
A Generic traits and the emancipating individual
B The individual within the community.

THE PREFACE 1918

Prefaces are usually skipped over quickly. Similarly with this one. But it is the rule with Steiner books, that Forewords and Prefaces are often the meatiest reading. So it will be found here, if not on the first study, then on the second or third time around.

Consider these two questions: CAN I BE CERTAIN OF ANYTHING or is all my knowledge subject to doubt? And the next: AM I A FREE AGENT or does some unknowable force pull my life strings?

Most of us have never even stopped and really faced these sphinx like riddles. They have a fearful quality, and if unprepared, they fix us sometimes. They can paralyse. This can happen, once an individual becomes inwardly productive. And the signs of such paralysis can be seen in some of these strange symptoms which take place in the souls of modern writers and artists.

The two modern forms of the Sphinx-riddle, WHAT IS MAN, occur in the very first paragraph of the Preface. And we discover that they are to become the themes of the two halves of the book itself.

When in ancient mystery tales, the crossing of the threshold was portrayed, there were always two such sphinxes to be placated. Or sometimes lions with or without wings. Architecturally: entrance lions are typical too, symbolically. Those guarding the New York Public Library, for instance, must seldom be fed by the learned entering there, judging by how little of living value emerges. So too, it is with the thought-edifice of this book - in itself a mystery structure in a way. Unless these two sphinx-like guardian questions are recognized and given their due, we can be sure the life of the book will escape us, and we will find nothing but difficult words and dry, abstract thoughts.

If the student wants to impress this Preface upon his memory, he may observe its polarity: three paragraphs on THEN - 1894 and three on NOW - 1918. In the first, the meaning of the two questions: a living knowledge of Man; in the second half, the value of the book as a foundation for the understanding of the later writings - Anthroposophy, the Spiritual Knowledge of Man. What could be more beautiful, and more memorable!

Many, of course, find the 'Philosophy' too difficult, or imagine they are philosophically inept, or find other reasons for avoiding it. They feel it unnecessary to come to grips with the nature of creative thinking or to know how the spirit permeates the human will today and yet leaves man free. Yet, these very people, though they may strive to become creatively productive within the movement, find their paths beset with obstacles. They lack the firm foundation on which to build and serve. Also, without this knowledge of Self as a thinking spiritual being, all perceptual forms of spiritual experience (clairvoyance) become of dubious value if not outright dangerous to health. KNOWLEDGE BEFORE EXPERIENCE is to be carved on every serious student's door. And that carving is done with the strength gained through this book. Or so these prefaced thoughts, it seems, can be interpreted.

A SKETCH OF THE THOUGHT WEB   THE ADDITIONS 1918

FRAMING THE MISINTERPRETATIONS   LAYOUT AND FORM
IN A NON-PROFESSIONAL VEIN

6. No good intellectual today can
admit his materialism. But without
spirit-science concepts he must
disguise his real nature.

5. A Sentient Soul problem: 7. A Soul conscious of Spirit
To confront the old Spirit   may inquire about: Higher pur-
of Contradiction. 'Der Doctor   poses such as Mission of Man-
hat gesagt' one thing and now   kind, of World Evolution, or
he says the very opposite!   Task of the Zeitgeist.

                    EGO ORGANIZATION
              Thinking things through to the End.

4. No warm True-Love   8. The Moral Astringency
without Intuitive-Thinking!   of Spiritual-Activity!
Arty-feelers & Good-deeders   Astral bodies purified,
take heed.   Doublegangers subdued by
                                     the Intuitive Mood.

3. On the Way to Reality: 9. For Modern Buddhists who
Widen your Idea of Perception   would be free-from Nature-will
But dont be fooled. Deepen   rather than permeate it with
your Intuition as well.   Intuitive Ideas.

2. Habit-Thinking: 10. This Book is a living
The Representation Mouse-trap.   organism and must like Man
Get yourself loose!   have a double-nature:
                                     Head and Heart.

      THREE BODILY-ASPECTS   THREE SPIRIT-ASPECTS
Intuitive-Thinking can reach   A Moral & Free Will is demonstrated
Reality if certain hindrances   possible for those who grasp
     are overcome.   Wesenhaft-Thinking.

1. THE READER'S PREREQUISITE: 11. THE AUTHOR'S INTENTION:

Before you begin, Brother,   To lay the Foundation for the
Get straight on Thinking!   Proper study of Anthroposophy.

        (Foreword)   (Afterword)

Appendix C
Meditation and the Value of Group Work

The Meditation
1. Perceive words and associated thoughts then forget
2. concentrate on thought pictures arising
3. see through pictures and meditate on beings

Imagination: seeing
Inspiration: hearing
Intuition: physical culmination
From a George O'Neil handout

First Meditation: The first meditation is the rhythmic reading of the text. As you read put a dot on the left side of the paragraph *where each sentence begins*. Breathe in before reading the next sentence. Thus put a dot with a lead pencil on left margin, breathe in, and then read sentence aloud:

> • Is the human being in his thought and action a spiritually *free* being, or is he compelled by the
> •iron necessity of purely natural law? Upon few questions has so much acute thought been
> •brought to bear as upon this one. The idea of the freehood of the human will has found warm
> •supporters and stubborn opponents in large numbers. There are people who, in their moral   fervor, label anyone a man of limited intelligence who dares deny so obvious a *fact* as freehood.

This three-fold rhythm creates a whole new way of reading and is particularly powerful when a group reads the text in this way. It has some resemblance to rowing. After you finishing reading the sentences, then count the dots and sentences to make sure you got it right.

Second Meditation: Make your synopsis and catch-words or -phrases. Look at the synopses as a whole.

Once you are finished condensing, say with chapter one, *Conscious Human Action*, you can start to 'member' or divide the text into parts. Find the middle paragraph and see how the two halves relate: paragraph 1-9 and 10 and 11-19. Paragraph 10 is the mid-point and defines freehood as following reason and decisions, the first affirmative answer to the freehood question in the chapter! The central paragraph(s) always play some important role in the content and mood of the thought-form.

Next sub-divide the 19 paragraphs to see where a theme begins/ends. One notices there is always nearly always a freehood question every seventh paragraph. There are three groups of seven paragraphs, each with a distinctive theme. Going from the whole to the parts you want to start subdividing the chapter from the title, to the two main parts, to three main parts, to six main parts finding catchword for each of the lager subdivisions.

The diagram below gives the first form of the contemplative meditation. See how the title (Conscious Human Action) points to the two halves and mid-point (question of knowing causes and what it mean to know the causes). Proceed to break it down further into the next mathematical/organic set of three curves. The three curves can be further subdivided into halves for a total of six parts, each consisting of four paragraphs. In this way you can quickly grasp how the form and content relate proportionately. By inter-relating these subdivisions at all levels (even into the individual paragraphs) you are entering into a seeing-thinking of meditation. You will create your own individual or group headings, subheading, and so on and the book will speak to you in a unique way. Follow this method with every chapter and you will learn a new capacity of thinking in wholes and parts. No text will ever make the same impression on you again when you grasp it in this way.

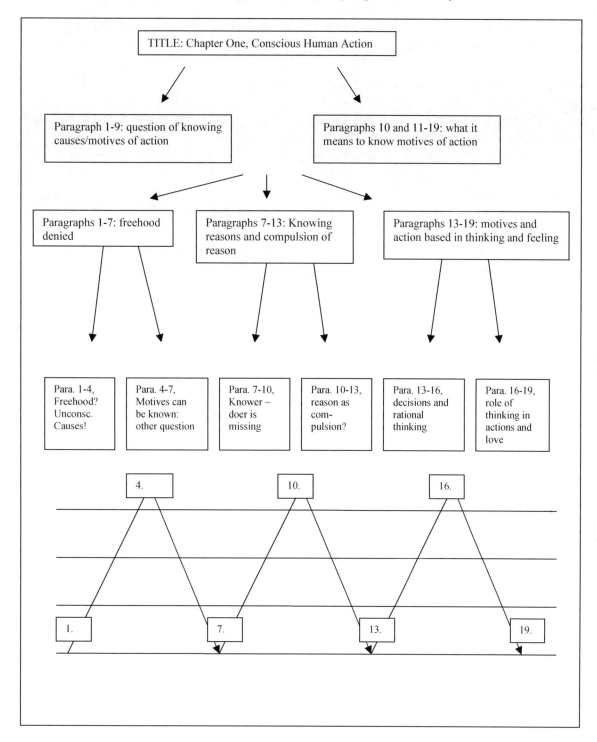

Third Meditation: A feel for the idea-content and gestalt is a solid beginning for organic-living meditation. So far we have our synopses and catchwords which we can enter into the wave forms. The next step is to practice the organic movements.

The four questions, what? how? why? and who?, represent the movement of enhancement (climb and swoop). One can repeat these questions aloud:

190

"What? Paragraph 1/14, the freehood question: there are opponents and supporters however, most attack free choice as an empty phantom although we know there is always a reason for choosing an action."

"How? Paragraph 2/10 the attacks against freehood: Spencer calls freehood the dogma of the liberty to choose, while Spinoza states that freehood only belongs to the nature of God not to his creations."

One would read each of the 19 paragraphs and their synopses in this way in order to get a feel for the levels and enhancements in the texts.

For the polarities you simply compare paragraphs 1/14 and 7/3, 2/10 and 6/6, 3/5 and 5/16. Read the results of your findings aloud:

"Paragraph 1 and 7 are polar in content. In paragraph 1 the topic is the freehood question and its supporters and opponents, while paragraph 7 deals not with the people, but only with the question of freehood and connected questions, and not with answers. Thus the polarity is contained in the fact that both discuss the freehood question: paragraph 1 with a broad focus, and 7 with a focus on reworking the question."

"The polarity between paragraph 2 and 6 consists of both having philosophers who are against freehood: paragraph 2 from a more external point of view (Spinoza) and paragraph 6 from a more internal point of view (Hartmann's characterlogical disposition). Steiner also captures the essence of the problem in 2 and corrects the problem in 6 by stating we can have knowledge of causes."

"Paragraph 3 and 5 are polar in that 3 presents Spinoza's rolling stone analogy against freehood and Steiner admonishes Spinoza's analogy in 5. Both paragraphs deal with Spinoza's analogy."

The polarities could look like this:

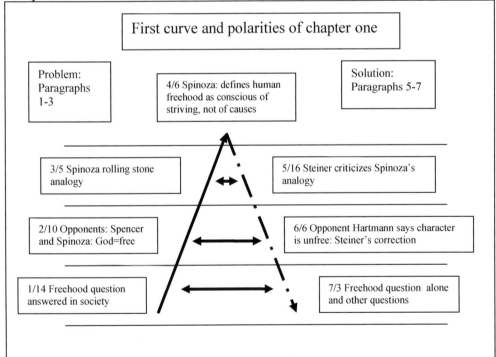

We begin to get a feel for the polarities in the text. We move back and forth finding similarities and differences training ourselves to think in a new way. Our mind raps itself around the rise and fall and polarities of the wave.

We can add to the enhancement and polarity the notion of inversion (turning-inside-out). Inversion can be seen as a logic extension of polarity but the emphasis is on how the thought-form transforms in the middle of the thought-structure. In the example above from the first curve in chapter one Spinoza says in paragraph 4/6: humans are conscious of their striving but not of the causes and believe themselves nevertheless to be free. The thought-form inverts because Spinoza looks inward and talks about self-consciousness and the rest of the paragraphs follow suit in that they discuss conscious motives. Inversion and polarity are intimately related, and it is hard to practice one without therewith practicing the other.

Fourth Meditation: At this point the content of the chapter should be familiar. You can now move freely through the form and content of the chapter when scanning it. Try to see the chapter without notes and see if you can locate the content of the paragraphs by their position and color! Paragraph 1, which is blue, discusses the freehood question; paragraph 2 is green and answers with the freehood question with a "no." Go through all 19 paragraphs *backwards and forwards* without looking at your notes. Of course in the beginning you will need them to refer to, but eventually you won't and you will "see" the whole chapter in your mind's eye as a living-painting-form.

You can experiment with your breathing by inhaling before entering into a new paragraph. In this way you give the chapter and its paragraphs a nice rhythm in which your whole being participates.

O'Neil suggests that at some point you can see through the text content, colors, and forms, and perceive the thought-beings behind each chapter. Alas, his notes have not been made available by his student Florin Lowndes who has kept his work a guarded secret. I am sure others will come along who will explore the new thinking meditations in new ways with new results and complete this unfinished work.

At this point it is safe to say that the higher type of meditation of the Philosophy of Freehood, that is, the type of meditation which is not yet understood, should wait until a person is very healthy in their soul life and can be told by the spiritual world how the higher meditation should be conducted for each individual. In part, George's work was eclipsed not because it was incorrect but because it is too early for people to practice safely. Thus the totality of his work must remain hidden to be rediscovered by each individual for himself.

The Joy of Text

Précis: Group study of Rudolf Steiner's work has declined worldwide. This section presents this author's personal experience with study groups and methods of reading Steiner texts, in particular the *Preface to the 1918 Revised Edition* of the Philosophy of Spiritual Activity. By changing the focus from 'what' Steiner said to 'how' he said it, seems to intensify and enliven the participants and give hope to a renewal of study.

Is there only one way to read a Steiner text? No, of course not. But are some ways more productive, more enhancing, and more fun? I think so. I enjoyed nearly all of the anthroposophical study groups I attended starting in 1991. Each one served its purpose in my search for the essential in Steiner's work.

The first group I attended was in Freiburg, Germany, with a Christian Community priest. It was uncomplicated: we chose a few bible chapters and discussed them in an open and friendly atmosphere.

My second group study experience was at the branch in New York City, and lasted for a whole year. We read the basic books (Knowledge of Higher Worlds, Theosophy, Building Stones etc.) in a circle of ten people and each week one of us retold the chapter, we had covered the week before. I enjoyed retelling the chapters and one time even prepared my own version of Trivial Pursuit cards for Theosophy, and had great fun quizzing the group on the contents. (Our group leader was even a little embarrassed that he enjoyed the challenge of answering the questions correctly.)

I attended a year-long anthroposophical intensive seminar in Steiner Haus in Stuttgart, Germany. The instructor's method was to show how the arguments Steiner makes in the Philosophy of Spiritual Activity or Theosophy are applicable to situations or problems in the world today. His lectures reflected a superior knowledge of the text; and he shared with us the fruits of his labor. Our discussion sessions with him gave the group confidence in their anthroposophical studies.

There are many different categories of groups that fall in between the three mentioned above, not all of them productive or fun. So far we have three ways of approaching a text: reading a passage and discussing (relaxed atmosphere), reading and retelling (activist mode), lecture and discussion (scholarly approach). In the next section is a description of the fourth method: reading a text for the joy of learning organic thinking.

Reading Steiner Organically:

My first encounter with organic study came when Florin Lowndes presented (to our Anthroposophical student group in Germany) suggestions on how to read a Steiner text for the purpose of learning Steiner's organic method of thinking. The simple steps outlined in these instructions on how to read the *Preface to the Revised 1918 Edition* to the Philosophy of Spiritual Activity gave our group an intensity and joy which I had never experienced in the other groups. The instructions were straightforward: first read for content, then for form.

This was the first method that required us to use colored pencils, to make diagrams, and to imitate *the way in which Steiner wrote*. Lowndes, being a professional painter, developed an artistic approach engaging the group on many different levels and points of view.

In comparison to other types of study groups, this approach has a clear agenda and the steps of the approach build upon one another. The activities in the study stimulate exploration, and a general mood of discovery pervaded the group. The organic laws of the text, when studied artistically and systematically, give the participants energy. Those already connected to Steiner will be amazed by some of thought-forms underlying his writings.

*

This approach proceeds from the notion that everything in the text has its meaning by its position in the text. Thus we read from the whole to the parts. Here are the main steps:

1) In the first meeting, we read the text lightly and made synopses of each paragraph in order to get a feel for the whole text.

2) In the second meeting, we underlined the main clauses and clarified subordinate clauses of sentences that were difficult to penetrate.

3) For homework for the next meeting, each participant prepared a rewrite of a paragraph in the *Preface*, and presented it to the group sentence for sentence within a designated amount of time. The goal of this exercise is not only to own the content, but also to clarify certain difficult sentences. Everyone, having done the same assignments, listened to the presenter and after each presentation offered feedback: did the presenter forget a sentence? Did they go over the time limit they allotted themselves? Did their rewrite make more sense than the way Steiner phrased it? We attempted to master the content by analyzing, rewriting, and presenting.

*

Reading for form is a slightly different story. Steiner composed his books, chapters, and sentences in organic forms resembling musical notation. The four levels of the four-fold human being are the basis of Steiner's organic method of writing. There are the four organic laws of rhythm, enhancement, polarity, and inversion, or simply put, the four laws of metamorphosis. Thus, when speaking about a "metamorphosed thinking" Steiner means a thinking which includes four new laws or relations.

Steiner wrote the *Preface to the Revised 1918 Edition* on the basis of these lawfulnesses. The *Preface* serves as an introductory text into this type of work. The goal is to study and practice the laws of metamorphosis and to go beyond what was said and to see how it was expressed. The steps for reading for form went as follows:

1) The group made a one- or two-sentence synopsis of each paragraph and put it on the chalkboard. By comparing the paragraphs to each other, a pattern emerges. First, one noticed symmetry in the themes of each paragraph, that is, the first three paragraphs mirror the last three. Second, one saw how each paragraph corresponded to the levels of the human being: physical, etheric, astral, and ego levels.

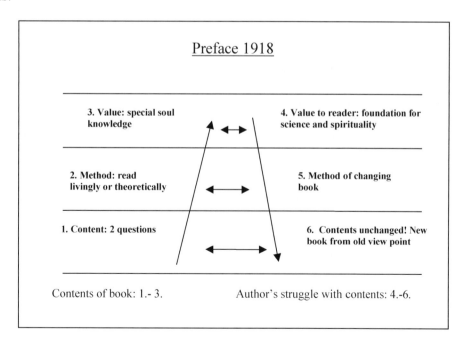

2) For homework participants prepared an analysis of the enhancement e.g., the intensification from paragraph 1, 2, and 3 or the polarity between paragraphs 2 and 5. We each chose, for example, a

time limit for our presentations, as we did with the content presentations mentioned above. The goal was to present what we prepared, and to do it with consciousness of time.

3) The process was repeated for the individual paragraphs at the sentence level. One begins to feel and understand the qualities of the levels even within the individual sentences. It is at this point one can start toying with the idea of writing one's own organic sentences.

4) The finale came when all participants could reproduce the entire thought-organism seeing it as a living whole. We were able to reproduce the whole text out of the colors and geometric forms, and to live freely in the content. This *Preface* became a thought-mantra, a dynamic meditational tool.

Value of Organic Practice:

One cannot do this method justice by simply writing about it. And this sort description cannot capture the intensity of this type of activity. The anthroposophical basis for this of work is that these laws of polarity and enhancement are worth practicing, and that repetitious practice brings changes in the soul life of the participants. This general organic approach to reading The Philosophy of Spiritual Activity leads to new faculties, even supersensible ones.

One democratic aspect of this type of work is that no matter how much one may know about Anthroposophy, everyone in the group starts off at the same level. The goal is to practice the laws as well as other analytic and social skills. Some will possess strong analytic skills; others will live easily into the process of organic thinking. These skills are: 1) learning clear thinking, 2) experiencing time as flexible, 3) exercising self-control, 4) listening skills, 5) inner transformation and joy, 6) seeing in pictures or whole- to-parts-thinking.

Clear thinking: Underlining main clauses, numbering sentences, clarifying subordinate clauses, and checking the translation against the original German text are activities which require participants to put aside (for the moment) what they feel or think, and live in the truth of the matter at hand. When participants agree on what was said, the way is clear for more creative and interpretative activities. A group cannot really function if the participants can't see the facts of the words of the page. Steiner used logic and grammar to express his thoughts in universal form. Their higher meaning, however, can only reveal itself to the individual when considered in the light of the organic laws and comparative thinking. When this exercise is done in depth, the grammatical structures in the German text reveal brilliant patterns in the form of main clause variations and emphasize with quasi-musical qualities.

Experiencing time as flexible: Presentations on content, polarity, and enhancement are opportunities for participants to practice their relationship with time. For example, if one has the assignment to present a 10-sentence paragraph sentence for sentence, how much time would one need? Would two minutes be enough time? Choosing a time - and sticking with it - is a real exercise. Some go over; some go under their allotted time. Eventually one experiences time *during* the presentation, as a 'flexible time,' since in this moment the god of time, Chronos, no longer dominates one's experience. Playing with time in a group study usually makes people giggle, as there is something strangely exciting when one is able to finish a presentation at the exact second, one chose for oneself. This exercise is fantastic for practicing the art of lecturing.

Self-control: Our logical nature associates and projects, ignoring reality. In organic study the opportunity is offered to think over-logically by learning about the inner nature of a text, as opposed to projecting meaning onto it. That's why presentations should be limited to the content and the lawfulness of polarity and enhancement. After a presentation, the other participants may compliment or critique the presenter's work. The presenters exercise self-control in that they listen to the other's critique quietly without qualifying themselves unless asked. *The unprepared cannot give critique*, for it happens nine times out of ten that the unprepared folks criticize and talk the most. The ideal participant, captured by

Schiller's description of the "beautiful soul," makes civility and self-control an art; and the beautiful should practices these qualities by being open to the text, giving and taking constructive criticism, and being prepared for group meetings.

Listening: A large part of organic study is listening to the presenters. When the group has worked sufficiently with the text, it may happen that some members are masters of rewriting the text in their own words. That is, they say the same thing Steiner did, but their choice of words is so different that the listeners loose, perhaps, their place during the presentation. Now, as the group progresses, something magical happens. Although the words are different than Steiner's, the group is able through a "higher listening" to follow the presentation with full understanding and appreciation of the rewrite. This higher listening is a bringing forth, as well as a receiving, in that it allows for the overcoming personal attachment to words, and for the opening of the soul to new possible meanings. This capacity humanity needs dearly, as most arguments are misunderstandings, not disagreements.

Inner transformation and joy: It is my experience in leading about ten different study groups (covering the *Preface to the Revised 1918 Edition*) that after about five meetings, the group begins to develop a new dynamic. The participants, in becoming familiar with the text and the laws of enhancement and polarity, begin to develop a warm bond. For whatever reason, Steiner's thought-forms, when shared organically in a group, seem to open the hearts of the participants. Also individuals, who considered themselves incapable of reading Steiner, find confidence in their new ability; while the incredible depth of the *Preface* humbles those with years of Steiner under their belt. In the Waldorf schools, the children are taught with healing organic pictures, and I believe this organic study to be an analogous healing activity for adults.

Whole-to-the-parts thinking: The parts have their meaning only in terms of the whole, a dogma of anthroposophy. But when does anyone practice it except maybe teaching the four mathematical signs in first grade Waldorf. (Musicians and artists are very close to this process as it is the basis of their work.) The diagrams of the organic approach give the reader the chance to see the whole text at once and to live in the spirit-laws of polarity. Of course one starts with diagrams and catchphrases of the paragraphs and sentences, but eventually one knows the content as color and form. The form now can bring forth the content, what Steiner had called "creating out of nothing."

Organic study requires a transition from purely logical thinking into an organic form of thinking. The work enlivens the individual; the rules are there to keep astral tendencies in check. Once groups get a feel for the organic thinking, they can make their own particular style of study, one that serves their wants. One would not want to study the whole Philosophy of Freehood at a snail's pace. The *Preface* and its sister text, the *Second Appendix*, contain all of the nine main thought-forms that Steiner used in his written works.

I can imagine many study groups would experience a completely different atmosphere if they would do this work. I know of no other approach that enters so deeply into Steiner's work. It will be hard for many veteran Anthroposophists to imagine that the organic form of Steiner's writing is essential to an understanding of the content. I do know that once one has read Steiner's basic books, one would like to go deeper. This approach facilitate this intensification of the work, and one should keep in mind that reading a Steiner text is about changing our thinking and feeling, not about acquiring new facts. You may very well know that in Steiner's first six books the same ideas are repeated over again, and even his spiritually oriented books contain much of the Philosophy of Freehood. The goal of studying Steiner is to learn his method, to individualize it, and to employ it, as situation and destiny require.

Appendix D
Fragments of Writings

A note about the forms: Beginners will often see forms everywhere. It is simply human nature to explore and enthusiastically "form-atize" everything. I myself applaud such enthusiasm, but new thinking is a science and discipline which has evolved over many decades of diligent study.

To superimpose a form on Steiner's chapters and paragraphs without having really explored and meditated and sketched it first is unhelpful. On the other hand, like poetry, new poetic forms have been created over the centuries and we need to keep an open mind. Thus let us respect the pioneering work of George O'Neil and Florin Lowndes by studying their hard-won results, while at the same time not closing our mind to new discoveries.

The coloring of the forms is dependent on whether a form is introverting of alternating. In Steiner's work often a form has several things going on at one. In Chapter three of the <u>Philosophy of Freehood</u> we see the typical buildup of A, B, C, D. Then there is the mirroring of 1the a, b, c, d, d^1, c^1, b^1, a^1

The basic thought-waves of the books: <u>The Philosophy of Freehood</u> has fourteen main chapters, a quasi-15th chapter, The Consequences of Monism, which is not numbered but nevertheless belongs to the main argument of the book. Steiner wrote a Preface and Second Appendix which contain all of the basic thought-forms of the whole book. And there is a First Appendix of which Steiner said: "They can leave this brief presentation unread." It is recommended to begin with an overview of the whole book and then go into the details. The Preface and Second Appendix are the primer texts, and because of their length lend themselves to a quick introduction.

The thought-waves come in many types. Each chapter introduces a different wave form. Even if a wave-form seems to be identical to others it often has a completely unique inner dynamic.

The waves are created by the ideas and subject matter moving through a series of points of view represented by the colors blue, green, red, and yellow. Like a wave, once the topic crests it descends down through the colors. These colors are qualitative points of view or questions: What? Blue; How? Green: Why? Red: Who? Yellow. Each wave starts from the concrete (what?) and moves into the dynamic (how?), into the feeling (why?), into the thinking level (who?).

Within the coloring of the four levels is also the coloring of the sections of the wave-form. The movement from blue to green to red and to yellow we call enhancement. Enhancement or the movement vertically and horizontally finds it completion in polarity. The first half of wave may be blue and the second half yellow in order to emphasize polarity or the contrast of outer and inner aspect of the ideas/subject matter. When there are, let us say, two waves the coloring may be blue, green, red, yellow emphasizing the enhancement instead of the polarity.

I have listed the forms of the <u>Philosophy of Freehood</u> in the colorings. Not to doubt the work of George and Florin Lowndes who have spent their lives testing and living with these forms, but to claim that this work is in a final form would be setting limitations on those who are seeking to take the work to new levels. When working in this way, one should not have the feeling that the forms presented here are the only way to organize the chapters.

Worth noting is the role of feeling. Steiner makes clear that "Knowledge of things, for the person who cares about totality, will go hand in hand with cultivation and development of his life of feelings." And in Steiner's sense, the thought-forms of the <u>Philosophy</u> could be called *feeling-forms* since the proper way to treat the conceptual aspect of the <u>Philosophy</u> is to bring feeling to the idea content.

Without this balance between feeling and the conceptual, the <u>Philosophy</u> becomes simply a head-book without any blood or emotion. The proper study of the <u>Philosophy</u> makes the wave-forms musical, that is, we sing the content of chapters in the same way a musician plays a score: feeling his way through the ups and downs, speeding up and slowing down, smiling and wincing. Half the work requires understanding the content and structure of the <u>Philosophy</u>; the other half requires bringing your individuality to personalize it.

How to ride them: What to do with these forms? When reading the <u>Philosophy of Freehood</u> start making little synopses of the paragraphs. You can choose whether you want first to discover the form of a chapter on your own, or simply go straight to the example and start practicing the one given.

Synopses usually start out a little long. The process of writing synopses is a personal one because some people need longer notes in order to recall the contents and tend to be more thorough. Depending on the length of the paragraph, the synopses could have one or two sentences which are then further represented by a catchword or catchphrase. These synopses and catchwords and phrases are transferred onto a diagram of the chapter.

When making synopses or condensing a chapter, you might want to see if your condensement fits the quality of the level. For example a blue paragraph will answer the question what? while a green paragraph will answer the question how? and so on. Thus in your condensement see to what extent the synopses have these qualities. Of course no paragraph is inherently blue or green but its quality is dependent on the interval between the levels as well as position in the whole text!

Once the synopses have been written in, you can test to what extent it harmonizes with the form. First see if the synopses fit the levels, colors, and questions. Then check the polarities: do the blue paragraphs relate to each other in outer/inner, knowledge/action, problem/solution contrast? Also note how on the one hand there is one consistent theme running through a whole chapter, while on the other hand, there are thematic breaks!

The purpose of the organic diagrams is to allow you to survey first the whole chapter, and from the whole enter into the parts seeing how they relate. By doing this you can begin to fix your synopses, and if necessary, consult the original text again in order to check how close your reading was. Now you are ready to enter into the meditative aspect of the work.

Read your synopses aloud. Speak the condensements according to their content and color. Listen to whether your synopses make any sense, whether you can tell the story of the chapter. Improve them where they don't sound right to you.

The next goal is to speak the chapters by gazing at only the catchwords, which means letting the catchwords lead you back to the synopses sentences and even to the paragraph itself. Eventually by just looking at the forms and colors without any notes you can recall all of the content. The form and the content have become one and now you can think in the pure form!

Background, text details, organic form, text numbering, dashes: Rudolf Steiner began his work on organic style in his teens. Throughout his career he changed some of the "rules" for organic style. A general rule seems to be that the significance of the grammar and punctuation in determining the organization of a text is dependent on the internal logic of that particular text. And I can say with certainty, not even as an expert in these matters, that Steiner purposely changed, is inconsistent in, made tricky the organization of his books including the <u>Philosophy of Freehood</u>.

A logical mind expects that the function of punctuation should be consistent. Steiner for example in his use of the dash varies greatly. A dash typically is used "to indicate a sudden break in thought, to set off parenthetical material, or to take the place of such expressions as *that is* and *namely*." Steiner uses the dash for yet another function: He puts dashes *in front of* sentences, sometimes indicating *a parenthetical sentence or even paragraph*! As a general rule dashes indicate parenthetical remarks if the book was published before 1901 as is the case with the Philosophy; however the addendum/additions to the Philosophy were written in 1918 and thus the dashes in the additions indicate new paragraphs, not parenthetical remarks as was the case in pre-1901 text. (The nature of the dash and the correct dates can be found in Florin Lowndes Das Erwecken des Herz-denkens.) Thus the book has two punctuation systems!

There are a number of places where Steiner uses good old fashion parentheses, not dashes. These true parentheses are not part of the sentence count and can be treated as footnotes. I have questions why Steiner used both. It seems that the parentheses contain remarks of a more personal nature for example: someone challenges Steiner fundamental conviction (Preface), no one should confuse Steiner's approach with rationalism (Consequences of Monism 2nd Addendum), and J. Rehmkes' is a completely different philosophy than Steiner's (First Appendix). Parentheses of a personal nature only appear in the sections written in 1918! Otherwise Steiner used them for references to texts including earlier sections of the book. This would confirm Steiner's intention that nothing of a personal nature was in his book.

There are several mysterious uses of punctuation in the book. In between the addendum in Consequences of Monism are three stars or asterisks whose function is not clear at all. There also appear several dashes at the end of a paragraph, which evidently in Steiner's day was used after a period to mark the end of a quotation. In one case, also in the addendum of Consequences, is a dash at the end of a paragraph whose function is mysterious. Are they typos?

In this translation, I kept all of the mysterious punctuation and added it where Wilson and other translators left it out. Lowndes has written about Steiner's punctuation and he has researched many grammatical questions such as the use of dashes in many of Steiner books. I am not sure why so few of Steiner's followers have interest in the organization of his books outside of George and Lowndes. In any case, the numbering of the text I got from Lowndes and any errors are mine own.

For the point of view of this translation, the form must be useful for organic study. The numbering of the text provides a structure out of which one can begin to work. There are nearly always substructures to a Steiner text as well as other mysterious goings-on. For example, one can follow how the concept of God changes in each chapter, or what animals, plants, words (love), and philosophers are mentioned. This study guide and translation are not intended to be exhaustive, but to provoke interest in a new method of communication.

Form and Quality: Here are several additional models to aid in analysis, understanding, and creation of organic thought-sequences. It should be noted here that those seeking to master organic thinking will study the main text of the Philosophy of Freehood and categorize Steiner's many literary devices. This would require a systematic study of all three-sentence paragraphs, four-sentence paragraphs, and so on. Here I want to give some tips about the forms.

Below is the *general* quality of each of the 12 main forms as they appear in chapters and paragraphs:

A one-sentence paragraph: profound; show stopper quality
A two-sentence paragraph: earth vs. heaven; concrete vs. abstract
A three-sentence paragraph: body, soul, and spirit; most readable organic rhythm
A four-sentence paragraph: clarity of an idea; well-developed
A five-sentence paragraph: dynamic and moving wave
A six-sentence paragraph: gentle contrast
A seven-sentence paragraph: archetypal
An eight-sentence paragraph: well-defined contrast
A nine-sentence paragraph: mysterious!
An eleven-sentence paragraph (a nine form with wings): very worthy of note

A twelve-sentence paragraph: ???

Sevenfold Model: It is important the reader have help in determining the quality of each chapter, paragraph, and sentence. O'Neil and Lowndes emphasized for the Anthroposophists that Steiner's method was based on the seven-fold human being consisting of four given bodies (physical, etheric, astral, and ego) and the three ennobled/purified members (spirit-self, life-spirit, and spirit-man). I find that so few Anthroposophists actually know the nine-fold or seven-fold human being there is almost no cause to use Steiner's old terminology.

One can find the list in Steiner's <u>Theosophy</u> the three bodily aspects (physical, etheric, and soul-body), and the three souls and their function (sentient soul, intellectual soul, and consciousness soul), and the three spirit-bodies (spirit-self, life-spirit, and spirit-man). It is more effect possibly to work with the universal inter-relationships of rhythm, enhancement, polarity, and inversion. There is a diagram below of the seven fold human being and its qualities.

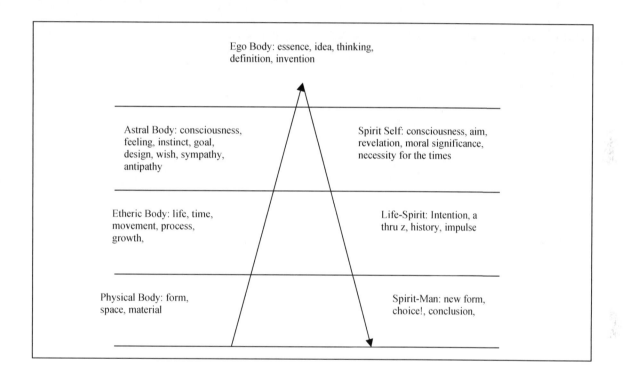

The nice thing about this chart is that it gives possibilities that one may not have considered in terms of polarities and enhancements.

The eight basic forms.

A nine-, ten-, and eleven-form. The eleven form introduces the concept
of wings which can be attached to any form

Two versions of the twelve-form, and one version of the thirteen-form.
The second version consists of three connected five-forms below.

A fifteen form consisting of 3x5forms.
The various kinds of connected five-
forms: 5, 9, 13 and so on.

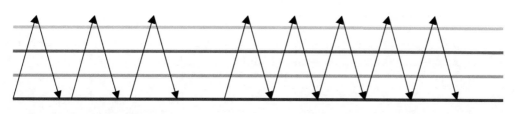

A twenty one form consisting of 3
x 7-forms. The various kinds of
connected 7-forms: 7-, 13-, 19- etc.

1.　　7.　　13.　　19.　　25.　　31.

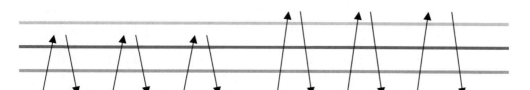

Six forms can make various forms consisting of 6, 12, 18, and so on. Eight-
forms create 8-, 16-, 24-, 32-forms and so on. Because some numbers overlap
one has to work hard to decipher whether the form consists of 6's or 8's. These
even-numbered forms are never connected for some reason.

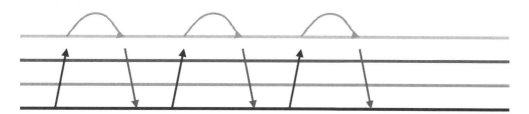

Nine-forms make 18-, 27-, 32-forms. The nine-forms
are also not connected for some reason.

There are some exceptional forms. Any form can be upside-down!
Included in this group could be the forms with wings (11-form and
chapter two of the Philosophy of Freehood).

202

Appendix E

Chapter I, Conscious Human Action [The Philosophy of Freehood] which is an exact translation of the German with the correct sentence and paragraph count.

1/14

1. Is the human being in his thought and action a spiritually *free* being, or is he compelled by the iron necessity of purely natural law?
2. Upon few questions has so much acute thought been brought to bear as upon this one.
3. The idea of the freehood of the human will has found warm supporters and stubborn opponents in large numbers.
4. There are people who, in their moral fervor, label anyone a man of limited intelligence who dares deny so obvious a *fact* as freehood.
5. Opposed to them are others who regard it as the height of unscientific thinking for anyone to believe that the lawfulness of nature is broken in the sphere of human action and thinking.
6. One and the same thing is thus proclaimed, once as the most precious possession of humanity, and again as its most fatal illusion.
7. Infinite subtlety has been employed to explain how human freehood can be consistent with the laws working in nature, of which the human being, after all, is a part.
8. No less is the trouble to which the other side has gone to make understandable how such a delusional idea as this could have arisen.
9. That we are dealing here with one of the most important questions for life, religion, praxis and science, must be felt by anyone who possesses any degree of thoroughness at all in his character.
10. It is one of the sad signs of the superficiality of present-day thought that a book which attempts to develop a "new faith" out of the results of recent scientific research (David Friedrich Strauss, The Old and the New Belief), has nothing more to say on this question than these words: "With the question of the freehood of the human will we are not concerned.
11. The alleged freehood of indifferent choice has been recognized as an empty illusion by every philosophy worthy of the name; the moral evaluation of human actions and attitudes, however, remains untouched by this problem."
12. Not because I consider that the book in which it occurs has any special importance do I quote this passage, but because it seems to me to express the view to which the thinking of most of our contemporaries manages to rise in this matter.
13. Today, everyone who claims to have grown beyond the elementary school level of science appears to know that freehood cannot consist in choosing, at one's pleasure, one or the other of two possible courses of action.
14. There is always, so we are told, a perfectly definite *reason* why one carries out just one particular action from a number of possible actions.

2/10

1. This seems obvious.
2. Nevertheless, down to the present day, the main attacks of the opponents of freehood direct themselves only against 'freedom of choice.'
3. Even Herbert Spencer, who lives in opinions which are gaining ground daily, says (Principles of Psychology): "*The fact that everyone is at liberty to desire or not to desire*, which is the real proposition involved in the dogma of free will, is negated as much by the analysis of consciousness, as by the contents of the preceding chapter (of Principles…)."
4. Others, too, start from the same point of view in combating the concept of free will.
5. The seeds of all the relevant arguments are to be found as early as Spinoza.

6. All that he brought forward in clear and simple language against the idea of freehood has since been repeated innumerable times, but as a rule shrouded in the most hair-splitting theoretical doctrines, so that it is difficult to recognize the straightforward train of thought - which is all that matters anyway.

7. Spinoza writes in a letter of October or November, 1674: "I call a thing *free* namely which exists and acts from the pure necessity of its nature, and *compelled* I call a thing which is determined in its being and action in a fixed and precise manner by something else.

8. Thus, for example, God exists freely, although with necessity, because he exists only through the necessity of his nature alone.

9. Similarly, God knows himself and all else freely, because it follows solely from the necessity of his nature that he knows all things.

10. You see, therefore, that I place freehood not in free decision, but in free necessity.

3/5

1. "But let us come down to created things which are all determined by external causes to exist and to act in a fixed and definite way.

2. In order to see this more clearly, let us imagine a perfectly simple case.

3. A stone, for example, receives from an external cause, after striking it, a certain quantity of motion, by reason of which, after the impact of the external cause has ceased, it necessarily continues to move.

4. The perseverance of the stone in its motion is due to compulsion, not to inner necessity, because it must be defined by the contact of an external cause.

5. What is true here for the stone is true also for every other particular thing, however complicated and multi-talented it may be, namely, that everything is necessarily determined by external causes to exist and to act in a fixed and definite manner.

4/6

1. "*Now, I ask you to suppose that this stone, while moving, thinks and knows that it is striving, as best as it can, to continue in motion.*

2. *This stone, which is conscious only of its striving and is by no means indifferent, will believe that it is absolutely free, and that it continues in motion for no other reason than because it wants to.*

3. *But this is precisely the human freehood that everybody claims to possess and which consists only in the fact that people are conscious of their desires, but do not know the causes by which they are determined.*

4. Thus the child believes that he desires milk freely, the angry boy that he desires vengeance freely, and the coward flight.

5. Further, the drunken man believes that he speaks of his own free will what, sober again, he would have rather left unsaid, and as this prejudice is innate in all people, one is not lightly freed from it.

6. For, although experience teaches us often enough that people are barely able to temper their desires, and that, moved by conflicting passions, they see the better and pursue the worse; yet they consider themselves free because there are some things which they desire less strongly, and some desires which they can easily inhibit through the recollection of something else which it is often possible to recall."

5/16

1. Because here a view is so clearly and definitely expressed, it is easy to detect the fundamental error that it contains.

2. Just as a stone carries out a particular movement in response to an impact, so does the human being, with the same necessity, carry out an action if he is driven by some reason or motive.

3. Only because a person is consciousness of his action, does he consider himself to be its originator.

4. But in so doing, he overlooks the fact that a cause drives him that he must follow unconditionally.

5. The error in this train of thought is soon discovered.

6. Spinoza, and all who think like him, overlooks the fact that the human being not only is conscious of his action, but also can be conscious of the causes by which he is led.

7. Nobody will argue that the child is *unfree* when he desires milk, or the drunken man when he says things which he later regrets.

8. Neither are aware of the causes, which are active in the depths of their organism, and which exercise irresistible control over them.

9. But is it justifiable to lump together actions of this kind with those in which a person is conscious not only of his actions but also of the reasons which cause him to act?

10. Are the actions of human beings really all of one kind?

11. Should the act of a soldier on the battlefield, of the scientific researcher in his laboratory, of the statesman in the most complicated diplomatic negotiations, be placed scientifically on the same level with that of the child when he desires milk?

12. It is no doubt true that it is best to seek the solution of a problem where the conditions are simplest.

13. But the inability to discriminate has before now caused endless confusion.

14. There is, after all, a far reaching difference whether I know why I do something, or whether that is not the case.

15. At first sight this seems to be a self-evident truth.

16. And yet the opponents of freehood never ask themselves whether a motive of my action which I recognize and see through, is to be regarded as compulsory for me in the same sense as the organic process which causes the child to cry for milk.

6/6

1. Eduard von Hartmann asserts in his Phenomenology of Moral Consciousness that the human will is dependent on two chief factors: motives and character.

2. If one regards human beings as all alike, or at least the differences between them as negligible, then their will appears as determined from *without*, namely, by the circumstances which come to meet them.

3. But if one bears in mind that various people make a mental picture into a motive of action, only if their character is such that through this mental picture a desire is aroused in them, then the human being appears to be determined from *within* and not from *without*.

4. Now a person believes - because, in accordance with his character, he must first adopt as a motive, a mental picture forced upon him from without, - that he is free, that is, independent of outside impulses.

5. The truth, however, according to Eduard von Hartmann, is that: "even though we ourselves first adopt a mental picture as a motive, we do so not arbitrarily, but according to the necessity of our characterological disposition, that is, we are *anything but free.*"

6. Here again the difference remains absolutely ignored between motives which I allow to influence me only after I have permeated them with my consciousness, and those which I follow without possessing any clear knowledge of them.

7/3

1. This leads us directly to the standpoint from which the subject shall be considered here on.

2. May the question of freehood of will be posed at all by itself, in a one-sided way?

3. And if not: with what other question must it necessarily be connected?

8/3

1. If there is a difference between a conscious motive of my action and an unconscious urge, then the conscious motive will result in an action which must be judged differently from one that springs from blind impulse.

2. The first question will concern this difference.

3. And what this question yields will then determine what position we have to take with respect to the actual question of freehood.

9/3

1. What does it mean to have *knowledge* of the reasons of one's actions?

2. One has paid too little attention to this question because, unfortunately, we have torn into two what is really an inseparable whole: the human being.

3. One has distinguished between the knower and the doer and has left out of account precisely the factor which comes before all other things: the one who acts out of knowledge.

10/2
1. It is said: the human being is free when he is solely under the dominion of his reason, and not of his animal passions.
2. Or again, that to be free means to be able to determine one's life and action according to purposes and deliberate decisions.

11/3
1. Nothing is gained by assertions of this type.
2. For the question is just whether reason, purposes, and decisions exercise the same kind of compulsion over a human being as his animal passions.
3. If without my co-operation, a rational decision emerges in me with the same necessity with which hunger and thirst arise, then I must by necessity obey it, and my freehood is an illusion.

12/2
1. Another form of expression runs: to be free does not mean to be able to *will* as one wills, but to be able to do as one wills.
2. The poet-philosopher <u>Robert Hamerling</u> expressed this thought with great clarity in his <u>Atomistic Theory Of The Will</u>: "the human being can certainly do as he wills, but he cannot will as he wills, because his will is determined by *motives*.

12a/10. -
1. He cannot will what he wills?
2. Let us consider these words more closely.
3. Have they any reasonable meaning?
4. Freehood of will would then mean being able to will without having a reason, without motive.
5. But what does willing mean if not *to have a reason* for doing, or trying to do, this rather than that?
6. To will something without reason or motive would be to will something *without willing it*.
7. The concept of will cannot be divorced from the concept of motive.
8. Without a determining motive the will is an empty *faculty*: only through the motive does it become active and real.
9. It is, therefore, quite true that the human will is not "free" inasmuch as its direction is always determined by the strongest motive.
10. But on the other hand it must be admitted that it is absurd, in contrast with this "unfreehood," to speak of a conceivable "freehood" of the will which would consist in being able to will what one does *not* will.

13/6
1. Here again, only motives in general are mentioned, without taking into account the differences between unconscious and conscious ones.
2. If a motive affects me, and I am compelled to follow it because it proves to be the "strongest" of its kind, then the thought of freehood ceases to have any meaning.
3. How should it matter to me whether I can do a thing or not, if I am *forced* by the motive to do it?
4. The primary question is not whether, when a motive has affected me, I can act upon it or not; but whether there are only such motives which impel with absolute necessity.
5. If I *must* want something, then I may well be absolutely indifferent as to whether I can also do it.
6. And if, through my character, or through circumstances prevailing in my environment, a motive is forced on me which to my thinking is unreasonable, then I should even have to be glad if I could not do what I will.

14/1
1. The question is not whether I can carry out a decision once made, but *how the decision comes about within me*.

15/13
1. What distinguishes man from all other organic beings arises from his rational thinking.
2. Activity he has in common with other organisms.

3. Nothing is gained by seeking analogies in the animal kingdom to elucidate the concept of freehood for the actions of human beings.
4. Modern science loves such analogies.
5. When scientists have succeeded in finding among animals something similar to human behavior, they believe they have touched on the most important question of the science of humankind.
6. To what misunderstandings this view leads is shown, for example, in the book Die Illusion der Willensfreiheit, 1885 by P. Rée, where the following remark on freehood appears: "It is easy to explain why the movement of a stone seems to us necessary, while the volition of a donkey does not.
7. The causes which set the stone in motion are external and visible.
8. But the causes which determine the donkey's volition are internal and invisible: between us and the place of their activity there is the skull of the ass. . . .
9. One cannot see the determining causes and therefore we judge that they are non-existent.
10. The will, it is explained, is, indeed, the cause of the donkey's turning round, but is itself independent; it is an absolute beginning."
11. Here again human actions in which there is a consciousness of the motives are simply ignored, for Rée declares that "between us and the place of their activity there is the skull of the ass."
12. Rée has not the slightest clue, judging from his words on this topic, that there are actions, not indeed of the ass, but of human beings, in which between us and the action lies the motive *that has become conscious*.
13. And he proves it again a few pages further on, with these words: "We do not perceive the *causes* by which our will is determined, hence we think it is not causally determined at all."

16/1
1. But enough of examples which prove that many argue against freehood without knowing in the least what freehood is.

17/6
1. It is completely obvious that an action which the agent does, without knowing why he does it, cannot be *free*.
2. But what about an action for which the reasons are known?
3. This leads us to the question of the origin and meaning of thinking.
4. For without the recognition of the *thinking* activity of the soul, it is impossible to form a concept of knowledge about anything, and certainly about an action.
5. When we know what thinking in general means, it will be easy to get clear about the role that thinking plays in human action.
6. "Thinking transforms the soul, with which animals are also endowed, into spirit," says Hegel correctly, "and hence it will also be thinking that gives to human action its characteristic stamp."

18/20
1. On no account should it be maintained that all our action springs only from the sober deliberations of our reason.
2. To call *human* in the highest sense only those actions that proceed from abstract judgment is far from my intention.
3. But as soon as our conduct rises above the sphere of the satisfying of purely animal desires, our motives are always permeated by thoughts.
4. Love, pity, and patriotism are mainsprings for actions which cannot be analyzed away into cold concepts of the intellect.
5. It is said: here the heart, the Gemüt hold sway.
6. Without question.
7. But the heart and the Gemüt do not create the motives of action.
8. They presuppose them and let them enter into their inner domain.
9. Pity enters my heart when the mental picture of a person who arouses pity appears in my consciousness.
10. The way to the heart is through the head.
11. Love is no exception.

12. Whenever it is not merely the expression of bare sexual instinct, it depends on the mental picture which we form of the loved one.
13. And the more idealistic these mental pictures are, just so much the more blessed is our love.
14. Here too, thought is the father of feeling.
15. One says: love makes us blind to the failings of the loved one.
16. But this can be considered the other way round and expressed: love opens the eyes just for these good qualities.
17. Many pass by these good qualities without noticing them.
18. One, however, perceives them, and thereby love awakens in his soul.
19. What else has he done but made a mental picture of what hundreds have failed to see?
20. Love is not theirs, because they lack the *mental picture*.

19/2
1. We may grasp the matter as we wish: it becomes more and more clear that the question of the nature of human action presupposes that of the origin of thinking.
2. I will turn next, therefore, to this question.

About my work:

There are several books which I cite in this study of Heart Logik. The Heart Logik work started with George O'Neil's manuscript on the <u>Philosophy of Freedom</u> which was printed on mimeographed sheets. One can borrow copies from the Steiner library. The generation now in their seventies in the Anthroposophical Society knew O'Neil's work but simply did not pursue it. These people run Waldorf education, and are in key positions in Anthroposophy. Only Florin Lowndes went on to publish a series of books based on O'Neil's papers and unpublished notes: <u>The Human Life</u> (Mercury Press), <u>The Enlivening of the Chakra of the Heart</u> (Rudolf Steiner Press), and <u>Das Erwecken des Herzdenkens</u> (Freies Geistesleben Verlag). More recently, Lowndes came out with colorful new editions of Steiner's basic texts called Code-X available for free on his website: www.heartthink.de. There is much left to do in the English language.

Some of the other books mentioned are *The Gospel Readings in the Cycle of the Year* (Floris Books) and Emil Bock's <u>Rhythm of the Christian Year</u> which both have much in terms of small gems for future research in organicism of the Christianity. A book worth mentioning is <u>The Burning Bush</u> by E. A. Smith because his book contains countless four-level diagrams of Steiner's cosmology.

My own work has consisted of my doctoral dissertation entitled <u>An Outline for a Renewal of Waldorf Education</u> which tried to show Waldorf educators how heart-thinking holds the Waldorf school together. In addition, I wrote a booklet (A Study Guide for Rudolf Steiner's Heart Thinking) for friends so they have a handy starter kit for the new thinking which is now available in Spanish and Romanian. I also did an experimental translation of Rudolf Steiner's essay *The Education of the Child* called <u>A Primer for Spiritually Thinking Educators</u>. I wanted to create a useful form of translation so that readers could have room to make synopses and study notes, to read actively.

In the near future I will come out with Heart Logik translation of Rudolf Steiner's <u>Theosophy</u> and <u>Philosophy of Freehood</u>. All of the translations of Steiner's work are all messed up with the wrong paragraph- and sentence-count, altered punctuation introduced by the translators. Unfortunately, most of which is written about these books is intellectual, not anthroposophical (spiritual) in the truest sense of the word. The anthroposophical presses are mainly responsible for the eclipse of the heart-thinking because their philosophy of translation is concerned with dumbing down the texts. It would be nice if a new generation would take seriously the organic form of Steiner's books and make translations that are useful for people practicing this heart-thinking.

The next project will be a new teachers college that brings the best elements of the heart thinking and academics, Waldorf education, and new types of spiritual training. Budding teachers should leave college having mastered academics and teaching, life skills (house building, cooking, farming, waste disposal,) and a healing or martial art. The current state of children requires a more curative approach to education and in this Steinerian tradition the teachers must be *awakened* first, then the children. Too much class time in American colleges, especially teachers colleges, is spent on useless theory and busy work, as opposed to those practical skills, interpersonal abilities, and types of meaningful knowledge that make human beings worthy teachers. The Heart Logik Teachers College will be founded someday.

In the meantime, I am offering three levels of Heart Logik training: the first level covering grounding in Heart Logik and body grounding; the second level having to do with thinking-practice and expansion as well as forgiveness; and the third level practicing more creative and intimate aspects of Heart Logik.

Since 2003 I have been involved in a very long training. During this training, I learned many things about grounding, expansion, and sexuality. Although my work and research is not complete, I have many things to share on this subject which I believe will revolutionize how we view and practice sexuality. My tentative book title is: "Loving Sexuality as a Healing Path". Where many authors have general principle about tantra, celibacy, I have concrete suggestions and troubleshooting that may just help those looking for a new sexuality. The thesis of the book is that loving sex can leads to difficult releases unless one knows how to navigate them.

Finally, I personally hope to be more active in disseminating this information by putting myself out there and trusting there are those who are ready for the transformative power of the heart-thinking.

Made in the USA
San Bernardino, CA
24 April 2016